Ecofeminism in Latin America

WOMEN FROM THE MARGINS

An Orbis Series Highlighting Women's Theological Voices

Women from the Margins is a series of books that present women's theological voices from around the world. As has long been recognized, women have shaped and continue to shape theology in distinctive ways that recognize both the particular challenges and the particular gifts that women bring to the world of theology and to ministry within the church. Their theological voices reflect the culture in which they live and the religious practices that permeate their lives.

Also in the Series:

Grant Me Justice! HIV/AIDS & Gender Readings of the Bible, Musa W. Dube and Musimbi Kanyoro, editors
Korean Women and God: Experiencing God in a Multi-religious Colonial Context, Choi Hee An

Ecofeminism
in Latin America

Mary Judith Ress

ORBIS BOOKS
Maryknoll, New York 10545

Founded in 1970, Orbis Books endeavors to publish works that enlighten the mind, nourish the spirit, and challenge the conscience. The publishing arm of the Maryknoll Fathers and Brothers, Orbis seeks to explore the global dimensions of the Christian faith and mission, to invite dialogue with diverse cultures and religious traditions, and to serve the cause of reconciliation and peace. The books published reflect the views of their authors and do not represent the official position of the Maryknoll Society. To learn more about Maryknoll and Orbis Books, please visit our website at www.maryknoll.org.

Published by Orbis Books, Maryknoll, New York 10545–0308.
Manufactured in the United States of America.
Manuscript editing and typesetting by Joan Weber Laflamme.

Library of Congress Cataloging-in-Publication Data

Ress, Mary Judith.
    Ecofeminism in Latin America / Mary Judith Ress.
        p. cm. — (Women from the margins series)
    Includes bibliographical references and index.
    ISBN-13: 978-1-57075-636-8 (pbk.)
    1. Ecofeminism—Religious aspects—Christianity. 2. Ecofeminism—Latin America. I. Title. II. Series.
    BT695.5.R47 2006
    270'.082'098—dc22

                                                              2005023630

In memory of Madonna Kolbenschlag (1935–2000)

Contents

Preface

The spiritual quest meets us at the borders of our soul, in our encounters and experiences, in the struggles and surprises within and without.
—MADONNA KOLBENSCHLAG, EASTWARD TOWARD EVE

Like many of my fellow human beings, I have searched for relevant images of the Godhead all my life in order to guide my way of being and acting in the world. At each stage I have found images that satisfied me, for a time at least, until I was prodded to seek out images that better reflected both a new stage of personal growth and a changing historical landscape.

While feminist theology over the years has provided me with the analytical tools to "suspect" the patriarchal underpinnings of our God images, it has not yet satisfactorily offered me more authentic images of Ultimate Mystery that incorporate the insights coming from the scientific discoveries of this rapidly changing world. Yet we human beings need constructs of meaning for building our lives and nurturing our spirits. "Without a vision, the people perish" (Prv 29:18). This seems ever more urgent to me. As I head into the later years of my life, I want images that make sense to me—and that not only make sense but also urge me, like Miriam of old, to lead the people in song and dance in praise and thanksgiving for the marvels that come with conscious awareness. In Carl Sagan's words, to celebrate "the local embodiment of a Cosmos grown to self-awareness."

As each day passes I am more convinced that humanity is "groaning" for a new definition of ourselves that perceives us as part of the Earth community rather than somehow apart from it or over it. This is a major conviction of ecofeminism, as I will

attempt to illustrate. While I am a North American and still claim
the United States as "home," since 1990, when I became a founding member of the Con-spirando Collective, a team of women
working in the areas of ecofeminist theology and spirituality in
Santiago, Chile, I have been deeply involved in the development
of Latin American ecofeminist thought and its theological, ethical, and spiritual perspectives. My hunch is that an emerging
ecofeminist world view can offer us, at this juncture in our history, a new cosmovision, a workable utopia for meeting the future. With that hunch in mind I designed this project as part of
my dissertation research for my doctorate in feminist theology.
The doctoral program was designed specifically for third-world
women by noted US feminist theologian Letty Russell. I also
want to acknowledge the guidance of Ivone Gebara, Latin
America's foremost ecofeminist theologian. Dr. Gebara, my dissertation advisor, is both friend and mentor. Much of this work
reflects her influence not only on my thought and practice but
on that of a growing number of Latin American women.

My hunch, which I have tried to substantiate over the past
decade, is this: In Latin America a growing number of activist,
faith-based women who had historically aligned themselves with
liberation theology and its practice during the 1990s are now
describing themselves as ecofeminist. This is evident in the way
they perceive themselves in relation to the rest of the Earth community and to the universe as a whole, in the way they are re-
imaging/re-naming Ultimate Mystery, in their beliefs about death
and rebirth, and in their spiritual and ethical practices.

To test this hunch I conducted in-depth interviews with twelve
women who have been active in the liberation theology move-
ments in Latin America. All twelve currently work in feminist the-
ology. They are Agamedilza Sales de Oliveira (Brazil), Marcia Moya
(Ecuador), Coca Trillini (Argentina), Sandra Duarte (Brazil), Fanny
Geymonat-Pantelís (Bolivia), Sandra Raquew (Brazil), Graciela
Pujol (Uruguay), Alcira Agreda (Bolivia), Clara Luz Ajo (Cuba),
Doris Muñoz (Chile), Gladys Parentelli (Venezuela), and Silvia
Regina de Lima (Costa Rica). My goal was to learn about their
theological and spiritual journeys toward ecofeminism.

Later, I brought these women together for a four-day workshop in Santiago, Chile, in April 2002 so that together they could draw conclusions from their histories, raise questions, set directions for Latin American ecofeminist theology, and perhaps challenge liberation theologians to incorporate these insights into their thought.

I published these interviews (which included many "right-brain" contributions from each woman, such as poetry, photographs, drawings, and in some cases excerpts from their own research) along with an introduction in which I contextualized the interviews and a prologue by Ivone Gebara describing the workshop in Santiago and its significance for the evolution of ecofeminist thought in Latin America. That book, published in Spanish, titled *Lluvia para florecer: Entrevistas sobre el ecofeminismo en América Latina* (Santiago, Chile: Colectivo Con-spirando, July 2002), is a primary resource for this new work.

My motivation for putting energy into this research rises from my firm belief in the need to lift up the voices of Latin American women whose faith-inspired commitment to the poor and oppressed is undisputed, but who are now forging a new theology, which is best described as ecofeminist. As such, this work is descriptive of a process rather than constructive theology in itself. I have no doubt that I am qualified to engage in this research—if for no other reason than the longevity of my immersion in the Latin American Catholic liberation milieu during the last quarter century. Indeed, it is high time that I systematized my reflections. I have been living and working in Latin America as a missionary, human rights advocate, journalist/editor, and feminist since 1970. Throughout the 1980s I was managing editor of *Latinamerica Press/Noticias Aliadas*, a weekly newsletter committed to reporting peoples' struggles through the lens of liberation theology. At the same time I have been involved with Christian feminism in Latin America from its beginnings and have participated in its development. Indeed, I am one of those "activist faith-based women" who, in the company of many others, is shifting from a faith rooted in the tenets of liberation theology to an ecofeminist perspective.

I am convinced that a number of Latin American "worlds" will be enriched by having these women's stories available: first and foremost, grassroots women's groups who may easily relate their own lives to these narratives; second, the region's theological world, especially those engaged in liberation theologies who, it is to be hoped, will delight in the expansion of theology proposed by the interviewees; third, religious women, pastors, and pastoral workers who will see these women as their companions on the journey and take heart; and fourth, young people, including my own sons, Peter, twenty-eight, and Benjamin, twenty-six, who are looking for some "anchors" for understanding the older generation's commitments. Perhaps other "worlds" will also be taken by surprise by these testimonies and experience a certain homecoming. That would be like "oil running down the beard, the beard of Aaron" (Ps 133:2).

Introduction

Our history, as well as our future, is intrinsically connected to the fate of the Earth. Past and future are also connected through insights coming from ecofeminism, a "remembering of who we are," which seems to offer a new utopian vision of what might lie ahead.

Ecofeminism insists that the *interdependence of all things* is a constitutive reality of the universe. Having just crossed the threshold of a millennium, we seem to find a new urgency to refashion ourselves as a species. Being "masters of the universe" leaves some of us with a bitter taste of being orphaned from the matrix from which we have evolved. Indeed, it is slowly dawning on us that while we are part of a greater whole, the greater whole is also part of us and it is precisely because of the evolution of the greater whole that we now realize how related we are to everything else.

Discoveries made in quantum physics and biology during the last twenty years have radically changed our definitions of the origin and scope of our universe. This major paradigm shift challenges our current mechanistic way of understanding the universe and entices us with the idea of an emerging cosmology. Today the material universe can be seen as a dynamic web of interrelated events.

Many feminist theologians, including myself, see ecofeminism as a new term for an ancient wisdom—a wisdom that lays dormant deep within our genetic memories. Certainly one of the greatest insights of ecofeminism is the dawning conviction that everything is connected—and therefore sacred. Ecofeminists make the connection that the devastation of the planet and the oppression of women and people of color are two forms of violence that reinforce and feed upon each other. They both come from a terribly misguided need to control, to dominate the other and that which is different. In short, this is a patriarchal mindset. From being the *source* of life, both the Earth and women have come to be regarded as *resources* to be used—and abused—as the power structures see fit.

Ecofeminists join with all those searching for a more holistic world view that recognizes and celebrates the web of all life. This ecofeminist posture places its advocates firmly in the postmodern debate as well as in the post-patriarchal quest for a more relevant and passionate understanding of who we human beings are in relation to the entire cosmos. This posture has engaged us in the struggle to redefine the divine as well as the human enterprise. We search for a more adequate cosmology, a more appropriate ethics, and a more inclusive spirituality.

This work attempts to flesh out the ecofeminist dream from a Latin American perspective. Chapter 1 tracks the development of feminist theology in the region, concentrating on its three stages as conceived by Elsa Tamez and Ivone Gebara, two of Latin America's widely known feminist theologians. My own theological journey, which I describe in some detail, parallels this evolution. It is in the third stage that ecofeminist theology comes to the fore and begins a critical dialogue with liberation theology.

Chapters 2 and 3 describe in detail the sources of ecofeminism. Chapter 2 treats both ancient wisdom traditions and the role of activist women as fundamental to the development of ecofeminism. Then ecofeminism's link with deep ecology, the new science, cybernetics, the new cosmology, and indigenous cosmologies is discussed, as well as the ecological vision of an economically sustainable world in which bioregionalism is a reality. Chapter 3 places ecofeminism within the larger feminist theoretical framework, examining the development of patriarchy through the lens of feminist anthropology. The influence of Jungian psychology on ecofeminism, the importance of the body as a source of wisdom, and the ecofeminist dream of forming post-patriarchal communities are also discussed.

Chapter 4 deals with the content of ecofeminist theology. Both post-Christian and Christian positions are examined briefly, before moving on to ecofeminist theology's development in Latin America. The thought of Brazilian ecofeminist Ivone Gebara is treated extensively because of her influence on a growing number of women who are "doing theology" in the region. Finally, the work of Con-spirando, the ecofeminist theological collective to which I belong, is described in detail.

Chapter 5 presents a sampling of how women in the region have evolved toward ecofeminism. This chapter summarizes my doctoral research in charting this evolution through in-depth interviews with twelve key Latin American women who have been working in the areas of liberation theology and feminist theology for many years and now identify—although some with reservations—with ecofeminist thought. I document their shifts in perception in three areas: changes in their self-understanding, changes in their understanding of the Divine, and changes in their beliefs surrounding life and death. I then show how these shifts are reshaping both their ethics and their spiritual practice.

Finally, Chapter 6 poses challenges for the future as well as presenting our hope for moving toward a post-patriarchal mindset that will be marked by a shift in consciousness. This shift in consciousness is becoming evident in the sense of who we are as humans, in our sense of the Sacred, in the movement of the locus of our epistemology from the head to the body, and in the way we celebrate our spirituality. These shifts have major implications for those of us involved in ministry.

I conclude with an epilogue that describes who, in the final analysis, I believe we are.

PART I

THE DEVELOPMENT
OF ECOFEMINISM

1

The Development of Feminist Theology in Latin America

Latin American feminist theology was born and matured within liberation theology, although today it is in critical dialogue with that theology. The evolution of Latin American feminist theology, which spans more than thirty years, can be divided into three stages paralleling the decades of the 1970s, 1980s, and 1990s.

Feminist consciousness within Latin American theology evolved from the total identification of women theologians and biblical scholars with liberation theology (first stage), to a growing awareness of—and discomfort with—liberation theology's patriarchal mindset (second stage), to challenging the patriarchal anthropology and cosmology present in liberation theology itself and calling for a total reconstruction of theology from a feminist perspective (third stage).

Scholarship on this evolution continues to grow. However, three Latin American feminist theologians have systematic studies of this historical development: Mexican feminist theologian María Pilar Aquino,[1] Costa Rican feminist scripture scholar Elsa Tamez,[2] and Brazilian ecofeminist theologian Ivone Gebara.[3] Aquino describes the first two stages in rich detail, using women's testimonies and women's group reflections throughout Latin America to substantiate her research. Tamez's periodization is the most systematic and succinct of the three; she describes each stage by setting it in the context of three congresses that gathered together Latin American women theologians in 1979 (Mexico),

1985 (Argentina), and 1993 (Brazil). In each stage she describes the political, economic, ecclesial, and theological context, the development of feminist consciousness, feminist hermeneutics, and the use of inclusive language. Gebara, while also describing the first two stages, concentrates on the third stage. Indeed, Tamez places Gebara's work on holistic ecofeminism at the center of third stage of Latin American feminist theology.[4]

Because of my focus on ecofeminism, which comes to the fore at the third stage in the 1990s, I will limit my summary of Latin American feminist theology to the schemas of Tamez and Gebara.

THE SCHEMA OF ELSA TAMEZ

Tamez first described the stages of feminist theology in Latin America in a lecture at the ecumenical congress of women theologians and biblical scholars and teachers held in Rio de Janeiro in December 1993. She continues to reflect upon and update her schema with rigor.[5]

While three fairly clear stages are observable in the evolution of feminist consciousness among women working in theology and biblical hermeneutics, Tamez insists: "It is important to recognize that the hermeneutical experiences of one decade do not cancel out those of another. Very often different, even conflicting experiences coexist, sometimes within the same person. . . . Nor is one phase to be treated as more important than another."[6]

Tamez describes the *first phase* of Latin American feminist theology (the decade of the 1970s) as an exciting period that saw the emergence of left-wing political parties and grassroots movements of *campesinos*, workers, and neighborhood and solidarity groups. In this same time period, however, the region's revolutionary struggles, which had coalesced a decade earlier, were severely repressed by military dictatorships in South America (Argentina, Bolivia, Brazil, Chile, Peru, and Uruguay). Military governments were already in place in Nicaragua, Guatemala, El Salvador, and Honduras in Central America. These dictatorships were infamous for their use of torture, assassination, and disappearances of activists. However, in the midst of this repression, there was an amazing growth in the number and strength of small Christian communities (CEBs), whose members were mostly urban slum dwellers. They gathered together in their small communities to reflect on biblical texts from their own experiences as militants. The book of Exodus, stories of the Babylonian captivity, and liberation texts from the Gospels were favorites.

During this decade women theologians and biblical scholars were enthusiastically committed to liberation theology's method and practice. They saw women as historical subjects in their own right, capable of being protagonists of liberation. They also lifted up the double oppression women suffer, that is, both as women and as members of an oppressed and impoverished class. Tamez notes, however, that there was practically no dialogue with either secular Latin American feminist organizations or with first-world feminist theologians. In those years most women working in theology saw feminism as simply another imperialistic invasion from the North, which could even be dangerous in that it diverted poor women from the primary contradiction of their economic and political oppression as a *class*. Women were seen as an implicit part of the category of the poor; therefore, the option for the poor meant the option for poor women. Time was spent studying Old and New Testament stories in which women were leaders (Deborah, Judith, the mother of the Maccabees), or renowned for their subversive acts (the midwives of Egypt), or women like Hagar, who was triply oppressed because of her class, race, and sex, and yet was blessed by God, who allowed her son to found a new people. Tamez underlines how reflections on these selected texts of liberation nourished hope in a new society based on socialist ideals, where it was assumed that egalitarian relations between the sexes would fall into place. However, in this period there was no awareness of the possibilities of inclusive language, and God was always addressed as masculine.

In the *second phase* (the decade of the 1980s) Tamez notes that an uneasiness was beginning to be felt by Latin American women theologians and biblicists about the affirmation that women were implicitly included in the category of the poor, and they began to see the need to read the Bible from the standpoint of women.

In this decade the political context shifted to Central America, where the Sandinistas came to power in Nicaragua and left-wing revolutionary struggles made headway in El Salvador and Guatemala. At the same time, most of the dictatorships in South America were replaced with restricted democracies in which the military remained vigilant watchdogs. In these years it became more and more evident that the foreign indebtedness of Latin American governments was sucking the lifeblood out of their peoples—so much so that the 1980s is seen as "the lost decade" in terms of the region's development.

This decade saw a right-wing backlash to liberation theology, especially from Rome. The Vatican's Congregation for the Doctrine of the Faith published a document warning against the dangers of liberation theology. Leonardo Boff, one of Latin America's most widely known liberation theologians, was summoned to Rome and subsequently silenced for a two-year period.

Theological reflection grappled with these realities by centering on themes of the kingdom of God and human history, a theology of life and of death, idolatry of the market, the discipleship of Christ, martyrdom, and a spirituality of liberation. At last, a dialogue began between male liberation theologians and their female counterparts on the oppression of women as women. Also, by the mid-1980s gatherings were taking place to reflect on black and indigenous theologies.

During these years more and more activist Christian women became involved in theological and biblical reflection. They gradually realized that liberation theology's discourse was tainted with androcentrism and patriarchal constructs, and they began to insist that theology done from the viewpoint of women's experience should reflect different cultural, biological, and historical experiences from those of men. Especially challenged was liberation theology's emphasis on economic oppression as it championed the option for the poor, often at the expense of cultural oppression and domestic violence. These were years of much creative theological production by women in liturgy, art, and poetry. Also, attempts were initiated to reach out to the region's feminist movements and to first-world feminist theologians.

With regard to hermeneutics, women began to search for female images of God and to refer to God as both mother and father. The Holy Spirit was seen as feminine. Women called not only for the practice of justice, but also for the need for tenderness, loving solidarity, and comfort toward those who suffer unjustly. Tamez, herself a biblical scholar, calls attention to three aspects of women's biblical work in these years. The first was the search for greater freedom in speaking about God, especially in the area of life's daily joys and sorrows. Second, there was a need for critical analysis of those biblical texts that were clearly patriarchal and discriminated against women. When a text did not allow for a more inclusive reinterpretation, it was dismissed as non-normative. This posture raised the question of the authority and inspiration of the Bible as the word of God. Third, there was also a need to affirm womanly virtues such as motherliness, unselfishness, and tenderness—virtues that historically society did not consider important. The virtues of commitment, resistance, and sacrifice were also seen as liberating.

God-language began to change in some circles because of the influence of some Christian feminists who began to address God as both father and mother. However, the word *feminist*, although widely accepted in some areas, was still shunned by many as an import from the North. "Doing theology from the standpoint of women" and reading the Bible "through women's eyes" were more acceptable.

The *third phase* (the decade of the 1990s to the present) is characterized by a radical, anti-patriarchal hermeneutical approach that proposes a new, inclusive, and non-patriarchal theology, indeed, a total reconstruction of theology itself. Ivone Gebara calls this phase "holistic ecofeminism."

During the 1990s progressive forces in Latin America were profoundly shaken by the collapse of the Communist governments of Eastern Europe and the demise of historical socialism. The defeat of the Sandinistas in Nicaragua also dampened the region's hope for an alternative to the capitalist order. Economically, the current neoliberal economic model, which gives supremacy to the demands of world markets, appears to be seen as the only viable alternative. Socially, once effervescent grassroots movements have stagnated, including the CEBs, which have gone into steep decline.[7] On the other hand, the inroads being made by Pentecostalism throughout Latin America are indeed remarkable. (A common phrase heard among Latin American pastoral agents these days is, "Liberation theology may have opted for the poor, but the poor have opted for Pentecostalism.") All this has affected the vibrancy of liberation theology, a topic that will be treated more thoroughly below.

One bright spot in an otherwise dismal political landscape has been the rise of the indigenous movement as a result of the five-hundredth anniversary in 1992 of the European invasion of the Americas. Indigenous theologians are calling for liberation theology's option for the poor to be expanded to include an option for the impoverished other, because the "otherness" of the continent's diversity needs to be taken into account along with economic disparities.

For a growing number of women, it has not been enough to speak of the feminine face of God. They find current theological discourse androcentric and patriarchal to the core and see their task as reconstructing the whole of theology from a feminist perspective. A major influence on these women has been the introduction of gender analysis into their theological and biblical work, along with new insights coming from feminist anthropology. In this area there is a much more open, welcoming attitude toward both Latin American feminism and colleagues in the first world.

One of the most forceful new hermeneutical categories for this feminist theological and biblical scholarship is the body. Concrete bodies of women and men are becoming a new locus for doing theology. Efforts are also being made to offer a non-sacrificial reading of redemption to free many poor women from accepting violence, especially domestic violence, as somehow "the will of God." New non-gender-specific names are emerging for the Divine, such as Grace, Compassion, and Energy. As Tamez concludes: "We are aware of the radical nature of this challenge, which means reworking, or rather reinventing, the whole of Christian theology. There is difficulty in re-reading the great theological themes such as Christology, the Trinity and ecclesiology because of their androcentrism. It is recognized that the implications of reconstruction take us beyond orthodoxy."[8] She ends her overview by emphasizing that the priority for feminist theologians and biblical scholars and teachers in Latin America is always to link their work to the basic concerns of the poor.[9]

THE SCHEMA OF IVONE GEBARA

While Gebara's systematization is not as detailed as that of Elsa Tamez, she also sees three stages in the development of Latin American feminist theology. She points out, however, that they are not necessarily chronological and that they often overlap, depending on historical circumstance and the level of feminist consciousness in a specific country or group. Gebara elaborated on this development in a course she taught in Chile in April 1993. When the course was finished, I interviewed her on these stages, focusing especially on the third stage.[10]

For Gebara, the *first stage* of feminist theology is characterized by women's discovery of their oppression as historical subjects—an oppression present in theology, the Bible, and the churches. She credits the secular feminist movement—not the churches—with nurturing this insight among Christian women. In this stage women rediscovered many women in the Bible, such as Sarah, Hagar, Miriam, Ruth, Esther, Judith, Mary, Magdalene, and the women at the empty tomb, and reclaimed them as key actors in the history of liberation. For Gebara, this was important but not sufficient in itself. She says that women tended to overvalue the feminine during this stage and to fall into the patriarchal trap of lifting up those domestic qualities historically associated with women, such as motherhood and the double-duty workday. Gebara also challenges work done in those years to hold up women liberators such as Judith as models without questioning the violent patriarchal framework in which the book of Judith is situated. She also believes that during this stage (which she also situates in the 1970s), women tended to think that they were the "good" gender and somehow spiritually superior to poor, weaker men. There was also a certain desire to "even the score" with their male counterparts.

Gebara calls the *second stage* the "feminization of theological concepts." This was a time when women theologians worked to rediscover the feminine, maternal face of God in biblical texts. She also notes that during those years (the decade of the 1980s), women were given a voice within the churches and within liberation theology so they could present "the women's perspective." This pleased progressive male theologians and pastors and particularly male liberation theologians who had always insisted that their ranks were open to women theologians. However, according to Tamez, Gebara has pointed out that what women had been doing was "patriarchal feminist theology."[11]

Gebara finds that liberation theology in general has not challenged the underlying patriarchal structure of Christianity itself. While she acknowledges that liberation theology offers a more collective understanding of God and stresses the social nature of sin and that God is a God of life and of justice who has a preferential option for the poor, she finds that its anthropology and cosmology remain riddled with patriarchy.

Gebara situates the *third stage* of Latin American feminist theology in the postmodern paradigm and invites us to consider what she calls "holistic ecofeminism." I will be dealing with Gebara's understanding of and contribution to ecofeminism in Chapter 3.

The schemas elaborated by Tamez and Gebara are very useful in describing the development of Latin American feminist theology, although both Gebara and Tamez insist that these are not fixed periods; often two phases can overlap in the same country or area or church. The following section combines the insights of both.

THE THREE PHASES
OF LATIN AMERICAN FEMINIST THEOLOGY

First Phase (1970–80)

Political/Economic Context
- effervescence of leftist political parties and popular movements (union, barrio, etc.)

- revolutionary struggles, which provoked military coups, followed by dictatorship
- repression through massacres, disappearances, torture, generalized human rights abuse

Ecclesiastical/Theological Context
- CEBs spring up all over Latin America
- grassroots reading and interpretation of the Bible *(lectura popular)*
- option for the poor; texts read with the "eyes of the poor"
- Medellín and Puebla documents
- ecumenism based on option for the poor, cutting through denominational lines
- theology of liberation comes into its own with its methodology of reflection based on praxis
- the poor become the theological locus
- key themes are the Exodus, the "valley of tears," the historical Jesus

Construction of Feminist Consciousness
- women theologians and biblical scholars identified totally with liberation theology
- women seen as oppressed historical subjects in the Bible, in theology, and in the churches
- women began to reclaim a more equal space within society
- theological point of departure became the double oppression of women based on both sex and class
- a tendency to overvalue the feminine and a certain wanting to "even the score" by making women the "good gender"
- almost no dialogue among feminist theologians from Latin America or between those from Latin America and the North (instead, a good deal of suspicion)

Hermeneutics
- biblical interpretation was both militant and grassroots-based
- liberation texts were emphasized over other texts
- the task was to rediscover biblical women as key players in the history of liberation (Sarah, Miriam, Ruth, Esther,

Deborah, Judith, Magdalene, Mary, the Egyptian midwives, Hagar), which took place without awareness of the patriarchal context of the text itself (for example, the history of Judith)

Inclusive Language
- no awareness of sexist language
- a masculine divinity
- the word *feminist* is rejected as a foreign concept, imported from the North

Second Phase (1980–90)

Political/Economic Context
- in Central America the Sandinista triumph, revolutionary movements in El Salvador, Guatemala
- in the southern cone dictatorships give way to restricted democracies
- Bush-Reagan era; Santa Fe documents
- foreign debt becomes a crushing weight on the poor

Ecclesiastical/Theological Context
- ideological polarization becomes acute (in Latin America, CLAI vs. CONELA)
- Vatican documents condemn liberation theology
- liberation theologians become interested in the "women's perspective"
- liberation theology becomes more receptive to the topic of "women" per se
- key themes are theology of life vs. theology of death; idolatry; martyrdom; spirituality of liberation

Construction of Feminist Consciousness
- growing commitment to see women's perspective at every turn
- growing critique of all theology for its anthropocentrism and patriarchal mindset

- starting point in women's experience, bringing a different discourse to theology because of biological, cultural, and historical influences
- efforts to rescue discourse related to God, for example, the maternal face of God
- efforts toward the feminization of theological concepts
- praxis of love and caring
- lots of innovation in liturgy
- openness to feminist contributions from both Latin American and northern feminists

Hermeneutics
- biblical interpretation sees every text from women's perspective
- search for feminine images of God (mother/father, Holy Spirit as feminine)
- commitment to feminize theology, to combine justice with tenderness
- biblical work centers on valuing the ordinary, pleasure, play; reinterpreting of virtues traditionally linked to women such as maternity, tenderness, sacrifice, commitment
- confrontation with patriarchal texts and insistence that they are not normative
- reconstruction of texts and questioning of sources of biblical authority

Inclusive Language
- God as mother/father; as he/she
- identification with the word *feminist* becomes more common

Third Phase (1990 and onward)

Political/Economic Context
- fall of the Berlin Wall, and with it, socialism as a model
- Gulf War, invasion of Panama, defeat of the Sandinistas
- neoliberal economic model firmly entrenched; market ideology reigns supreme

- state as benefactor of people is dismantled
- popular movements in general are weakened, lackluster interest in reform

Ecclesiastical/Theological Context
- CEBs stagnate
- ecclesial crisis within both Protestantism and Catholicism
- Santo Domingo document (Catholic) is weak
- CLAI III document (Protestant) is weak
- amazing growth of Pentecostalism
- new energies coming from indigenous movement (anniversary of five hundred years)
- Chiapas becomes a rallying cry, "a society where all fit!"
- women's movement gains strength, as well as the black movement
- key themes are the market and the gods of sacrifice, the new evangelization, ecology and the land, dialogue with other religions
- option for the poor evolves into option for the impoverished other

Construction of Feminist Consciousness
- feeling of being "boxed in" with no room to expand
- need to reconstruct all theology from a feminist perspective
- use of gender theory to analyze situation of oppression
- growing contributions from black and indigenous women
- new theories coming from the anthropology of symbolism
- challenge to confront the patriarchal structures latent in Christianity itself
- challenge to confront the patriarchal anthropology and cosmovision present in liberation theology
- calls for redefinition of both the human and the Divine
- openness to holistic ecofeminism (Ivone Gebara is key figure)

Hermeneutics
- body and the ordinary are considered hermeneutic categories

- call for a non-sacrificial reading of redemption
- key themes are the fiesta, joy, embodiedness, sexuality
- gender theory is applied to biblical texts
- creative reconstruction of texts to hear the lost voices of women
- major challenge is to reinvent all Christian theology in relation to the concepts of God, Jesus, Trinity, sin, and redemption, going beyond what is currently considered orthodox
- key question being raised is how to articulate a feminist hermeneutic that takes into account the basic problems of impoverished peoples

Inclusive Language
- non-sexist names for the Divinity (Energy, Mercy, Infinite Compassion, Grace)
- terms *feminist* and *ecofeminist* now commonly accepted

MY PERSONAL JOURNEY TO FEMINIST THEOLOGY

In 1996 Elsa Tamez's systematization of feminist theology inspired me to review my own life journey, which, curiously enough, closely parallels the three stages of feminist theology in Latin America described by Elsa Tamez and Ivone Gebara. Since the key starting point for doing feminist theology is one's own experience, I thought it appropriate to share my own journey. In writing this brief account of my journey, I was also struck by how closely it resembles or fits into the ecclesiology and theology of the times.

I was born on a May morning in 1942 to a close-knit family in a small US Midwestern town famous for its high school football team. My grandparents and all their children and grandchildren lived on the same short street. We all went to the same parish, which also provided most of our social life. I went to Catholic grade and high schools, where I found myself incredibly attracted to the sisters who taught me.

After high school I entered a convent and spent three years as a novice at the motherhouse farm in western Pennsylvania.

During those years my prayer was "Dear God, let me just keep up with this dedicated bunch." My fellow novices (forty of us!) were a healthy, happy crowd, and the sisters in charge of our formation were warm and caring. I will always link my continual searching for community to my experience among the Sisters of the Humility of Mary. I belonged to this community for fourteen years.

After the novitiate I was sent to college, destined to become a high school teacher. Many of us entered an academic track to major or minor in Spanish because the community, responding to Pope John XXIII's call to re-Christianize our "sister continent" of Latin America, had just opened a mission in Temuco, Chile, to work with Mapuche women.

After graduation from college I taught Spanish and social studies for four years in one of the community's flagship schools for wealthy young women. I "wore lots of hats" in those very busy years, but two events in particular stand out. The first was when we took students across the country on a school bus to live with Cesar Chavez and the migrant farm workers for a month. The second was also a trip; we took a small group of girls to Mexico for summers (and one summer in Spain) to study Spanish.

By my third year as a high school teacher, I found myself getting restless. In 1969 I applied for and was awarded a fifteen-month East to West grant to study at the University of Hawaii, including three months of fieldwork in India. However, about a month after receiving the grant, the mother superior of my community called to say that one of the sisters was leaving the school. She asked me to postpone my grant and reapply the following year so I could take her place. I did as asked, but to my great disappointment I did not receive the grant the following year. On the rebound, I decided to join the Cleveland Mission Team to El Salvador. Throughout the ensuing years I've mulled over my being denied the chance to study in India and ending up instead in El Salvador, as that decision has so shaped my life. Since 1970, with only some short intermissions, I've been living and working in Latin America.

As I moved about—from teaching in a Catholic high school to doing mission work in Latin America—my ideas of the Divine also moved from where they had been. They seem always to be closely connected with the women with whom I'm working. Having grown up in the pre–Vatican II Catholic tradition of the 1950s, my earliest image of the Divine was Mary, Mother of God and Mother of Christ. Mary was truly my mother: I went to her to be comforted when I was hurt or confused. All my prayers of petition were to her, because—as the popular theology of the times taught—"to Jesus through Mary." She was the mediatrix par excellence; how could Christ refuse anything asked in his dear mother's name? As a young girl, God the Father was some remote being. (I supposed he looked like Michelangelo's old man with the beard, but I never had a very vivid vision or much interest in this faraway force.) Jesus, of course, was Jesus, and I trotted faithfully behind him through the liturgical cycle of his birth, boyhood, public life, suffering, death, and resurrection. But, if the truth be known, although Jesus was God's son and thus somehow also God, he was, in the end, the child of Mary. It was Mary who really mattered.

I cannot stress enough the importance of Mary as my *root image* of the Divine. My childhood was marked by May crownings, May altars, and novenas to Mary—all in the context of the liturgical cycle of my parish, St. Mary's, which was known for celebrating all the Marian feasts with great gusto. As a teenager I joined the Sodality, an organization whose members consecrate themselves in a special way to Mary, and became one of its leaders. Through the Sodality I felt called to serve the poor and less fortunate in the spirit of Mary (and her son) and engaged in a variety of apostolic services. All through these years there were strong female models in my life whose devotion to Mary—and love of life—continually inspired me.

The religious congregation I entered also had a special devotion to Mary. For several months during my novitiate I even consecrated myself secretly as a slave of Mary (a rather macabre series of observances taught by the French saint Louis de Montfort) until my novice mistress found out and forbade my "slavery." Today, given the wealth of feminist research about patriarchal repressions of the goddess image in our history, I am much better able to put my Marian devotion into perspective. At the time, it was extremely attractive to me and to many other novices.

However, my religious training in the convent introduced me to more rigorous study of the Jesus of the Gospels and to a more enlightened understanding of trinitarian theology. Jesus became more pivotal: it was he who introduced us to his Father as Abba; it was he who left us his Spirit to be with us always. But not only did Jesus become an attractive historical figure, he also became my "spouse." (My convent formation was right on the cusp that divided a more scripture-based Vatican II theology from a more pietistic theology where vowed religious women became "brides of Christ.") I clearly remember the day of my first vows, when I had a mystical experience of being wed forever to this God-bride-groom, who, because he loved me in such a special way, would be most demanding of me ("to whom much is given, much will be asked"). And so, at the age of twenty-one, wearing his betrothal ring, I set out to save the world for Christ.

While the Second Vatican Council was taking place, an erup-tion of Catholic social encyclicals from Pope John XXIII and Pope Paul VI called the church to "open the windows" to let in the Spirit of justice and compassion. Key to those times was the conviction that the church was not a structure or an institution but the people of God on a journey. Ever a product of my times, I became an enthusiastic Vatican II Catholic, preaching, teach-ing, and trying to put into practice the new social doctrine of the church. Nourished by a simpler, more understandable liturgical cycle in which the Mass became a meal shared among friends, I found myself involved in the civil rights movement, in the anti-war movement, and in the grape boycott to promote justice for the migrant farm workers. Radical to the core, my habit and veil gradually changed to jeans and a sweatshirt. By 1970 (not en-tirely altruistically, having just lost the chance to go to Hawaii and India) I had decided that the most authentic way to live out the gospel was to become a missionary in Latin America.

The First Stage: The 1970s

Living in El Salvador in 1970 was a major change from teach-ing at an upper-class girls' school. Tremendous poverty, heat, government corruption and violence, and the growing political restlessness of the people overwhelmed me. I was twenty-eight years old, and my only qualifications as a missionary were that I was a high-school Spanish teacher and that I had been deeply "converted" to establishing peace and justice in the world by taking to heart the social doctrine of the church!

I still remember the evening I arrived in El Salvador. Some of my future colleagues met me at the airport in a jeep. After what seemed like hours of bouncing over dark mountain roads in a downpour, we arrived at what appeared to be the end of the world. I descended from the jeep and found myself knee deep in mud. Dressed as I was in my Sunday best "cool nun duds," the villagers in the tiny hamlet of Chirrilagua must have thought I was a creature from another planet. I was so relieved to have finally arrived that I didn't cry over my mud bath. However, when folks amiably conversing outside my window awakened me at 4:30 the next morning, I did weep. I quickly learned that because of the heat, the best hours for socializing are those of the very early morning. I soon found myself rising in those cool predawn hours to stroll in the refreshing breeze and visit with folks—all of whom were up and ready for a new day.

I went to El Salvador as an idealistic young nun ready to serve the poor. Since I had been a popular high school teacher back home, I assumed I would be equally successful working with teenagers in the barrios. Very quickly, however, I realized I was in a different world, a world where poverty was so acute that children really did die of hunger and disease. I learned that in El Salvador unjust structures were so embedded in the very air we breathed that only something like a revolution could change the stifling status quo.

I only lasted two years. During that time I formed a youth center in La Union that brought together most of the town's young people. It lasted until the local bishop—who was also the chaplain of the local military barracks—shut it down for being "subversive." After that major setback I began working to solidify the several CEBs that the mission team was forming both in La Union and in the outlying *cantones*. Another sister and myself developed a group-dynamics program for rural women because it soon became evident to us that women needed to be able to express what they were feeling, but were timid about speaking out in a group.

I clearly remember the *campesinos* with whom I worked. As they discovered their dignity and their power through a militant reading of scripture, they would often tell us that they would rather "die on their feet than live on their knees." Engraved in my memory forever is the moment during those first CEB meetings when we pastoral agents would ask: "Brothers and sisters, is there injustice in our world?" A long pause, then, finally, *Sí, madre, hay mucha injusticia en nuestro mundo*. And then the process of what Brazilian educator Paulo Freire called *concientización* would begin. It was in these CEB meetings that I too discovered a new way of reading scripture. I discovered a Jesus who took sides with the oppressed and downtrodden in their struggles for a more just society. However, I couldn't see a role for myself in this struggle: I was a naive *gringa* who couldn't even play the guitar. I also realized that the same injustices and class divisions in society that cried out for vengeance also existed within the church, which was polarized around the causes of the extreme poverty of El Salvador's majority. I was fortunate to meet Archbishop Oscar Romero—and this was before his conversion when he was still known for being a conservative. He visited a course I was giving for young *campesinas*. I have a vivid recollection of his frayed cassock, his kindness, and his real concern for the girls.

I left El Salvador in 1972, disillusioned about the possibility that the kingdom of God might come to this suffering people—at least during my lifetime. I left convinced that I had seen what liberation theologians called social sin—the exploitation, torture, hatred, and utter disrespect that the wealthy and powerful aimed at the poor. I felt I had confronted the "powers and principalities" of a dominant class so entrenched in its position of privilege that it would never willingly relinquish anything that would compromise that position. I became more sympathetic to armed struggle because I saw no way out other than some sort of violent revolution.

I must note that the woman who replaced me on the mission team in El Salvador was Ursuline Sister Dorothy Kazel. She was murdered in 1980, along with three other religious women, by the Salvadoran security forces. "There but for you, go I." This has had and continues to have a great impact on the meaning and direction of my life.

I returned to the United States in crisis regarding both faith and identity. I left religious life. I felt I had been a failure as a missionary. I went to Chicago where I roomed with a good friend who had left the community a year before. Almost immediately, I fell in love with a theology professor at Loyola—an ex-Jesuit seminarian. When the relationship did not develop, I spent a rather dreary year as a "single."

Then one day I saw an ad in the *National Catholic Reporter* inviting people to be a part of a missionary team to a small village in the Peruvian Andes. After several letters back and forth, I met David, the priest coordinating the effort, and agreed to be a part of his team. I spent the next three years (1973–76) living at an altitude of ten thousand feet and working as a pastoral agent in Huarochiri, a small town with a population of two thousand. I taught school, worked with a women's group, and helped form a consumer's cooperative. I grew to know firsthand the church of the poor and those working in liberation theology. We were committed to Paulo Freire's method of conscientization and to the "see, judge, act" method of praxis to delve into the roots of oppression. In those years I came to know Gustavo Gutiérrez and his circle of Christians who were developing liberation theology and its practice. David was deeply involved in the progressive priests' movement, ONIS, and we were both committed to what we all called a new way of being church. For me, the years in Huarochiri were also a time of contemplation because of the absolutely breathtaking beauty of the Andes. Also, because the villagers went to their fields around six in the morning and came home around six in the evening, it was hard to do much organizing, so I would walk the hills and valleys of this majestic part of Peru. Little by little I drew close to a people and a culture very rich in history and tradition. This period has left a lifelong mark.

With hindsight, I realize that I was quite dogmatic in those years. My letters home to my family and friends were filled with revolutionary zeal and condemnations of capitalism. I stubbornly wore my "revolutionary uniform" of jeans, poncho, and boots everywhere. I identified with my biblical namesake, Judith, who killed the oppressor Holofernes to save her people.

My relationship with David also deepened during this time, but he was very committed to the priesthood, as it was understood by liberation theologians in those days. Many regarded the Colombian guerrilla priest Camilo Torres as a heroic figure. In 1976, however, the bishop of our area, a member of Opus Dei, dismissed all the priests, sisters, and pastoral agents working in the six parishes up and down the valley and replaced us with missionaries from Spain. This caused a major crisis, for us and also for the Peruvian church. In the end, after succumbing to a bad case of hepatitis, I went back to the United States. David, although he had left his community, continued to work as a priest in the mining camps in southern Peru.

Back in the United States, I was at my lowest ebb. I made a retreat with a good friend, while trying to let go of David and my life in Peru. In the fall of 1976 I enrolled in the Graduate School of Social Research in New York and earned a master's degree in economics. I learned from friends at Maryknoll that Sergio Torres, a Chilean priest and liberation theologian in exile, was trying to organize groups who were doing liberation theology in the United States. I took a position as Sergio's bilingual secretary and assistant in the Theology in the Americas office (which would eventually also become the office for EATWOT, the Ecumenical Association of Third World Theologians). I worked during the day and studied at night—until one day in October when David called to propose marriage.

Many who had been "brought up" on liberation theology frowned on marriage as a step that would lead to "abandoning the struggle." Inevitably, they felt, one became bourgeois and forgot the option for the poor. But we married in 1977. The songs at our wedding reflected our determination to continue accompanying the oppressed "as long as we both shall live." On our honeymoon we went to Appalachia, where we thought we might find meaningful work. Midway through our trip, however, we received word from the American Friends Service Committee

(AFSC)—the Quakers—that the committee would like to interview us about being their representatives in Chile.

We arrived in Chile in October 1977. I was seven months pregnant, and our first son, Peter, was born on Christmas Day. Our second son, Benjamin, was born in Chile in 1979. I loved being a mother, and my maternal sentiments awakened a surprising link to the struggle against Chile's dictatorship. I felt a deep connection to the mothers whose loved ones had been "disappeared." I became more aware of the role that women—as women—were playing in the resistance movement. Although I had worked closely with women's groups in both El Salvador and in Huarochiri, my overriding commitment was to the class struggle. Although I was still firmly within the liberation framework of class analysis, in my last year in Chile I began to read about feminism.

The four years we spent in Chile (1977–81) were intense. This was the height of the Pinochet dictatorship, and our work involved supporting human rights groups, soup kitchens, artisan groups, and Mapuche groups, as well as sending reports monitoring the human rights situation back to AFSC headquarters. We worked closely with the Catholic church's Vicariate of Solidarity and also participated actively in a CEB located in a shantytown on Santiago's west side. In June 1981 David was arrested and interrogated by Chile's secret intelligence service for twenty-four hours. After some negotiation he was allowed to stay in Chile until October, when we agreed to leave the country.

The Second Stage: The 1980s

I spent much of this decade trying to make sense of all that happened to me in El Salvador and Peru and in Chile under the Pinochet dictatorship. In early 1982 we arrived in Lima to work with the weekly *Latinamerica Press/Noticias Aliadas*. David served as director, and I was managing editor. We spent seven years reporting on the church and the world of the poor in Latin America—always from the perspective of liberation theology.

This was a privileged time. We were in contact with the key actors struggling for structural change in the 1980s, working for a viable socialism that would take into account the idiosyncrasies of Latin America. I interviewed many of the key liberation theologians in those years, including Gustavo Gutiérrez, Leonardo and Clodovis Boff, Jon Sobrino, Sergio Torres, Diego Irrarázaval, and Ronaldo Muñoz. I also interviewed *comandantes* in the liberated areas of El Salvador, women who were searching for their disappeared loved ones, pastoral workers, and religious sisters and priests who were committed to a new way of being church among the poor. We worked to show the region's "other face," which was ignored by the mainline media.

In 1983 I joined several women who had participated in a workshop entitled "Patriarchy and the Church" at a meeting of Latin American feminists. At our meeting on the outskirts of Lima we formed what would become the Circle of Christian Feminists (Talitha Cumi), a collective of women committed to a feminist perspective on issues of faith and society. Two of Talitha's founders, Maryknoll sisters Rose Timothy Gavin and Rose Dominic Trapasso (the famous Roses of Lima), became mentors for me. Working with these women, I began to see the implications of patriarchy—especially as it exists within the Catholic church and even within liberation theology. I also began to search for more relevant images of the Sacred to nourish my spirituality. I started to question the obvious absence of women among the liberation theologians and the absence of concern within liberation theology about issues involving the lives of poor women, such as domestic violence. By the end of the decade I was deeply engaged in proposals coming from feminist theology and its challenges to liberation theology. And, in the end, I had become tired of so much martyrdom and so many calls for sacrifice to bring about a revolution that never seemed to come.

We left Lima in 1989 and went to Rome, where David became executive secretary of IDOC, an international documentation center, and I was named editor of the bimonthly magazine *IDOC Internazionale*. We were supposed to turn a dying organization around, but, in the end, it couldn't be done. My work there was exciting, though, because my mandate was to give the magazine a new focus—a fusion of ecology and theology from a third-world perspective. Slowly I began to rethink my world view and my place within the larger story of the universe.

The Third Stage: The 1990s to the Present

David and I had been close to the Maryknoll missioners for many years. In 1990 we decided to leave Rome and return to Latin America through Maryknoll's lay mission program. As lay missioners, we returned to Chile in early 1991, and our two sons, now teenagers, rediscovered their Chilean roots.

I returned to Chile as a convinced feminist and as a budding ecologist. In Rome I had devoured books and articles dealing with discoveries from what has come to be called the new science. Basic to this conversion was Thomas Berry's *The Dream of the Earth*. Berry, along with authors such as Brian Swimme, Charlene Spretnak, and Starhawk, captivated me with their new understanding of the universe as an ever more complex, transformational cosmogenesis. I began to realize that everything is—and always has been—interconnected, but that somewhere during our development as a species we managed to forget that basic fact. It seemed that our thought processes and systems were themselves permeated with dualism and patriarchy. My feminism evolved toward ecofeminism, and my theological questions veered toward more cosmological quests. Today I am comfortable describing the developing Mystery in which we live as "the call of the future," because it is compatible with my understanding of cosmogenesis.

I searched for a community in Chile like the one I had experienced in Lima with Talitha Cumi. Such a Christian feminist organization did not yet exist in Santiago, but several women expressed interest in forming a group where we could celebrate our lives and our spiritualities without fear of being criticized. This is how the Con-spirando Collective was born.

In 1993 Ivone Gebara came to Chile and gave a course on holistic ecofeminism. Her insights were like rain on dry land. I felt she was naming and contextualizing my questions and doubts about how to define God, the place of Jesus in my life today, and how to be faithful to the option for the poor and to the struggle for a better world when I no longer have the revolutionary fervor of the previous decades.

Compared with the 1970s and 1980s, I seem to have no "great project" to struggle for, although I admit being drawn to the idea of being part of a bioregion, an ecological village, a "shared garden." I continue to search for a sustainable economic and cultural model that can be an alternative to current neoliberal capitalism. We try to eat lower on the food chain; to commit to recycling, composting, organic gardening; and to use the bus more and the car less. David is much more diligent at this than I am. I do focus on planning and celebrating rituals to capture where we are on our journey. Over time these rituals have become less verbal and more embodied through a freer use of dance and movement.

I still am searching for ever more authentic answers to the meaning of life. Although I have grown tremendously uncomfortable with the androcentrism and anthropocentrism of the central doctrines of Christianity, I do not consider myself post-Christian. I am a pilgrim who, along with many others, is searching for post-patriarchal theological *and* cosmological answers that will give us energy and pleasure in being alive at this time in history in this small corner of the planet.

In the end all of us, our history and our future, are radically connected to the fate of this fragile green planet we call home. We are entering a new epoch where we humans need to engage in a profound listening to voices long forgotten: those of the sea, the rivers, the mountains, the forests, the stars, the moon; those arising from our genetic memory—our ancestors, both human and otherwise; those of our own bodies—mine, yours, the friend who has been abused, the new baby, the youngster, the old woman now wrinkled and worn, the Earth itself. Key to this is a broader sense of kinship. In a very real way there is no "other"; the other is myself, because we all come from the same source.

THE CURRENT STATUS OF LIBERATION THEOLOGY

While Latin American feminist and ecofeminist theologies grew out of liberation theology, they now take a more critical view of several of liberation theology's key tenets. A review of the current status of liberation theology can be helpful. A heated debate is now taking place within liberation theology as to whether or not it is in crisis, given what appears to be the collapse of historical socialism. Some theologians, like Gustavo Gutiérrez, continue to insist that the end of the communist world does not affect liberation theology because its commitment was never to Marxism but to the poor. He argues that liberation theology is more urgently needed than ever in the face of neoliberal capitalism, which has aggravated the disparities between rich and poor.[12] Gutiérrez reaffirms the preferential option for the poor, reminding us that poverty has human and socioeconomic causes. While he acknowledges that liberation theology may have overemphasized economic factors, he insists that in its description of the poor as the "insignificant ones of history," women, especially poor women, as well as ethnic minorities were always implicitly included. He particularly welcomes current reinterpretations of the Bible from a women's perspective.[13]

Juan-José Tamayo, a Spanish liberation theologian who has written and taught extensively on Latin American liberation theology for more than thirty years, is one of the more enthusiastic protagonists of including emerging Latin American theologies under the general heading of liberation theology. Tamayo believes that while at first liberation theology emphasized the socioeconomic aspects of poverty and class conflict, now, conscious of its own reductionism, it has opened itself to the new faces of the poor—marginal races and ethnic groups, cultures that have been overlooked, religions that have been outlawed, doubly and in many cases triply oppressed women, oppressed nature, abandoned street children, entirely excluded peoples and countries, and so on.[14] Convinced that liberation theology must grapple with the major changes of the twenty-first century, he welcomes challenges coming from "new faces."

Tamayo is also aware of the discomfort feminist theologians feel about the androcentrism of much of liberation theology, and he lauds feminist theologians' use of the hermeneutics of suspicion to deconstruct categories that exclude women not only from theological discussion but from the Christian experience itself. He underlines the work feminist theologians are doing in initiating a post-patriarchal reconstruction of Christianity. Familiar with the ecofeminist posture of Con-spirando, he sees ecofeminism as a logical development in the search to discover the root causes of women's oppression and the destruction of the Earth. Tamayo views these as exciting, viable themes that liberation theology must address, and he speaks of both feminist and ecofeminist liberation theology.[15]

However, some leading Latin American liberation theologians are not as enthusiastically open to these new faces. Tension was evident at the theological congress sponsored by the Sociedad de Teología y Ciencias de la Religión (SOTER) held in Brazil in July 2000, where many of the "fathers" of liberation theology were present. It became evident during the congress that humanity is not only facing a major change in epoch but an end to a theological era "characterized by fragmentation and a search for new theological spaces, an enormously complex time in its pluralism, but at the same time promising and fruitful in its resources."[16]

It was neither feminist nor ecofeminist theology that produced a heated debate at the congress, but rather Leonardo Boff's work in the area of ecological theology. In his presentation Boff expanded his definition of the option for the poor. In the 1960s, he said, liberation theology emphasized the economically and politically poor; in the 1970s the definition was extended to the culturally poor and included indigenous peoples, blacks, and other discriminated minorities; in the 1980s emphasis was given to the question of gender and the oppression of women; and now in the 1990s, liberation theology had begun to hear the cry of the earth,

> also impoverished because it is unjustly despoiled and exploited systematically. For each concrete oppression, we responded by developing a corresponding strategy and liberating pedagogy. Never has the Theology of Liberation fallen victim to an impoverished concept of the poor. It always tried to deepen its understanding of the complex reality of any poverty imposed unjustly.[17]

The great "poor" at this time, then, is the Earth itself, which humanity can collectively destroy. We must change, or we will perish, Boff warns, using the metaphor of the spaceship with a few first-class passengers and many poor, the latter confined to the baggage department. But both groups depend on the welfare of the ship. There will be no Noah's ark this time round to save a few while the rest perish.[18]

Boff calls upon liberation theology to situate its reflection in the context of the new cosmology that has emerged from the latest scientific discoveries and that contemplates a broader understanding of evolution. He argues that all of us are being held hostage by a way of living and ways of production and by relations with the environment that imply systematic violence against persons, social classes, countries, ecosystems, and the Earth itself. He concludes:

> The option for the poor—the hallmark of Theology of Liberation—must be integral: all the poor with all their many faces, and the great poor one, the Earth, known as Gaia, Pachamama, and Great Mother. It is important to free all. But there are priorities. First is the urgent need to liberate the Earth through a real revolution in our paradigm of relationality with her. . . . This suggests a holistic paradigm based on reverence, respect and care for her biodiversity, integrity, and beauty.[19]

Boff's expansion of the option for the poor to include the Earth itself caused a major altercation between him and his brother Clodovis at one of the plenary sessions. Clodovis Boff represents those liberation theologians who find Leonardo Boff's embracing of the new cosmology dangerous to liberation theology's traditional commitment to poor and downtrodden *people*. In Gustavo Gutiérrez's words, *¿Dónde dormirán los pobres?* (Where will the poor sleep?). It is the poor majorities of Latin America who have always been the central focus of liberation theology. There is a growing fear among some liberation theologians that the concrete lives of the poor will no longer be the locus of their theology and that the issue of the poor seems to be losing its theological and ethical prominence.[20] There is also fear that the traditional concerns of liberation theology will be watered down by new paradigms, such as the new cosmology. It seems likely that this debate will continue.

José Comblin, another of liberation theology's pioneers, is more blunt in his assessment of liberation theology's future: "Liberation theology is at a standstill," he says, "because Catholic theology and Christian theology in general are at a standstill; nothing new is coming out . . . there is no more interest in theology."[21] Comblin is pessimistic about liberation theology's accomplishments. Now eighty, he feels free to be blunt. He says that the major reason there has been stagnation in people's willingness to participate in CEBs is the arrival of television. Even more pointedly, he says that the CEB movement arose not from the people but from pastoral agents who saw in them a new form of church and the promise of a new society. When such hopes were frustrated, pastoral agents often gave up.[22] He finds the CEBs riddled with clericalism and therefore condemned to wither on the vine. He notes that Catholics, along with everyone else, are consulting other wisdom traditions and constructing their own belief syntheses.

Comblin believes that if liberation theology had been grounded in a strong autonomous culture, it too could have been autonomous. But given the current state of Latin American culture, he notes, such a situation is still a dream. He asks: "Where is Latin American liberation theology taught today? Who reads it? In Latin America, a tiny minority of the educated religious public. Rejection has produced an isolation, the upshot of which is that liberation theology is better known and more read in Europe and the United States than in Latin America itself."[23] For Comblin, the value of liberation theology is that it questions theology as a whole. It directs Christian thinking beyond traditional Scholastic theology and the church's traditional social teaching inspired by that theology.[24] However, he challenges some of liberation theology's most prized affirmations. For instance, he says that the "irruption of the poor" happened only in the sense that the church became aware of the poor. He also argues that while liberation theologians and pastoral workers were proposing radical change, most of the poor simply wanted to improve their lives. The real revolution, in his opinion, took place in the second half of the twentieth century with the migration of millions of *campesinos* to the cities. That migration meant moving from one civilization to another.[25] He also criticizes consciousness-raising as "injecting ideology into the mind of the popular classes: a task of instilling doctrine so that the people would learn to feel what the theory said that they ought to feel and to want what the theory said that they should want."[26]

Comblin notes that the last stronghold of Christianity was the family. But with the sexual revolution and the discovery of effective means of birth control, women were able to cut the cords of total economic dependency on their male partners. He marks other effects of the sexual revolution: the manifestation of those "repressions, fantasies, and taboos—an unconscious or semiconscious world that had never been brought to awareness. . . . For many women, the sexual revolution was—and still is—experienced as the most visible and most vital manifestation of personal freedom."[27]

Comblin concludes that women, indigenous people, and blacks have been unwilling to be assimilated into liberation theology, and rightly so; the starting point for feminist theology has been a questioning of almost the entire history of humanity from the perspective of patriarchy. "For women, it is not enough to return to early Christianity: the solution will not be found there. And it is not very likely that the issue of women will be resolved through a theology, because it has much deeper roots which go beyond the domain of Christianity."[28]

Comblin's frank evaluation concurs with what other analyses have pointed out. Although the problems of poverty, marginality, and inequitable income distribution have been exacerbated in recent decades, there is a growing shift in consciousness. The current situation does not result from capitalism alone but from a system, which today we name patriarchy, that goes back more than five thousand years. Although liberation theology has been persecuted by an increasingly conservative papacy, this is not the major cause for its apparent demise. The collapse of historical socialism has meant the loss of a utopian horizon, without which it becomes difficult to focus, mobilize, and sustain a struggle for a different, more just world. That world must be able to be imagined, and at this juncture of history, it cannot be. No revolution can survive without a utopian vision, and today, the old words and symbols that once energized a generation of liberation theology activists no longer evoke such revolutionary energy. It appears that a deep historical shift is taking place.

Some would see this shift as a call to go deeper and address issues neglected by liberation theology and to seek new paradigms and new sources of inspiration. Many liberation theologians see this as an enriching experience, while others maintain that questions coming from feminist and cosmological perspectives go beyond the basic commitment of liberation theology to the poor. New issues include analyzing not only neoliberal capitalism as the cause of oppression but also the older oppression of patriarchy; questioning the traditional theism of an omnipotent, anthropomorphic Creator; and addressing the lingering dualism that separates mind from matter, natural from supernatural, and the human from the rest of the life community. At the same time it is important to stress that liberation theology has opened the door for those who have gone on to newer theological perspectives—indeed, it unveiled the possibility of dreaming in new ways. It is also necessary to acknowledge that the realities of poverty, injustice, and oppression that liberation theology addressed in the 1970s and 1980s have not gone away and that the blood of the martyrs still cries out. But the new millennium brings urgent new challenges and questions to be addressed:

- Can we speak of the poor and their children inheriting the Earth if it is devastated and poisoned, bereft of so many soulful presences?
- Can we live out an option for the poor without rediscovering our deep kinship with all living beings, our spiritual belonging to the wildly creative, deeply spiritual, unfathomably interdependent network we call the cosmos?
- Can we be of service to the Latin American poor, mostly *mestizos*, without more deeply imbibing the religious wisdom of their largely forgotten indigenous heritage?

- Can love for the people be sustained without a profound re-discovery of our bodies, of the healing and animating power of tenderness and sensuality?
- Can we expect the poor to be empowered while failing to deal with our gender issues, our hierarchical habits, our Western craving for control?
- Can our solidarity bear fruit if our allegiance is to an immutable anthropomorphic deity with a ready-made plan for the human future?
- Can the God-images of traditional theism fill us with the energy, the burning passion required to face these historic challenges?[29]

THE FEMINIST AND ECOFEMINIST CRITIQUE OF LIBERATION THEOLOGY

Although Latin American feminist and ecofeminist theologians do not dispute their origins in liberation theology they are now experiencing varying degrees of ambiguity about whether they are still doing liberation theology, or if their criticisms of patriarchal theology place them outside this playing field. While most feminist theologians are increasingly critical of liberation theology's ingrained androcentrism, many first-generation liberation theologians—and most are clerics—have been the teachers of today's feminist and ecofeminist theologians. Thus there is a long history of friendship and a certain reluctance to criticize one's mentors. In addition to these strong personal relationships, feminist theologians still agree with much of liberation theology's analysis, especially regarding the devastating effects of the current neoliberal economic model on the region's poor. They ask, "What can feminist theology from Latin America and the Caribbean contribute to the knowledge, criticism, and defeat of this globalized, neo-liberal economy?"[30] They also engage in theology from the locus of the poor, focusing on poor women and continually deepening their analysis of the feminization of poverty in a globalized world.[31]

One of the severest criticisms feminist and ecofeminist theologians level against historical liberation theology is its avoidance of the issues of sexual and reproductive rights, especially as they affect poor women. Finnish feminist scholar Elina Vuola has examined this gap in her book *Limits of Liberation*. She charges that the stances of Latin American liberation theologians on sexual ethics have not moved from traditional Catholic teaching, which reflects the church's misogynist view of women. She notes, "One of the first causes of death for women of reproductive age all over the Third World, including Latin America, is the complications after an illegal abortion, [but] preventing the death of poor women has not been an explicit part of liberation theologians' 'agenda' of defending the poor."[32]

Vuola views the concept of the poor in liberation theology as vague and homogenized. Until recently the poor were defined principally in economic terms and as productive and political subjects.[33] She points out that "there has been a yawning gap in LT [liberation theology] which has to do with human corporality, sexuality and sexual ethics. The right of a female subject to her body and 'bodiliness' has been absent."[34] There seems to be an inability to see "domestic" problems as "real" problems, given the supposedly more pressing survival struggles of the poor majorities. Furthermore, the unequal power struggles existing between men and women have been largely ignored. This, Vuola charges, underlines liberation theology's disconnection between theory and practice: "Nothing is said of the reality of illegal abortions and the high rates of domestic violence and households headed by women, which are some of the most burning problems for Latin American women."[35] She concludes that sexual ethics is an area in which liberation theologians are far from their stated ideals and method as a praxis-oriented theology that considers ethical reasoning and action key. She insists that defending poor women has not been part of liberation theology's priorities. The reason is that "'the poor' are seen mainly as productive subjects, understood in the framework of Marxist class analysis, and not as bodily, gendered, and reproductive subjects as well."[36]

Mexican feminist theologian María Pilar Aquino argues the same point:

> The masculine theological focus has covered up the oppressive relations lived in the private area, and concealed relationships of domination exercised in the domestic sphere, where it is women who always endure the worse part. Ordinary daily life for an androcentric vision does not have epistemological value, nor does it form part of its attempts to understand the horizon of reality, that is, it does not influence the doing of theology. What, in effect, happens here is that the masculine theological focus grants a character of *naturality* to private, everyday life.[37]

Criticism of liberation theology's androcentric vision has come to the fore in the third phase of feminist theology. Ecofeminist theologian Ivone Gebara argues that while feminist theology embraces liberation theology's critique of Euro-centered universalism, liberation theology is guilty of a similar masculine and androcentric universalism—the result of the education and formation of most male liberation theologians (primarily clerics, she stresses) in Aristotelian and Thomistic philosophy and theology. This, she says, is where the two perspectives are most in conflict. Ecofeminist theology relies on different philosophical sources and conducts its research outside clerical circles and at the margins of ecclesial centers of power.[38] Liberation theology's frame of reference continues to be one of underlining the discontinuity between God's life and human life. Gebara argues that

> the fundamentally anthropocentric and androcentric character of liberation theology appears unquestionable. It speaks of God in human history, a God who in the end remains the Creator and Lord. . . . It senses no need to reexamine the cosmological and anthropological foundations of the Christian faith. It reaffirms the goodness and justice of God's being without raising questions about the

repercussions, throughout human history, of traditional or historically conditioned images of God.[39]

I will return to these arguments in Chapter 3 when I review Gebara's understanding of ecofeminism.

FEMINIST BIBLICAL HERMENEUTICS

There are two very clear currents within the third stage of Latin American feminist theology: holistic ecofeminism and feminist biblical hermeneutics. The two are not exclusive and can indeed complement one another. But those feminist scholars working to reinterpret biblical texts from the standpoint of feminist hermeneutics are, perhaps, more committed than their ecofeminist counterparts to redeeming biblical traditions from their patriarchal interpretations.[40] According to Colombian feminist biblicist, Carmiña Navia Velasco, feminist biblical scholarship is alive and well in Latin America. She reports that today it is not just a question of rereading texts with a critical feminist eye but also of searching for and examining the scriptures on topics that range from themes such as the body to violence and peace. She mentions feminist biblicists such as Alicia Winters, Tania Sampaio, Elsa Tamez, Irene Foulkes, and herself, among others, and cites the biblical journal *RIBLA*, published in Costa Rica, as a major publisher for their work.[41]

Navia Velasco says that ecofeminism in Latin America is especially rich in offering a more vibrant spirituality, including "a full reconciliation with one's being born a woman; a rediscovery of one's female genealogy and the role played by mothers, grandmothers, aunts, etc. in transmitting the faith; a joyful and full reconciliation with our bodies; a search for alternative forms of tenderness; and above all, a recovery and reworking of traditional symbols of the sacred."[42] Here she mentions the contributions of Ivone Gebara and the Con-spirando Collective.

This second current, ecofeminism, along with its implications for theology, ethics, and spirituality, will be explored in the following chapters.

I sense that "all creation is groaning" for a new vision of who we are. We are in a time of Great Turning, of the Great-in-Between, some would say even a dark time. We are experiencing the waning days of some larger historical period but cannot yet glimpse the rebirth to come. Who are we? What do we want? What appears to be happening at the psychic level to many of us? I have no answers, only intimations, most of which come from a more holistic perspective offered by ecofeminism. So, along with a growing number of Latin American women, I invite you to consider ecofeminism, its theory and its practice.

2

Sources
of Ecofeminism

All beings at some time have been my mother.
　　　　　　—BUDDHIST TEACHING

There is a story—both ancient and new—that we are earth-lings, that both our past and our future are radically connected to the fate of this fragile green planet we call home. Ecofeminism is simply a radical remembering of this—of who we are. Ecofeminists insist that the interdependence of all things is the *constitutive reality* of the universe. Now, in the opening years of a new millennium, there appears to be an urgency to refashion ourselves as a species. Discoveries made during the last twenty years in quantum physics and in biology have radically changed our definitions of the origin and scope of our universe as well as who we are as a species. This major paradigm shift challenges our current understanding of the universe and draws us toward the idea of an emerging cosmology in which the material universe is seen as a dynamic web of interrelated events.

Many fields of study that explore these interconnections, including the new science and cybernetics, are discussed in this chapter. Ecofeminism has also gained insights from radical or cultural feminism, the subject of Chapter 3.

ANCIENT WISDOM TRADITIONS

Although *ecofeminism* is a relatively new term, it describes a deep intuition that has been present in many wisdom traditions, including medieval Christian mysticism, Buddhism, and Shamanism, to name only three. These traditions affirm communion with nature and describe the Divine in terms that are other than masculine or heaven centered. While it is not possible to examine these ancient roots here, it is worth noting the renewed interest among ecofeminist theologians in the life and work of Hildegard of Bingen, a twelfth-century German mystic. Hildegard's reflections on God's "greening" as that vital energy present in all creation are closely linked to deep ecology's belief that all matter is bio-spiritual.

Among more contemporary influences are four precursors who have influenced current ecofeminist thought, especially my own. In 1962 Thomas Kuhn, in his now classic *The Structure of Scientific Revolutions*, described the concept of paradigm as "a constellation of achievements—concepts, values, techniques, etc.—shared by a scientific community and used by that community to define legitimate problems and solutions."[1] According to Kuhn, shifts in paradigms occur in rapid, discontinuous, and revolutionary breaks. Now, forty years after he described the paradigm shift taking place within the scientific world through quantum physics, we are aware that this was part of a much larger shift in cultural transformation, as we shall see below.

Another precursor is Albert Einstein, that great human being of the last century who developed the theory of relativity. We now know that the universe is expanding and therefore had a beginning, and this discovery opened the doors for other scientists to begin to question earlier ways of thinking. In the second half of the twentieth century quantum physicists began to see that there is no such thing as an "essential building block of life" because matter at the subatomic level dissolves into wave patterns that can behave in an infinite number of ways. Nature, it seems, is made up of a complex web of relationships that compose, in the end, a unified whole. This has caused a revolution in the scientific world and changed the definitions of the material basis for life.

A third precursor is marine biologist Rachel Carson, whom many have dubbed the first ecofeminist. In 1962 she wrote *Silent Spring*, now considered the first alert to the industrialized world about the interconnectedness of all life. She was a leading voice against the use of DDT, one of the "dirty dozen" pesticides. DDT was routinely sprayed on some of the richest agricultural lands in California to rid crops of insects. Carson pointed out that one cannot kill the insects without killing the songbirds, and one cannot kill the songbirds without poisoning the children. Carson argued that pesticides make their way through the food chain, seeping into the water supply and into the soil; chemicals spread on crops poison the birds and animals and humans and thus create a "silent spring." The chemical industry's response to Carson was to mock her as a "spinster in galoshes who worried about birds."[2]

A final precursor is the French Jesuit paleontologist Pierre Teilhard de Chardin, who first raised the possibility that the cosmos was conscious (the noosphere) and therefore sacred. It was he who first told us that we live in a self-transforming universe or "cosmogenesis." His books *The Phenomenon of Man* and *The Divine Milieu* nourished a whole generation of seekers within the Catholic world and beyond.

WOMEN ACTIVISTS

Ecofeminism in Latin America is quite new; indeed, its philosophy and theology are only now becoming known and accepted, and the environmental activism of women is not seen necessarily as ecofeminist practice. However, in other parts of the Third World—especially in India—ecofeminist activists have been raising their voices since the 1970s.

Credit for coining the word *ecofeminism* is given to French feminist Françoise d'Eaubonne, who argued in 1974 that male control of production and of women's sexuality brought the twin horsemen of environmental destruction and overpopulation. She called for "a planet in the female gender."[3]

During the late 1970s and early 1980s the term *ecofeminist* was used to describe activist women who organized to protect themselves and their families from environmental disasters. Classic examples often cited include:

- The Chipko movement in India, a movement of poor women who protected large swatches of forest in the Himalayan mountains against clear-cutting by "hugging trees" (*chipko* in the native language) in defiance of the loggers' advance, causing them to retreat. The Chipko movement has been documented by Indian ecofeminist Vandana Shiva in her book *Staying Alive*, in which she relates how poor rural women's link with the natural world is the reality of their daily lives. She argues that "maldevelopment," which is synonymous with the violation of nature and women, has been created by the North as it imposes its model of development on other parts of the world.[4]
- The Green Belt movement in Kenya, led by anatomy teacher Wangari Maathai, which has galvanized hundreds of rural women to engage in extensive tree-planting to resolve firewood shortages as well as to prevent desertification and soil erosion by surrounding their villages with a "green belt." In 2004 Dr. Maathai won the Nobel Peace Prize for her work.
- The Love Canal protest in Niagara Falls, New York, led by housewife Lois Gibbs, who exposed the fact that for many years government officials had been using an abandoned canal trench as a chemical dump. It had been covered over and a school had been built on the site. The chemicals had also seeped into the town's water supply. Gibbs began documenting the relationship between the town's inordinately high number of birth defects and miscarriages and the chemical dump. No one believed this "hysterical housewife" until Gibbs found a scientist to translate her "housewife data" into legitimate scientific jargon.[5]

In Latin America, one of the most dynamic movements is the ecology movement. The majority of its members are women and young people. Worldwide, women form 60 to 80 percent of the membership in grassroots environmental organizations, even though the leadership profile does not reflect this phenomenon.[6]

While ecofeminism has firm theoretical underpinnings, it is important to note that ecofeminist practices usually emerge in a very practical manner from the critical demands of life—the imperatives of a particular historical setting—and not from any set theory. When women protest against the destruction of their environment, they usually make the connection between what is happening to their surroundings and the fact that they are women. They experience two kinds of violence—that waged against the environment and that, which perhaps they had not really noticed before, leveled against them because they are poor women (rural women in the case of India and Kenya or "hysterical housewives" in the case of the United States). In the last fifteen years a growing number of women—most of whom have not been politically active before—have become either indignant or terrified at what is happening to their environment along with the resulting ill effects on the health and well-being of their families. They recognize their vulnerability to increasing environmental disasters and their lack of access to the centers of power responsible for the disasters. This has led many women to critique the present model of development.

Ecofeminist theory continues to evolve from this activism and search. Women sense that there is a way to understand what is happening to the planet, and, in many cases, they also are looking for a spirituality that will nurture their struggles. Today, ecofeminism provides such a theoretical framework.

DEEP ECOLOGY

Deep ecology is an approach to environmental study that does not separate humans from the natural environment but conceives the planet as a network of phenomena that are fundamentally interconnected and interdependent. Deep ecology recognizes the intrinsic value of all living beings and views humans as only one particular strand in the web of life.[7]

Deep ecology is both a philosophical school and a global grassroots movement. It was founded by Norwegian philosopher Arne Naess in the early 1970s. Naess distinguished between "shallow" and "deep" ecology, characterizing shallow ecology as anthropocentric in that it views humans as above or outside nature, as the source of all value. Only by recognizing that humanity is no more but also no less important that the rest of the Earth community can humans learn to dwell within their own environmental niche and allow other species to flourish. For deep ecologists, anthropocentric hierarchies would be replaced by biocentric or ecocentric egalitarianism. Such a perspective views the world as an intrinsically dynamic web of relations in which there are no absolute dividing lines between the living and the nonliving, the animate and the inanimate, or the human and the nonhuman.[8] Deep ecology is passionately committed to overturning mindsets such as anthropocentrism, dualism, atomism, hierarchalism, rigid autonomy, and abstract nationalism, all of which seem partially responsible for humanity's destruction of the biosphere.[9] A mature humanity, deep ecologists agree, would understand its interrelationship with everything else.

For physicist Fritjof Capra, one of today's leading deep ecologists, deep ecology is ultimately committed to a deepening spiritual awareness: "When the concept of the human spirit is understood as the mode of consciousness in which the individual feels a sense of belonging, of connectedness to the cosmos as a whole, it becomes clear that ecological awareness is spiritual in its deepest essence."[10] Capra and others underline the paradigm shift in values that is taking place. They note the spiritual, psychological experience (as opposed to a more logical approach) that nature and the self are one. They point to a change in the perception of the self that gradually widens to identify with other beings. Michael Dowd summarizes the possibilities deep ecology offers:

> It offers reconnection to our genetic memory and billions of years of evolutionary wisdom. Its application can empower us to live in synergistic cooperation and harmony

with the rest of the body of Life. . . . We can begin to experience a consciousness of heavenly rapport with all of life. Timely as it may be, the message of deep ecology must . . . be put into fervent daily practice in every area of our lives. The planet is calling us to create communities that live and love ecologically. This is essential for the salvation of millions of species, especially our own.[11]

Deep ecologist Joanna Macy is a leading voice in this extended understanding of the self. I first encountered Macy's work through reading about a ritual she and ecologist John Seed developed called "The Council of All Beings."[12] Later, I heard about a series of "despair workshops" Macy was holding and felt a deep empathy with her. Macy, a Buddhist, is convinced that at this time we humans are feeling a profound despair that we try, unsuccessfully, to keep at bay. Nevertheless, we are being bombarded by data that question the survival of our culture, our species, and even our planet as a viable home for conscious life. Despair comes from our loss of the assumption that our species will inevitably pull thorough. Macy's "despair workshops" focus on acknowledging that inner pain and grief.

Macy maintains that until we can grieve for our planet and its future inhabitants, we cannot fully feel or enact our love for them. Such grief is frequently suppressed. At the root of this suppression lies a dysfunctional notion of the self as an isolated and fragile entity. So long as we see ourselves as essentially separate, competitive, and ego-identified beings, it is difficult to respect the validity of our social despair, deriving as it does from our interconnectedness. Macy believes that the acknowledgment of despair, like faith, is a letting go of the assumption that conscious ego can or should control all events.[13]

Macy sees four particular ways people on spiritual paths look at the world. First, the world is a *battlefield* where good and evil are pitted against each other. Such a view arouses courage and engenders a sense of certainty. This view is very strong among monotheistic religions. Second, the world is a *trap* from which we must disentangle ourselves and escape. This stance is based on a hierarchical view of reality, where mind is seen as higher than matter and spirit is set over and above nature. There is contempt for the material and a great emphasis on detachment from the tough work of social change. Third, the world is *lover.* Instead of a stage set for our moral battles or a prison from which to escape, the world is beheld as an intimate and gratifying partner. Desire plays a creative, world-manifesting role here; one feels embraced in the primal play of life. When we see the world as lover, every being, every phenomenon, can become an expression of that ongoing, erotic impulse. And fourth, the world is *self.* Hunger for this union springs from a deep knowing, to which mystics of all traditions give voice. For Macy, once the bonds of our limited egos are broken, the individual heart becomes one with its world.[14]

To experience the world as an extended self and its story as our own extended story does not necessitate a surrender of our individual self. Having gained distance and a certain sophistication of perception, Macy says that we can now recognize who we have been all along. Now we can realize that we are "our world knowing itself"—and thus relinquish our separateness:

> We have all gone that long journey, and now, richer for it, we come home to our mutual belonging. We return to experience, as we never could before, that we are both the self of our world and its cherished lover. We are not doomed to destroy it by the cravings of the separate ego and the technologies it fashioned. We can wake up to who we really are, and allow the waters of the Rhine to flow clean once more, and the trees to grow green along its banks.[15]

One of Macy's most compelling concepts is her notion of the "ecological self," or the "greening of the self," which she describes as that wider construct of identity and self-interest that is coextensive with other beings and the life of the planet. Macy believes that what is taking place is a shift in identification caused by three converging developments. First, the conventional small self, or ego-self, is being impinged upon by the psychological and spiritual effects brought on by the dangers of mass annihilation. Second, a new way of dismantling the ego-self is arising out of science itself, which now calls for a systems approach to every-thing. From the perspective of the new science, life is seen as dynamically composed of self-organizing systems, patterns that are sustained in and by their relationships. Third is the resurgence in our time of non-dualistic spiritualities. For Macy,

> the ecological self, like any notion of selfhood, is a meta-phoric construct and a dynamic one. It involves choice: choices can be made to identify at different moments, with different dimensions or aspects of our systemically interre-lated existence—be they hunted whales or homeless humans or the planet itself. In doing this, the extended self brings into play wider resources—courage, endurance, and inge-nuity—like a nerve cell in a neural net opening to the charge of the other neurons. *There is the sense of being acted through and sustained by those very beings on whose behalf one acts. This is very close to the religious concept of grace. In systems language we can talk about it as synergy.* With this extension, this green-ing of the self, we can find a sense of buoyancy and resil-ience that comes from letting flow through us strengths and resources that come to us with continuous surprise and sense of blessing.[16]

Insights coming from deep ecology have led activists to put their own lives at risk in defense of the planet's forests, oceans, rivers, and wildlife sanctuaries. A recent example is Julie "Butter-fly" Hill, who, beginning in 1998, spent two years living in a two-hundred-foot old-growth redwood tree in northern Cali-fornia to stop loggers from cutting it down. Hill spoke of her experience living in Luna (her name for the tree), described how she and the tree mystically became as one, and how in storms Luna actually protected her from thunder and lightning. She witnessed how living in Luna changed her entire perspective of the relatedness of all things.

However, while ecofeminists and deep ecologists share much in common and would generally agree that nature must be seen as alive and having its own agency, their emphasis is different. Ecofeminists' central criticism of deep ecology is that while it condemns anthropocentrism (human-centeredness), it ignores the role that androcentrism (male-centeredness) plays in ecological destruction. As ecofeminist Mary Mellor has pointed out, "The question of whether humanity as a whole should be held account-able for the ecological crisis, or some aspect of its internal orga-nization such as patriarchy, has given rise to a prolonged debate between ecofeminists and deep ecologists."[17] Ecofeminists see many male deep ecologists as remarkably sexist in their approach to saving the planet, with stress placed on male individualist val-ues such as reclaiming the "wild man" or the "noble man con-fronting nature," or the "freedom to roam the forests as the pe-rennial backpacker."[18] They call upon deep ecologists to embrace a "lived awareness that we experience in relation to particular beings as well as to the larger whole." They also call for a more grounded approach to human-nature relations, which include the issue of sex/gender relations and the particularity of women's lives.[19]

Ecofeminist Marti Kheel is especially clear on this point: "Whereas the anthropocentric world view perceives humans as the center or apex of the natural world, the androcentric analysis suggests that this world view is unique to men." Kheel questions whether deep ecologists' search for an expanded self is "a way of transcending the concrete world of particularity."[20] She reminds us that, under patriarchy, women's identities, unlike those of men, have been identified with the devalued natural world. This issue will be addressed more fully below.

THE NEW SCIENCE

Deep ecology owes much of its shift in world view to scien-tific discoveries in the later part of the twentieth century. While a detailed discussion of these discoveries is impossible here, an overview can show the enormity of the changes. Excellent sum-maries of these discoveries can be found in the writings of Tho-mas Berry and Brian Swimme, Fritjof Capra's *The Web of Life*, and Irish priest and sociologist Diarmuid O'Murchu's *Quan-tum Theology*.[21] These authors point to a paradigm shift from a mechanistic and reductionist way of understanding the universe, one that concentrated on the parts that make up the whole, to an emphasis on the whole, or on what has come to be called systems thinking. As Capra explains: "A system has come to mean an integrated whole whose essential properties arise from the relationships between its parts and 'systems thinking' is the understanding of a phenomenon within the context of a larger whole."[22] Systems thinking began among organic biologists who observed that the essential properties of an organism are the essential properties of the whole that none of the parts has unto itself. These properties arise from the *relationships* among the parts and can only be understood within the context of the larger whole. This shift in perception created a profound revolution in the way scientists think.

The next science to have its world view shaken was physics. The reductionist view had been that all physical phenomena could be reduced to the smallest "building block" or particle. However, the principles of quantum physics demonstrated that there are no building blocks at the subatomic level but only wave-like patterns of probabilities of interconnections. The amazing discovery here was that "sub-atomic particles have no meaning as isolated entities but can be understood only as interconnections, or correlations. . . . In other words, sub-atomic particles are not 'things' but interconnections among things and these, in turn, are interconnections among other things, and so on. In quantum theory we never end up with any 'things'; we always deal with interconnections."[23] As Werner Heisenberg, one of the founders of quantum theory, puts it, "The world thus appears as a complicated tissue of events, in which connections of different kinds alternate or overlap or combine and thereby determine the texture of the whole."[24]

Systems thinking uses the concept of a network to describe living systems. At each level the parts of one network turn out to be smaller networks. Thus networks nest within other networks. Seen in another way, the new science posits that our universe is a sphere of belonging—indeed, there are "horizons of belonging," which biologist Rupert Sheldrake calls "fields."

Sheldrake believes we belong to something greater than ourselves, something that is forever unfolding and evolving.[25]

Beginning with Einstein's development of the theory of relativity, then, the mechanistic world view that had dominated scientific thought for two hundred years began to unravel. This world view began in the sixteenth and seventeenth centuries when the earlier notion of the universe as an organic, living being was replaced by the idea that the world was a machine. René Descartes and Isaac Newton were both significant figures within the Enlightenment's scientific revolution. Descartes was responsible for the method of analytic thinking, which consisted of breaking everything into pieces in order to understand the whole by understanding the properties of its parts. Descartes viewed the world as a perfect machine governed by mathematical laws. Newton applied this same reasoning to the solar system, concluding that the universe was a large mechanical system running according to laws of motion that were entirely predictable and deterministic. The metaphor was that of a clock, with God as the Great Timekeeper who wound the clock and then sat back and let the universe tick on its own.

However, with the advent of systems thinking, today's scientific revolution has returned to an earlier, more organic view of the universe. For instance, scientists have learned that time and space are not two separate entities but that together they form a space-time continuum, and that energy and mass are, in fact, part of the same phenomenon and must be understood in relation to each other. This theory was extended to include gravity, the mutual attraction of all bodies with mass, which has the effect of curving space and time. Thus our universe is not a flat plane but a curved one—and it is this curvature that effectively holds everything in place and enables the universal life process to function as a whole.

Following Einstein's lead, scientists began to question the determinist laws of nature of Descartes, Newton, and their followers and to posit—again—a living universe. They discovered that radiation (either light or heat) is not emitted continuously but in the form of quanta, energy packets that could be either particles or waves depending on how and in what medium they were observed. Quantum physics has revolutionized the way scientists understand the subatomic world. It appears that there is no basic building block but only probabilities. As Diarmuid O'Murchu summarizes:

> It is at a perceptual level that the theory evokes a new way of viewing and understanding our world. In essence, it states that everything we perceive and experience is a great deal more than the initial, external impression we may obtain, that we experience life, not in isolated segments, but in wholes (quanta); that these bundles of energy which impinge upon us are not inert, lifeless pieces of matter, but living energies; that our naming of the living reality we experience will at least be a probability-guess at what its real essence is (an essence best understood by interacting with it experientially rather than trying to conceptualize it at an "objective" distance).[26]

Basic to the paradigm shift from the mechanistic view (the whole equals the sum of its parts) is that the whole is *greater* than the sum of its parts; furthermore, the whole is also contained in each of its parts. Thus the concept of *holon* (Greek for whole) is beginning to emerge as a new metaphor to name this shift, and we now speak of a hologram as that key feature whereby each part contains information about the whole object.

David Bohm, a physicist who worked with Einstein, has proposed that the universe itself is a hologram. All that unfolds before our eyes is but an external, fragmentary manifestation of an underlying unbroken wholeness that he calls an "implicit order." Bohm holds that all matter can be discussed in terms of folding and unfolding. Every part of the universe is related to every other part but in different degrees. Our primary reality, according to Bohm, is the implicit order, which is the subtle, universal reservoir of all life, the wellspring of all possibility, and the source of all meaning. The explicit order, that which is visible, is the product of the implicit order. The primary reality is not the external, visible sensory world but the invisible, enfolded realm of potential and possibility.[27]

What we perceive, then, is not a landscape of facts or objects but one of events, process, movement, and energy. Bohm saw in this creative flow that past, present, and future are one. Each creation of matter is a recapitulation of all past creation and carries an inherent propensity to become something more than it is at any present moment. Moreover, the universe seems to be knit together by a type of memory network that builds matter around itself in various forms ranging from molecules to plants, to stars and galaxies, to our own species. O'Murchu, influenced by Bohm, concludes: "Wholeness, which is largely unmanifest and dynamic (not stable) in nature, is the wellspring of all possibility. In seeking to understand life, we begin with the whole, which is always greater than the sum of the parts; paradoxically, the whole is contained in each part, and yet no whole is complete in itself."[28]

This change in the perception of reality is affecting not only physics and biology but also astronomy, geology, chemistry, and mathematics. It is not surprising that a new language for understanding the complex, highly integrative systems of life has emerged as well, including terms such as *dynamic systems theory, theory of complexity, nonlinear dynamics, network dynamics,* and so on. The list of pioneers in the "new science" grows every day as scientists bring their expertise to bear on the conviction described by biologist Elisabet Sahtouris: "Our planet and its creatures constitute a single self-regulating system that is in fact a great living being, or organism."[29]

CYBERNETICS

Additional insights come from the field of cybernetics, the study of the patterns of organization. These insights tend to break down former dualisms between mind and body and thus contribute to the paradigm shift taking place in the scientific world.

The most widely known cyberneticist is Gregory Bateson. Bateson thought of himself primarily as a biologist and saw the many fields he became involved with—anthropology, epistemology, psychiatry, cybernetics—as branches of biology. His lifelong aim was to discover common principles of organization in their diversity, or, as he put it "the pattern that connects." Although Bateson is hard for most non-scientists to understand, he is unquestionably a seminal thinker of our times. His systems approach has made significant contributions in the area of family therapy; he has also developed a cybernetic model of alcoholism and authored the double-bind theory of schizophrenia.[30] However, Bateson's most important contribution to science and philosophy is a concept of Mind based on cybernetic principles. His thinking, which opened the door to understanding the nature of Mind as a systems phenomenon, was the first successful attempt in science to overcome the Cartesian division between mind and body.

Batesonian holism posits that:

- fact and value are inseparable
- nature is revealed in our relations with it, and phenomena can be known only in context
- unconscious mind is primary
- quality takes precedence over quantity
- mind/body, subject/object are each two aspects of the same process
- circuitry rather than infinite, linear progress is the norm
- single variables in the system cannot be maximized
- we cannot know more than a fraction of reality
- logic is dialectical and requires both/and
- process, form, and relationship are primary
- wholes have properties that parts do not have
- living systems, or Minds, are not reducible to their components
- nature is alive[31]

Bateson was convinced that it was possible to find the same sort of laws at work in the structure of a crystal as in the structure of society. He believed that all phenomena, including individuals and societies, are organized entities that are "coded" in a coherent

manner. Immersed as he was in cybernetic theory, Bateson saw
that we live in a world of circuit structures and that we know a
thing only in context, in relation to other things. He developed
an epistemology that holds that there are always Minds within
Minds:

> A man himself is a Mind, but once he picks up an ax and
> starts to chop down a tree, he is part of a larger Mind. The
> forest around him is a larger Mind still, and so on. In this
> series of hierarchical levels, the homeostasis of the largest
> unit must be the issue. Thus "person" or "organism" has to
> be seen as a sub-Mind, not as an independent unit. West-
> ern individualism is based on a confusion between Sub-Mind
> and Mind. It regards the human mind as the only mind
> around, free to maximize any variables it chooses, free to
> ignore the homeostasis of the larger unit.[32]

For Bateson, there is no "self" cutting down a tree "out there."
Rather, a relationship is taking place, a systemic circuit, a Mind.
The whole situation is alive, not just the human being, and this
aliveness is immanent in the circuit, not transcendent to it. What
is going around this circuit—tree-eyes-brain-muscles-ax-stroke-
tree—is information. This circuit of information is the Mind,
the self-corrective unit, now seen to be a network of pathways
not bounded by the conscious intent of the man cutting down
the tree but extended to include the pathways of all unconscious
thought as well as all the pathways along which information can
travel. Clearly, then, as we can see from this example, large parts
of the thinking network lie outside the human body.

Another example Bateson uses is that of the pollution of Lake
Erie. Lake Erie, beginning in the 1950s, was so contaminated
with lead and other chemicals from local industry that it was referred to as a "dead" lake. However, a major cleanup was undertaken in the late 1970s, and today Lake Erie is once again "alive."
Since Mind is immanent in the ecosystem—and indeed in the
total evolutionary structure of the universe—if we pollute Lake
Erie until "it loses its mind," we too will also go somewhat in-
sane, because we are a Sub-Mind in a larger Mind that we have

driven a bit crazy. The resulting insanity becomes part of our thought and experience. Furthermore, says Bateson, there are clear limits to how many times we can create such situations before the planet, or the larger Mind, reacts and does something to save itself.[33]

For Bateson, a mental system, or Mind, can behave in two possible ways: self-correcting or runaway. In a self-corrective system the results of past actions are fed back into the system and these new bits of information enable the system to maintain something close to its optimal state. A runaway system, on the other hand, becomes increasingly distorted over time. Bateson points to addiction as an example of a runaway system; the addict needs an increasingly larger fix. Addiction, he says, characterizes all aspects of industrial society in its effort to control everything. Any system that maximizes certain variables (such as fossil fuels, for example) violates the natural steady-state conditions that would optimize those variables and is by definition runaway. Bateson insists that there is no escaping self-corrective feedback, even if it takes the form of the total disintegration of the entire culture. As Bateson puts it, "If you fight the ecology of a system, you lose—especially when you win."[34]

Two parallel schools of thought support and deepen Bateson's thinking: the research of Humberto Maturana in Santiago, Chile, and the Gaia Hypothesis developed by James Lovelock and Lynn Margulis. Both schools point to a self-organizing principle at the heart of the universe. Maturana, a biologist, has coined the term *autopoisis* to describe the ability of living systems to renew themselves continuously and to regulate this process in such a way that the integrity of their structure is maintained and continuously enhanced. This "will to life" stretches into infinity.[35]

Lovelock, an atmospheric chemist, and Margulis, a biologist, have posited the theory that the Earth (*Gaia* is the Greek word for Earth) creates the conditions for its own existence. They have identified a complex network that points to the self-regulation of our planetary system. They found that the Earth's entire cycle—which links volcanoes to rock weathering, to soil bacteria, to oceanic algae, to limestone sediments, and back to volcanoes—acts as a giant loop that helps regulate the Earth's temperature. The heat of the sun stimulates bacterial action in the soil, which increases the rate of rock weathering. This, in turn, pumps more carbon dioxide out of the atmosphere and thus cools the planet. According to Lovelock and Margulis, similar feedback cycles—interlinking plants and rocks, animals and atmospheric gases, microorganisms and the oceans—regulate the Earth's climate, the salinity of its oceans, and other important planetary conditions.[36]

THE NEW COSMOLOGY

These new perceptions of interconnectedness also affect theology. As many prefer to phrase it, a new cosmology is being born.

As can be seen from the brief overview of the new science, the quantum view maintains that the reality of our universe does not need an external, supernatural *raison d'être* to uncover what is real. The laws governing the universe are such that matter and energy can organize themselves into the complex forms and systems that make up the ongoing evolutionary process. Indeed, opposite concepts, such as beginning or end, inside or outside, become outmoded.

According to physicist Paul Davies:

The picture we obtain for the universe is a remarkable one. At some finite instant in the past, the universe of space, time and matter is bounded by a space-time singularity. The coming-into-being of the universe is therefore represented not only by the abrupt appearance of matter, but of space and time as well. The significance of this result cannot be overstressed. People often ask: Where did the Big Bang occur? The Bang did not occur at a point in space at all. Space itself came into existence with the Big Bang. There is a similar difficulty over the question: What happened before the Big Bang? The answer is: There was no "before."[37]

Diarmuid O'Murchu, struggling to respond theologically to the quantum paradigm shift, develops a set of twelve principles. The first is this: "Life is sustained by a creative energy, fundamentally benign in nature, with a tendency to manifest and express itself in movement, rhythm, and pattern. Creation is sustained by a superhuman, pulsating restlessness, a type of resonance vibrating throughout time and eternity."[38] He describes Ultimate Mystery (he shies away from using the words *God* or *the Divinity*) as a creative energy that is constantly changing, evolving, and transforming itself into ever-greater complexity. This energy is the substance of life, the unrelenting wellspring of pure possibility, the symmetry within all.

Geologian Thomas Berry, a priest and cultural historian, and his disciple, physicist Brian Swimme, are two interlocutors who have wrestled with insights coming from deep ecology, the new science, and cybernetics, confronting those findings with Christian thought. Although other voices also call humanity toward a new cosmology, the insights of Berry and Swimme are particularly significant.

Reading Thomas Berry's *The Dream of the Earth* in 1989 was illuminating for me; it provided me with a meaningful framework to describe what I had vaguely intuited but had not been able to express in any coherent way. Berry offers what he terms a *new story*—a functional cosmology—to guide us toward what he believes is a dawning ecological age. This involves a deeper understanding of the relationship between the human community and the Earth. "A truly human intimacy with the Earth and with the entire natural world is needed," he says. "We need to present ourselves to the planet as the planet presents itself to us. In an evocatory rather than a dominating relationship."[39] He points out that

> this re-enchantment with the earth as a living reality is the condition for our rescue of the earth from the impending destruction that we are imposing upon it. To carry this out effectively, we must . . . reinvent the human as a species within the community of life species. Our sense of reality and of value must consciously shift from an anthropocentric to a biocentric norm of reference.[40]

Berry reminds us that we cannot live without a myth, a story that tells us who we are. He says that the deepest crisis experienced by any people is that moment when its story is no longer adequate for the times. The human species, he maintains, is now at that moment in our history. Berry holds out hope, however, and believes that we are discovering a new origins story, which is the story of the universe as an emergent evolutionary process:

> The story of the universe is the story of the emergence of a galactic system in which each new level of expression emerges through the urgency of self-transcendence. Hydrogen in the presence of some millions of degrees of heat emerges into helium. After the stars take shape as oceans of fire in the heavens, they go through a sequence of transformations. Some eventually explode into the stardust out of which the solar system and the Earth take shape. Earth gives unique expression of itself in its rock and crystalline structures and in the variety and splendor of living forms, until humans appear as the moment in which the unfolding universe becomes conscious of itself. The human emerges not only as an earthling, but also as a worldling. We bear the universe in our beings as the universe bears us in its being. The two have a total presence to each other and to that deeper mystery out of which both the universe and ourselves have emerged. . . . This might be considered a new revelatory experience; a new paradigm of what it is to be human emerges.[41]

For Berry, history is governed by the overarching movements that give shape and meaning to life by relating the human venture to the larger destinies of the universe. Creating such a movement might be called the "Great Work" of a people, the title of his latest book.[42] The Great Work now, as we move into a new millennium, is to carry out the transition from a period of human devastation of the Earth to a period when humans will be present to the planet in a manner that is mutually beneficial. Berry emphasizes that the deepest cause of the Earth's present devastation is to be found in the radical *discontinuity* between the human and other modes of being—along with the bestowal of all rights on the human. He invites us to a new understanding of the Earth based on deep feelings of wonder at its magnificence and mystery. He calls us to move from our human-centeredness to an Earth-centered understanding of who we are. He insists that the Earth as a bio-spiritual planet must become for us the basic referent for our future. For Berry, we are in desperate need of a new revelatory experience wherein human consciousness awakens to the grandeur of the Earth:

> This awakening is our human participation in the dream of the Earth, the dream that is carried in its integrity not in any of the Earth's cultural expressions but in the depths of our genetic coding. Therein the Earth functions at a depth beyond our capacity for active thought. . . . We probably have not had such participation in the dream of the Earth since earlier shamanic times, but therein lies our hope for the future for ourselves and for the entire Earth community.[43]

Berry believes that as the Earth's physical resources become less available, psychic energy will be key to supporting the human project. The universe will be experienced as the Great Self. Each is fulfilled in the other: the Great Self is fulfilled in the individual self; the individual self is fulfilled in the Great Self. Thus new fields of energy will become available to support us as we go into the future. He also reminds us that we have a fourfold wisdom to guide us into the future: the wisdom of indigenous peoples; the wisdom of women; the wisdom of the classical traditions, including Judeo-Christian thought; and the wisdom of science. For Berry, the essential flaw in our Judeo-Christian heritage is the belief in a personal male deity, creator of a universe that is clearly distinct from himself. Supposedly, we have direct communication from this supreme personal deity, who appeared in human form as teacher and savior. The historical dynamism of this tradition has driven the course of the Western world. This tradition holds that the entire human community is being led to fulfillment in a divine kingdom, a kingdom with a fulfillment here on Earth in historical time (a time when peace and justice reign once and for all and, as recorded in Isaiah 11:6, the "lion shall lie down with the lamb") and a post-historical fulfillment in an eternal transcendental mode of being (heaven). Berry argues that because we see ourselves as a transcendent mode of being, we have a hard time believing that we really belong to the Earth, that we are indeed earthlings. This, he stresses over and over again, is a deeply ingrained pathology that has led to our understanding that we have a destiny beyond that of the Earth's. This theological context has given us permission to use the Earth as we see fit because "it is not our true home." Berry also finds that Christianity's stress on redemption—that we are a "fallen race" in need of a savior who came and "saved" us so that we might return to some heavenly paradise—neglects the primary revelatory experience of the natural world.[44]

Yet Berry has always been an optimist. He tells us that we are experiencing a moment of grace at the beginning of the twenty-first century. He is convinced that a comprehensive change of consciousness is coming over the human community:

> We are now experiencing a moment of significance far beyond what any of us can imagine. What can be said is that the foundations of a new historical period, the Ecozoic era, have been established in every realm of human affairs. The mythic vision has been set into place. The distorted dream of an industrial technological paradise is being replaced by the more viable dream of a mutually enhancing human presence within an ever-renewing organic-based Earth community.[45]

Brian Swimme is Berry's foremost disciple. In 1994 they wrote *The Universe Story*, now a classic. Swimme also uses the medium of video to transmit his development of the new story.[46] Swimme's first video series, "The Canticle to the Cosmos," is the attempt of a physicist to give flesh to and expand Berry's insights into the workings of the cosmos as the primary revelation. He resituates the scientific quest as a sacred journey and invites his fellow scientists to step away from an uninvolved rationalism and move toward a participatory consciousness in the scientific enterprise. This series develops each of Berry's twelve cosmological principles:

1. The universe, the solar system, and the planet Earth in themselves and in their evolutionary emergence constitute for the human community the primary revelation of that Ultimate Mystery whence all things emerge into being.

2. The universe is a unity, an interacting and genetically related community of beings bound together in an inseparable relationship in space and time. The unity of the planet Earth is especially clear; each being of the planet is profoundly implicated in the existence and functioning of every other being of the planet.

3. From its beginning the universe is a psychic as well as a physical reality.

4. The three basic laws of the universe at all levels of reality are differentiation, subjectivity, and communion. These laws identify the reality of the universe, the values of the universe, and the direction in which the universe is proceeding.

5. The universe has a violent as well as a harmonious aspect, but it is consistently creative in the larger arc of its development.

6. The Earth, within the solar system, is a self-emergent, self-propagating, self-nourishing, self-educating, self-governing, self-healing, self-fulfilling community. All particular life forms must integrate their functioning within this larger complex of mutually dependent Earth systems.

7. The genetic-coding process is the process through which the world of the living articulates itself in its being and its activities. The great wonder is the creative interaction of the multiple codings among themselves.

8. The human is that being in whom the universe activates, reflects upon, and celebrates itself in conscious self-awareness.

9. At the human level, genetic coding mandates a further trans-genetic cultural coding by which specific human qualities find expression. Cultural coding is carried on by educational processes.

10. The emergent process of the universe is irreversible and non-repeatable in the existing world order. The movement from non-life to life on the planet Earth is a one-time event. So, too, the movement from life to the human form of consciousness. So also the transition from the earlier to the later forms of human culture.

11. The historical sequence of cultural periods can be identified as the tribal-shamanistic period, the Neolithic-village period, the classical civilizational period, the scientific-technological period, and the emerging Ecozoic era.

12. The main task of the immediate future is to assist in activating the inter-communion of all the living and nonliving components of the Earth community in what can be considered the emerging Ecozoic era of Earth development.[47]

In his 1998 video series, "The Earth's Imagination," Swimme develops further Berry's conviction that we are at a decisive moment in the development of human consciousness and that we are, indeed, on the threshold of reinventing ourselves as a species.[48] In this series Swimme explores how the human mind developed. For Swimme, the fundamental way to understand the human being—from the context of the universe as a whole—is as a transformation of the dynamics of evolution.

Swimme argues that there is a fundamental difference in looking at the human from an evolutionary perspective as opposed to more classical or even modern philosophical approaches that appear to posit the human mind as somehow *other* than the Earth. In fact, he points out, much energy in Western civilization has been invested in showing the human mind as different, distinct, higher, and special. And yet we too are geological formations.

From an evolutionary perspective, our minds are largely the same as the other minds in the primate world. We arrived out of a billion-year shaping process with very particular kinds of minds, very particular kinds of consciousness. The nature of the primate mind, in terms of synergy, is twofold: first, there is a deep focus on the level of the organizing mind, on the level of sentience, on sexual reproduction, creating the largest possible number of offspring; second, this focus takes place within emotionally bonded groups, either within the family or with closely related kin. The difference between other primates and the human is that the rate of development slowed down in the human, which enabled the development of the imagination. It is the imagination in particular that distinguishes the human from other primates. Although all primates have an imagination, in the human it became a huge capacity. The imagination, then, is the root of what it means to be human. For Swimme, imagination is the ability to seize possibilities that are otherwise invisible. And that made all the difference in what we have become:

> So then we invented flint and we invented grinding tools, and then the screwdriver and the compass, then we drew in the power of the wind and of the tides; then we had the steam engine. Then we had nuclear energy, then we had recombinant DNA. Each time the human, through the imagination, is drawing a new power of the Universe into the human project. The human then, through the imagination, draws in all the powers of the Universe, all the powers of the Earth community. And yet dealing with this we are using the same old primate mind. There has been no time for a change in anatomy; it has taken place that fast. . . . That goes far beyond the capacity of the life process to stay with it or to catch up. So the human has become this planetary power, yet it does not have the understanding or the wisdom to organize this power within the total life complex.[49]

For Swimme, we are in a transition from a time when life was shaped by natural selection to a time when life itself begins to be shaped by something like conscious selection. Comprehensive compassion is beginning to take hold of the life process, through the human being. Although it is not possible to predict what will take place, certain intuitions are emerging. Swimme describes this as "the emergence of a vibrant Earth community." Swimme is convinced that just as our imagination ultimately determines, personally, our life and our character, in the same way, for the species as a whole, what fascinates the human imagination will shape life. The question, then, is what goals, what purposes, what aims are we going to choose as humans? Whatever we choose will become a central shaping power of the life process. Swimme is convinced that our true destiny lies in what deeply fascinates us.

Swimme is also convinced that in order to develop what he calls "macrophase wisdom," we humans need the self-understanding that we are a mode of the universe, of life itself, of evolutionary dynamics, as opposed to our prevalent understanding of ourselves as individuals. This would move us into another form of humanity. We would begin to create ourselves by a vision that arrives out of the future, out of the "not yet." The more we become fascinated by that possibility, the more we would actually become that reality. We would change from a fixation on the human project to a fascination with the Earth project. And the first step toward accomplishing the change would be to cease our industrial assault on the rest of the Earth community. Drawing back our destructive imposition would immediately set into motion strategies that have been worked out over billions of years. Our withdrawal from destruction would bring a deep delight, because we would see the Earth's ecosystems burst forth with life. On a deeper level we would share in these ecosystems' own fulfillment; their blossoming would be our own.

Swimme suggests a second step, which involves the invention and discovery of new forms of synergy within the Earth community so that the wolves, the fish, the humans, and the trees all feed abundantly on the Earth community in mutually enhancing relationships. While it is difficult for us to imagine a form of interaction with the encompassing community that is truly mutually enhancing, Thomas Berry remind us that "the dream drives the action."

These seminal ideas of Thomas Berry and Brian Swimme concerning how we view ourselves in relation to the wider Earth community continue to influence profoundly ecofeminist thought.

INDIGENOUS COSMOLOGIES

Many recent discoveries of the new science confirm what the original peoples of the Earth have long known: the Earth is a living "mother" and all creatures, great and small, are her children. We are all related. Indigenous cosmologies are once again being studied and embraced, not as mere folklore but as extraordinarily creative ways in which humanity tells its story. Furthermore, their traditional love and care for the Earth can lead the rest of us to a deeper understanding of the land and its ecosystems. As Berry points out: "One of the significant historical roles of the primal peoples of the world is not simply to sustain their own traditions, but to call the entire civilized world back to a more authentic mode of being. Our only hope is in a renewal of those primordial experiences out of which the shaping of our more sublime human qualities could take place."[50]

Indigenous peoples everywhere are among the world's poorest; this is especially true of indigenous women.[51] This situation will probably not improve until non-indigenous viewpoints of superiority and assimilation give way to respect and recognition of the value of indigenous lifestyles. However, the very structure of our technological civilization prevents us from communicating in depth with native peoples. There is also a tendency among some spiritual seekers to trivialize and exploit indigenous spiritualities. Cherokee Andy Smith writes:

The New Age movement has sparked a new interest in Native American traditional spirituality among white women who claim to be feminists. Indian spirituality, with its respect for nature and the interconnectedness of all things, is often presented as the panacea for all individual and global problems. Not surprisingly, many white "feminists" see the opportunity to make a great profit from this new craze. They sell sweat lodges or sacred pipe ceremonies, which promise to bring individual and global healing. . . . Our spirituality is not for sale.[52]

Non-indigenous peoples are thus warned to differentiate between appropriating indigenous spirituality and learning from its insights. Berry, as a cultural historian, has studied North American Indians for many years. "Awareness of a numinous presence throughout the entire cosmic order establishes among these peoples one of the most integral forms of spirituality known to us," he writes.[53] He also underscores indigenous peoples' interior communion with the archetypal world of the collective unconscious as revealed in their vision quests, the guidance they seek in dreams, and their connection with their own psychic powers in general—something most modern non-indigenous peoples have lost:

Indigenous wisdom is distinguished by its intimacy with and participation in the functioning of the natural world. The dawn and sunset are moments when the numinous source of all existence is experienced with special sensitivity. . . . This ever-renewing sequence of sunrise and sunset, of seasonal succession, constitutes a pattern of life, a great liturgy, a celebration of existence. In this context early humans discovered their food and sheltered themselves from the elements. Above all they developed an interpretation of life and pain and suffering and death, along with a feeling of security and joy in existence. A native wisdom was passed down through the generations, a wisdom carried in the lives of the people, in their thoughts and speech; in their customs, songs, and rituals; in their arts, their poetry; and in their stories not in any written form. In a special manner this wisdom is carried by the sacred personalities: the elders—both men and women, the chiefs, the shamans.[54]

Latin America has seen a resurgence of indigenous militancy since the quincentennial in 1992 of the European invasion of the Americas. The Zapatistas in Chiapas, Mexico, the Maya in Guatemala, the Quechua and Aymara of the Andean countries, and the Mapuche of southern Chile and Argentina have all mobilized in recent years to demand the return of their territorial lands, which were usurped by colonial powers. This struggle is based upon a renewed sense of their own history as native peoples and in their own cosmovisions, which were often hidden or syncretized with the imposition of Christianity by the *conquistadors*. As Diego Irarrázaval, a Chilean priest working among the Aymara and Quechua peoples of Peru, writes:

> [These people] seek to survive within a cosmic harmony and wisdom. Such human groups are at the far edges of the modern world. They feel the sacred in their entire existence; they interact intensively with their ancestors and with benign and evil spirits; they see woman as a socializing and spiritual center; and they have devised warm rituals and mythical accounts having to do with life and death. . . . In doing so, they implicitly question a modernity that plunders nature and splits persons.[55]

Irarrázaval goes on to describe how very much alive this cosmic presence is, especially through ritual and celebration. There is ongoing interaction with those who have died, a sacred relationship with the surrounding living and inanimate beings, and a close relationship between bodiliness and spiritual energy. He calls attention to the relationship between ritual and healing, noting that "much of the activity of believers has to do with handling illnesses and pain, with recovering emotional, bodily, communal, and mystical equilibrium."[56] These beliefs continue to flourish, despite their condemnation as demonic by colonial Christianity.

For some time now, I have been wrestling with Latin America's indigenous heritage from a feminist perspective. Several years ago I wrote an article entitled "After Five Centuries of Mixings, Who Are We? Walking with Our Dark Grandmothers' Feet,"[57] in which I attempted to summarize how the women of Con-spirando felt about being a "mix" between European and indigenous peoples. In light of the five-hundred-year anniversary of the supposed "discovery" of Latin America, we were trying to redefine Latin

American identity. Our primary question was, "Who are Latin American women after five hundred years of resistance, adaptation, and accommodation to wave after wave of foreign 'invasions'?"

We concluded that we are a mix of European and indigenous peoples, and that we are also a mix of mixes—the descendants of Spanish, Portuguese, German, British, and Irish men (who arrived alone, without women from their own culture) with Mapuche, Aymara, Quechua, and Aztec women, and also of Chinese and African male slaves with women from the first mixture. Neither white nor black nor indigenous, Latin Americans are a new race, a new synthesis.

Given our *mestizaje*—our mix of mixtures—Con-spirando member Elena Aguila asked: "What is my responsibility to my ancestors, to my white as well as to my dark grandmother? I am a woman of both worlds; I refuse to deny one and adopt the other. I feel the urgent need to dialogue with the voices of all my grandmothers."[58] Aguila then asked why so many Latin American women ignore their indigenous roots and raise up those of their European ancestors. Her answer: Because being white is synonymous with power, meaning economic, political, and cultural power. It has also included the power to formulate theological questions and suggest answers, the power to present an image as holy, the power to institutionalize religious practices, and the power to establish myths and rituals for an entire culture.

On the other hand, being indigenous has meant oppression, poverty, and a life of hardship. (It is undeniable that the greatest poverty in Latin America is among the still-existing indigenous communities.) Aguila challenged Latin American women to rediscover the power in the mixture—without denying "the plurality written on our faces—to vindicate the wrinkles and scars of our dark grandmothers, because who knows what wisdom, power and secrets lie hidden there."[59]

Mestiza Latin American women recognize that the cosmologies of their Mapuche, Aymara, and Mayan ancestors profoundly color their emerging theology and spirituality. At the same time, research and experience lead us to conclude that, although it appears to be true that indigenous communities were more ecologically sensitive to their environments than our Western societies, these native communities cannot be construed as "paradise lost." Even by the time the Spanish colonizers arrived, some of them, such as the Aztec and the Inca empires, had degenerated into a period of war, expansionism, and rigid hierarchies. Although women were esteemed and deities were both masculine and feminine, men governed.

Latin American women as a rule have no romantic illusions about returning to the past. However, this is a time of great change that requires a new synthesis, along with new energies, symbols, and initiatives. Thus, what might we learn from these "dark" grandmothers? What do they whisper about our origins as well as our destiny? Perhaps an even more crucial question might be how their ancient beliefs—so long repressed as paganism by their European counterparts—challenge and reshape Christianity.

The rituals and practices of Con-spirando reflect this need. We are attracted to holding our rituals under the trees; we feel moved to dance and sing to the sound of the drums, while we try to feel the rhythms of Mother Earth, known to the Aymara and Quechua as Pachamama, in our bodies. We are attracted to the many modern-day *machis* (Mapuche holy women) and *curanderas* (healers) who walk our streets—wise old aunts and grannies who counsel us about what to do when our children suffer from asthma or some other ailment or when we have a migraine or a "woman's problem." The sense of interconnection with the Mapuche and Aymara traditions and the need to reinstall the Aymara practice of reciprocity—to return to the Earth what we take from her— feel right to us. We believe that failure to do so is one of the causes of our current ecological crisis.

We are just beginning this process of recovering our origins, of journeying with our dark grandmothers' feet. However, as pointed out above, any perspective of the indigenous past must be accompanied by caution against falling into fantasies of re-covering a long-lost world, of simplistic stereotypes that often surround reengaging the wisdom of indigenous cultures. With so much of the context lost, how do we decipher and interpret the few images and artifacts that still exist? How can we extract a more truthful understanding of indigenous myths and legends while not over-idealizing the indigenous past? How can we do this while not dismissing it as "savage"? How can we begin a process of simply accepting these ancestors as part of ourselves? How can we let these ancient women speak to us today through our bodies, through our lives? This search will engage us for some time to come.

ECONOMIC SUSTAINABILITY/BIOREGIONALISM

Deep ecologists, armed with insights from the new science and cybernetics, inspired by the new story coming from cosmologists, and reclaiming the Earth-based wisdom traditions of indigenous peoples, put their vision into practice by trying to "come home to place."

Planet Earth, of course, is not a uniform reality but a highly complex web of differentiated bioregions that support local life communities. Again, quoting Berry: "A bioregion is an identifiable geographical area of interacting life systems that is relatively self-sustaining in the ever-renewing processes of nature. The full diversity of life functions is carried out as a community that includes the physical as well as the organic components of the region. Each of the component life systems must integrate its own functioning within this community to survive in any effective manner."[60] Bioregionalism, an alternative to viewing the planet as a collection of nation-states, can be described as a community that maintains a certain numerical balance in species and members; is self-sustaining in food and well-being for all its members; can regenerate and adjust to seasonal changes; and has an inflow and outflow of energy that sustains the community over an indefinite period of time.

For ecofeminist Judith Plant, a leader in the bioregional movement in Canada, "bioregionalism means learning to become native to place, fitting ourselves to a particular place, not fitting a place to our predetermined tastes. It is living within the limits and the gifts provided by a place, creating a way of life that can be passed on to future generations."[61]

Such a perspective makes it clear that our current industrial economy is not sustainable. Industrial technologies are becoming more and more destructive of the Earth's natural processes. All modern economic systems—whether socialist or capitalist—are anthropocentric, seeing the Earth as a container of resources for human use instead of a finely tuned web of ecosystems into which human beings, as one species among many, must fit.

David Korten, author of *When Corporations Rule the World*, maintains that social and environmental disintegration is accelerating everywhere on the planet. "The continued quest for economic growth as the organizing principle of public policy is accelerating the breakdown of the ecosystem's regenerative capacities and the social fabric that sustains human community; at the same time, it is intensifying the competition of resources between the rich and the poor—a competition that the poor invariably lose."[62] For Korten, this growth is based on short-term financial gain for a handful of powerful corporations that claim consumerism is the path to happiness—a myth propagated by the media, established political and economic systems, and indeed, by the very "air we breathe" in order to justify greed.

> In the name of modernity we are creating dysfunctional societies that are breeding pathological behavior—violence, extreme competitiveness, suicide, drug abuse, greed, and environmental degradation. Such behavior is an inevitable consequence when a society fails to meet the needs of its members for social bonding, trust, affection and a shared sacred meaning. . . . Healthy societies depend on healthy, empowered local communities that build caring relationships among people and help us connect to a particular piece of the living Earth with which our lives are intertwined.[63]

According to economist Herman Daly, environmentally sustainable societies must satisfy three conditions: (1) the use of renewable resources must be based on a given ecosystem's ability to regenerate them; (2) the consumption of nonrenewable resources must not exceed rates as which renewable substitutes are developed and put to use; and (3) rates of pollution emission into the environment cannot exceed the ecosystem's ability to absorb them.[64]

As more and more of Earth's people become grounded once again in their local bioregional communities, perhaps the creativity of imagining new possibilities for sustainability predicted by Brian Swimme will flourish and the Ecozoic age envisioned by Thomas Berry will indeed dawn. This is also a hope of ecofeminism.

3

Ecofeminism's Roots
in Other Feminist Movements

Ecofeminism has deep roots within the broader feminist tradition, sometimes called radical or cultural feminism.[1] Both radical and cultural feminism arose as part of the "second wave" of feminism in the 1960s and 1970s principally, although not exclusively, within the United States. The "first wave," occurring mainly in the first half of the twentieth century, is defined as women's struggles to gain the right to vote. In the second wave of feminism, women continued to struggle for a broadening of their civil, political, and economic rights, and they also introduced feminist studies as a new academic discipline. While a variety of perspectives emerged within feminism, they can be broken down into four major types:

- Liberal feminism emphasizes civil rights, including the right of women to make decisions freely about their own sexual and reproductive health; it also seeks full equality of women with men in all facets of societal life, especially in economic and political life.
- Cultural or spiritual feminism emphasizes the moral superiority of women over men and the values traditionally associated with women, such as compassion, nurturance, and peacemaking; it seeks to better society by stressing the contributions made by women. It is sometimes associated with women's separatist movements.

- Radical feminism emphasizes the pervasiveness of male domination, which is seen as the cause of all societal problems, and the importance of women-centered culture, which is characterized by nurture, closeness to nature, and compassion; it seeks to eliminate patriarchy in order to liberate women from male control in every facet of life.
- Socialist feminism emphasizes white male domination in the class struggles of capitalist societies and believes that this dominance results in the division of labor according to sex and race and the devaluing of women's work, especially the work of raising children; it seeks to end the economic dependence of women upon men and to achieve major social reforms that will end class divisions and enable all women and men to have equal opportunity to be gainfully employed and to be actively involved in parenting.[2]

The "third wave" of feminism, beginning in the 1980s and continuing to the present, seeks to attend to differences among women from different parts of the globe and build alliances that extend across these lines of differences. (Nowhere was this diversity more visible than at the United Nation's Fourth Conference on the Status of Women held in Beijing in 1995.) Ecofeminism, which is part of this third wave, brings together concern for the domination of women and other subjugated groups with concern for the exploitation of the Earth.

Ecofeminism clearly flows out of radical feminism; both identify patriarchy as the main source of global ecological destruction. However, ecofeminism's relationship with cultural and spiritual feminism is less clear. Some ecofeminists tend to stress male domination per se as the cause of behavior that is ecologically destructive and socially oppressive, while holding up women's "ways of knowing" as more ecologically sound. Such cultural and spiritual ecofeminists tend to stress an elemental connection between women and nature, which has led to charges of essentialism.

Ecofeminists coming from a socialist feminist background would argue that the division of power between men and women results in unsustainable patterns of development. (Most socialist feminists do not embrace ecofeminist thought, charging that ecofeminism diverts energies from the struggle against the major oppression of economic exploitation of capitalism.)

Ecofeminism is fairly critical of liberal feminism because ecofeminists maintain that there is no purpose in fighting for equal opportunities within the present political and economic system. As ecofeminist Ynestra King has written: "The piece of the pie that women have only begun to sample as a result of the feminist movement is rotten and carcinogenic. . . . What is the point of partaking equally in a system that is killing us all?"[3]

Ecofeminist Charlene Spretnak, in a now classic essay entitled "Ecofeminism: Our Roots and Flowering," maps three different paths women have taken toward ecofeminism.[4] The *first path* included the study of Marxist political theory in the 1960s and dominance theories in the 1970s by radical and cultural feminists. They rejected the Marxist assertion that domination is based solely on economic oppression and class exploitation, pointing out that the most universally dominated class was women. Their studies of dominance theory included an exploration of the roots of patriarchy, identifying the dynamics of fear and resentment behind male dominance.

The *second path* was exposure to nature-based religion. In the mid-1970s many radical/cultural feminists, examining historical and archeological studies, discovered pre-patriarchal myths and goddess cults that honored the female and portrayed the divine as immanent. Spretnak notes that this discovery "was utterly earthshaking for us Judeo-Christian women of a thoroughly modern culture . . . and inspired rituals of our own creation that express our deepest feelings of a spirituality infused with ecological wisdom and wholeness."[5]

A *third path* is through environmentalism and/or green politics, where women encounter theories of ecofeminism or deep ecology, which give their activism a more coherent philosophy.

Spretnak identifies many variations on these three paths, but she finds that ecofeminism's promise lies not only in addressing "the interlinked dynamics in patriarchal culture of the terror of nature and the terror of the elemental power of the female, but also the ways out of the mesmerizing conditioning that keeps women and men so cut off from our grounding in the natural world, so alienated from our larger sense of self in the unfolding story of the universe."[6]

Ynestra King concludes:

> In ecofeminism, nature is the central category of analysis. An analysis of the interrelated dominations of nature—psyche and sexuality, human oppression, and nonhuman nature—and the historic position of women in relation to those forms of domination is the starting point of ecofeminist theory. We share with cultural feminism the necessity of a politics with heart and a beloved community, recognizing our connection with each other—and with nonhuman nature. Socialist feminism has given us a powerful critical perspective with which to understand, and transform, history. Separately, they perpetuate the dualism of "mind" and "nature." Together they make possible a new ecological relationship between nature and culture, in which mind and nature, heart and reason, join forces to transform the systems of domination, internal and external, that threaten the existence of life on Earth.[7]

THE DEVELOPMENT OF PATRIARCHY

All ecofeminists agree that patriarchy is the root cause of our present unsustainable situation. Patriarchy can be defined as

> the social construction of reality and of thinking that is based on domination of women and of all groups considered inferior because of race, gender, class, sexual orientation, disability, etc. These structures of domination and subordination are woven into a *double web of oppression* created by structures of political, economic, cultural and intellectual power distribution in society, and of a dualistic system of thought that justifies this unjust distribution of power.[8]

A patriarchal culture has several characteristics:

- appropriation and control over goods, persons (especially women), and nature.
- a culture of domination, centered on authority, obedience, and the use of force. (Males develop a kind of psychological armor that manifests "strong" emotions like anger and aggression and expresses contempt for "soft" emotions such as love, compassion, and tenderness. Self-control is strongly emphasized, and sensuality and pleasure are seen as sinful or as expressions of weakness. Pain and fear are used as central motivators.)
- justification of appropriation and control through appropriation of the truth. (Insistence that there is only one correct way in religion, politics, and the social order. Alternative ways of thinking and acting are regarded as threats and are duly punished: "I am a jealous God" [Yahweh] and "Error hath no rights" [Saint Augustine].)
- hierarchical relationships in all areas: church, politics (monarchy), economic institutions, educational institutions, and the family. (Everything is ranked and compared; competition is a way of life. There are hierarchies of wealth and power, of strength and intelligence, of beauty, and even of merit and sanctity. Each person's dignity and worth tend to be related to the person's position in the "pecking order" rather than in his or her intrinsic human qualities.
- linear rather than process thinking and action. (Even God is seen as having a fixed, linear "plan" for creation.)
- patriarchal religion based on a monarchical God, clothed in patriarchal robes, who is a warrior God (Lord God of hosts), a judge who metes out severe punishments, a distant and immutable deity. (In keeping with its need for control and self-control, this religion may emphasize asceticism or even self-mutilation.)
- controlled and suppressed violence. (Peace is found only in domination: Pax Romana or Pax Americana. There is peace only when everything is under control.)[9]

The development of patriarchy can be summarized in four stages.[10] *The Paleolithic or Hunter-Gatherer Stage*, present from

2 million to 10,000 BCE, comprised 99 percent of human history. Some thirty thousand years ago *homo sapiens* had spread to all parts of the planet and lived in tribes of twenty-five to thirty people. These peoples were nomadic and had few possessions. Although there were occasional fights among tribes, wars of conquest were unknown. Men hunted larger animals, while women, who were in charge of the children, stayed closer to the campsite. Much time was devoted to religious ceremony.

Members of these tribes were animists who conceived everything as a complex of interconnecting spiritual forces: the mountain, the river, and every living being had its own spirit or totem. This was a world of profound participation, magic, and intuition. And all was a manifestation of the Great Mother, the source of life to which they believed they would return. The Medicine Wheel (still seen in many indigenous cultures) expressed the primary experience of living in a world of amazing fecundity with its sequence of seasons and a cyclical autumn dying and spring rising. To this generosity of the Earth the tribes responded with gratitude. There was no distinction between nature and spirit, between religious and "ordinary" life. The first images of early religious sensibilities were expressed in the multitude of Venus figures found around the planet—the image of the pregnant or fertile woman, the symbol of the origin of life. To the Paleolithic mind, the Great Mother was manifest in the body of a woman. Sexuality, birth, death, and resurrection were all of one piece, both natural and spiritual.

The Neolithic Revolution: The Age of Agriculture began around 10,000 BCE and lasted until 3500 BCE. Human beings gradually began to domesticate plants and animals. With the development of agriculture, they moved from a wild planet to a domesticated one, resulting in a change in relationship on the entire planet. More food was cultivated in a small space, flocks of animals were controlled, and small villages of about 150 people developed. There was a growing division of labor: women domesticated plants and small animals and were in the forefront of subsistence agriculture. Men were more associated with plow agriculture and with pasturing and herding animals. With the development of agriculture, accumulation became possible; surplus food allowed some individuals to dedicate themselves to tasks other than agriculture and herding. There was growing specialization in ceramics, art, architecture, weaving, and ritual.

In terms of psychic development, major spiritual energies continued to be expressed in complex feelings of both gratitude and fear of the Great Mother—her power both to give life and to bring death. Sexual unions between men and women were seen as a sacred ritual reflecting those mysterious powers that sustain life. The *hieros gamos*, a "sacred marriage," a public enactment of a sexual union, was considered the most important yearly rite of the Neolithic period. In imitation of the Earth, the ritual honored the source of life by partaking in sexual pleasure with joy and gratitude. Sexual pleasure was considered sacred and pleasing to the Great Mother.

A growing body of evidence suggests that between 4300 and 2800 BCE at least three waves of invasions dramatically altered earlier Neolithic societies around the Fertile Crescent. Pastoral but warlike tribes from what is now northern Europe and the Russian steppes began to invade these agricultural settlements in search of food and fertile women. They came on horseback and sacked the villages, killing the men and capturing the women. The invaders apparently had an altogether different psychic experience from that of inhabitants of the more matristic villages; they also had a different relationship with the Earth than did the agriculturalists. They had learned to domesticate animals and turn them into herds, which also meant protecting them from other animals, such as wolves, now seen as enemies.

Procreation, rather than sexual union for pleasure, became an overriding value. More than their agrarian counterparts, herders valued the ability of women and animals to procreate and sought to control that procreation. The gradual appropriation of women's ability to reproduce offspring changed what had been a more egalitarian relationship between the sexes. Fertile women came to be seen as a highly prized resource and were often exchanged or captured. Men, as a group, began to have a power over women; women, as a group, had no equivalent power over men.

Exposed to the vastness of the plains, the immensity of the heavens, and the harshness of the climate, herding peoples felt awe and fear in the presence of powerful, invisible forces in the cosmos. Total submission to these forces was seen as the only possible response. In the end, as is recorded in the many myths of the ancient world, the patrifocal invaders subdued the more matristic world, and their gods overthrew the Great Mother.

The Classical Civilizations, from 3500 BCE to 1500 CE, were marked by major leaps in production and technology, especially in fertile valleys where large surpluses allowed greater specialization. This was the age of bronze and iron, marked also by the rise of the ancient classical cities. It was the age of the wheel, development in transportation by land and sea for exchange of goods, the movements of migrations, and the age of the great temples. Division among social classes was based on property ownership. Kings ruled empires and recruited armies both for defense and to conquer other empires. War became chronic. The patriarchal family became the norm, with the patriarch owning his wife, children, slaves, and property. The subordination of women was viewed as natural and was institutionalized in the religious and legal codes. The Earth was a resource to be exploited by humans, and accumulation provided a sense of security. Hierarchical, militaristic societies governed by religious and/ or political elites became the norm around the planet. The earlier sense of coming from and returning to the Great Mother was replaced by belief in deities representing the patriarchal "power over" mindset.

The Modern Period, which arose around 1500, has been characterized by the rise of empirical science and technology, and by the appearance of movements that have challenged the four patriarchal dominations described above: the appropriation of most economic resources by a small elite, the political-military rule of kings and emperors, male domination over women and children, and the domination and exploitation of the Earth.

While emancipation movements have not yet successfully eliminated these dominations (some actually intensified under the colonial system, with the application of fossil fuel–based technology to the exploitation of the Earth, and with the increasing power of transnational corporations), they point to a new awareness of the problems and have unleashed enormous energy and growing expectations that change will come about. Patriarchal structures and values are being questioned all over the world, and growing masses of people have become aware that these structures and values need not last forever.

FORMING A FEMINIST ANTHROPOLOGY

Ecofeminism is, above all, a movement that focuses on spirituality, namely, a spirituality that is Earth based. Immersion in this spirituality of the connectedness of all things provides ecofeminists with the energy to chart new directions. One of the sources of this energy comes from the realization that before the male, monolithic God of the Judeo-Christian tradition, there were countless representations of the divinity in female form.

Nowhere has this discovery been more clearly documented than in the work of feminist archeologist Marija Gimbutas. Gimbutas devoted her life to an exhaustive study of images and symbols to discover their inner coherence. After she had directed several excavations where 90 percent of the images dug up were female, she realized that something was missing in traditional theories about religion and culture in the Neolithic period. She widened the scope of descriptive archeology, an expanded approach she called "archeomythology," which incorporated the study of linguistics, mythology, comparative religion, and historical records. Using this meta-language, Gimbutas discovered a sacred relationship between human society and the natural world, and she concluded that the female form, expressed in thousands of images, reflects the centrality of women in religious and cultural life.[11] As ecofeminist scholar Carol Christ writes: "The work of Marija Gimbutas has the potential to bring about a paradigm shift in the way we study religion: it pushes the time of cultural and religious origins far back before the Sumerians, the Hebrews, or the Greeks and challenges us to rethink the roles of women and of female symbolism in religion."[12]

Goddess Images

Gimbutas was the first scholar to present an overview of Neolithic cultures on a pan-European scale and the first to articulate the differences between the matristic Old European system and the patriarchal Indo-European system. In her view, these contrasting systems underwent a hybridization that determined the development of all subsequent European cultures. In her major work, *The Civilization of the Goddess*, a summary of her life's work that names Old Europe as a civilization without war or male domination, Gimbutas provides an essential key for deciphering the sources of contrasting cultural elements that became tangled and fused over time.[13] She writes: "Celebration of life is the leading motif in Old European ideology and art. There is no stagnation; life energy is constantly moving as a serpent, a spiral, or whirl. . . . One form dissolves into another. . . . There was no simple death, only death and regeneration. And this was the key to the hymn of life reflected in their art."[14]

Gimbutas's theory describes three stages:

1. There flourished in Neolithic Europe (6500–3000 BCE) a pre-Indo-European goddess civilization that was matristic, socially egalitarian, communal, peaceful, highly artistic, and primarily goddess worshiping.
2. This indigenous European civilization was overrun and dominated by patriarchal, horse-riding, Indo-European, sky-god-worshiping invaders (named Kurgans for their burial mounds) from the Russian steppes in three successive waves, beginning around 4400 BCE, 3500 BCE, and 3000 BCE, respectively.
3. The subsequent culture of Europe was a hybridization of the Indo-European and Old European cultures—the dominant patriarchal warrior culture and the peaceful matristic culture. The latter was partially destroyed, partially subordinated, and partially assimilated.[15]

Gimbutas maintains that while the symbolic structures of the Indo-Europeans prevailed, those of Old Europe survived as an undercurrent. She further maintains that without this insight into different symbolic structures, it is difficult to make sense of the ideologies of European peoples and the genesis and meaning of their symbols, beliefs, and myths.

Gimbutas believes that women played central roles in the religion and society of Old Europe. Evidence from graves shows no great disparities among individuals or between women and men. This stands in sharp contrast to the royal graves of later periods and suggests that members of the societies of Old Europe were equal. The clearest marks of patriarchal societies—implements of war, the celebration of warriors, warrior kings, and a warrior God—are lacking. Gimbutas interprets the civilization of Old Europe as "matrifocal," worshiping the Goddess and honoring women, and probably also matrilineal, with family ties traced through the female line. However, Gimbutas does *not* call Old European civilization "matriarchal," because this would imply that women dominated men. She insists that men played important and valued roles within the culture, especially with regard to trade:

> The Old European culture took keen delight in the natural wonders of *this* world. Its people did not produce lethal weapons or build forts in inaccessible places, as their successors did, even when they were acquainted with metallurgy. Instead, they built magnificent tomb-shrines and temples, comfortable houses in moderately sized villages, and created superb pottery and sculptures. This was a long-lasting period of remarkable creativity and stability, an age free of strife. Their culture was a culture of art.[16]

Gimbutas maintains that it is very difficult for those of us from modern European-based cultures to understand the religion and culture of Old Europe because our world views have been shaped by the ideas of those who overthrew Old Europe. She believes that we are still living under the sway of an aggressive male invasion that began around 4400 BCE. We are only now discovering our long alienation from our authentic European heritage, which was "gylanic, nonviolent and earth-centered."[17] Recently,

Gimbutas's theory of Kurgan invasions from the Russian steppes into eastern Europe has been corroborated by the work of Italian geneticist Luigi Cavalli-Sforza, who has discovered genetic evidence for a population expansion into what is now Europe stemming from an area that closely matches Gimbutas's projection for the center of Kurgan culture.[18]

The research of Gimbutas has come under fire from more orthodox anthropologists because she did not find what she should have found in Old Europe, that is, an inferior, primitive, barbarian prelude to civilization. Instead, Gimbutas argued that embedded in the symbolic language of Old Europe is a culture and a world view that are not only comprehensible but also civilized. Old Europe was nonhierarchical, in tune with nature, peaceful, highly artistic, and in many ways superior to the cultures and world views that followed it in Europe. She rejects the assumption that civilization refers only to androcentric warrior societies and maintains that it is a gross misunderstanding to contend that warfare is endemic to the human condition.

Carol Christ suggests that we should look at the deeper reasons why some scholars are uncomfortable with claims that the culture of Old Europe was violently destroyed. Christ points out that the conquest of the Americas demonstrates that better-armed, well-trained armies can easily defeat less well-armed, less militaristic populations and, over several generations, may also succeed in largely eradicating traditional values. Nonetheless, proponents of the myth of progress insist that cultures proceed onward and upward by a kind of internal logic, with new and superior ideas replacing old and inferior ones. Christ notes: "Most of us continue to think that Christianity became the dominant religion of Europe owing to the inherent superiority of its ideas about human life and because paganism was in decline and decadent, rather than because it took control by the sword and by violent suppression of the practitioners of all other forms of religion."[19]

Gimbutas caused further discomfort among scholars when she placed the female at the center of her work. She believed that at the root of Old Europe's artistic creations and at the heart of its ability to live in harmony for thousands of years was a spiritual world view anchored in an understanding of the Goddess as giver, taker, and renewer of life.

The Goddess as giver of life was symbolized as a bird, a chevron (V), water, stream, zigzags (M), meanders, water birds, breasts, eyes, mouth, beak, spinner, metalworker, music maker, ram, net, the power of three, vulva, birth giver, deer, bear, and snake.

As taker and regenerator of life the Goddess was symbolized as vulture, owl, cuckoo, hawk, dove, boar, the Stiff White Lady (bone), a stiff nude, an egg, the column of life, the regenerative vulva, a triangle, an hourglass, a bird claw, a ship of renewal, a frog, a hedgehog, a fish, a bull, a bee, and a butterfly.

As renewing and eternal Earth she was Earth mother, a pregnant goddess, lozenge and triangle with dots, sow, sacred bread, hill and stone as omphalos (belly), tomb as womb, holed stones, the power of two and doubling. As energy and unfolding she was spiral, lunar cycle, snake coil, hook and ax, opposed spiral, caterpillar, snake head, whirls, comb and brush, standing stone, and circle.[20]

Gimbutas has inspired a whole new generation of feminist researchers to look with new eyes at so-called pre-history and to document that there was God the woman before God the Father. Gimbutas was the first to connect archeology with mythology and scientific research with spirituality. Her findings are remarkably consonant with the new science of physicists, biologists, mathematicians, systems theorists, eco-psychologists, ecofeminists, and others as they come to terms with the mysterious interface of mind and matter, body and spirit, reason and intuition. Gimbutas herself addresses the relevance of her discoveries to contemporary life: "This material, when acknowledged, may affect our vision of the past as well as our sense of potential for the present and future. We must refocus our collective memory. The necessity for this has never been greater as we discover that the path of 'progress' is extinguishing the very conditions for life on earth."[21]

Another view of why the Goddess has been displaced was put forward recently by Dr. Leonard Shlain, a vascular surgeon and chief of laparoscopic surgery at California-Pacific Medical Center in San Francisco. Shlain posits that with the invention of writing the great Goddess began to lose power:

> In their attempts to solve the mystery of the Goddess's dethronement, various authors have implicated foreign invaders, the invention of private property, the formation of archaic states, the creation of surplus wealth and the educational disadvantaging of women. While any or all of these influences may have contributed, I propose another: the decline of the Goddess began when some clever Sumerian first pressed a sharp stick into wet clay and invented writing. The relentless spread of the alphabet two thousand years later spelled Her demise. The introduction of the written word, and then the alphabet, into the social intercourse of humans initiated a fundamental change in the way newly literate cultures understood their reality. It was this dramatic change in mind-set, I propose, that was primarily responsible for fostering patriarchy.[22]

Shlain holds that the Goddess's demise is also related to the development of monotheistic religions that offer an imageless Father deity whose authority rests on his word ("in the beginning was the Word"). Conceiving a deity with no concrete image, he contends, prepared the way for the abstract thinking found in law codes, dualistic philosophy, and mechanistic science. He finds that wherever a culture elevates the written word at the expense of the image, patriarchy dominates; when images are more important than the written word, feminine and egalitarian values flourish.[23]

Shlain's work contributes to the work of feminist scholars to rewrite history from a feminist viewpoint. Today, there is overwhelming archeological and historical evidence that during a long period of our history we worshiped goddess figures as manifestations of the Great Mother. In Sumer, she was Inanna; in Egypt, Isis; in Canaan, Asherah; in Syria, Astarte; in Greece, Demeter; in the Andean cultures, Pachamama. Throughout the world she was recognized as the creatrix of life, nurturer of the young, and source of vitality for both animals and humans; she presided over the great mysteries of living, dying, and rebirth.

Many women feel there is a tremendous allure and joy in discovering the lost mystical world where women were honored as the givers of life. As Charlene Spretnak so poetically writes:

> What was cosmologically wholesome and healing was the discovery of the Divine as immanent and around us. What was intriguing was the sacred link between the Goddess in her many guises and totemic animals and plants, sacred groves, and womblike caves, in the moon-rhythm blood of the menses, the ecstatic dance—the experience of knowing Gaia, her voluptuous contours and fertile plains, her flowing waters that give life, her animal teachers.[24]

Ecofeminists from the Christian tradition, like myself, do not take the discovery of the pre-patriarchal goddess tradition as a call to a literal return to worship her. Rather, this discovery invites us toward liberating ourselves from the ultimacy of the biblical image of the patriarchal God. A growing number of women who have gone through a process of realizing that there was an evolution in our root image of the Holy—that is, that before God there was a more primal image of the Goddess—look for new images more appropriate to how we might now image Ultimate Mystery. Emphasis on the Goddess as a symbol leads to a revaluation of our bodies as women and of the Earth. Carol Christ reminds us that we have a deep human need for symbols and rituals that enable us to cope with evil and suffering and to help us pass through life's key transition moments of birth, sexuality, and death. When the key image of the Divine is the Goddess, women are tremendously empowered, finding "the fierce new love of the divine in themselves."[25] Christ continues:

> For me the divine/Goddess/God/Earth/Life/It symbolizes the whole of which we are a part. This whole is the Earth and sky, the ground on which we stand, and all the animals, plants, and other beings to which we are related. We come

from our mothers and fathers and are rooted in community. We come from the Earth and to the Earth we shall return. Life feeds on life. We live because others die, and we will die so that others may live. The divinity that shapes our ends is life, death, and change, understood both literally and as metaphor for our daily lives.[26]

Jungian Psychology

To understand the importance of the Goddess as a symbol, many ecofeminists have been influenced by the work of Swiss psychiatrist Carl Jung and his work on archetypes. Two years of work in a study group on Jung have dramatically widened my horizons and my awareness of who we are as humans. I have discovered that I am acting on a much larger stage than that of which I was previously aware. I have become more attuned to the components (archetypes) that have entered my psyche without any direct line or tradition. Jung teaches that the *imago dei* in the human psyche is a symbol of our quest for psychic wholeness. I have also learned that we (our bodies as well as our psyches) emerge from the unconscious and return to it, linking us with those who have gone before us as well as with those who will come after us. We are both memory and possibility.

In contrast to Freud, who held that each person is a unique, independent phenomenon, Jung believed that people are unique not in their own right but in terms of the larger entities to which they belong. Although all of us are products of our relationships, Jung held that our interconnectedness is not simply interpersonal but also cosmic. Based on this insight, he offered his idea of the *collective unconscious*, which he saw as a vital force permeating all creation, an energy containing all the thoughts, feelings, and dreams of the past and all the hopes and aspirations of the future, even the evolutionary "aspirations" of the universe itself.

Jung distinguishes between the personal unconscious—things we simply do not remember or that we repress—and the collective unconscious, qualities that are not individually acquired but inherited, such as instincts, impulses, and archetypes. The collective unconscious forms an "omnipresent, unchanging and everywhere identical *quality or substrate of the psyche per se.*"[27]

Jung's notion of the collective unconscious is part of the paradigm shift affecting science. Jung worked closely with physicist Wolfgang Pauli, who pointed out that the idea of the evolution of life requires a revision that would take into account the interrelation between the unconscious psyche and biological processes. Marie Louise von Franz, one of Jung's closest collaborators, believed that the most promising field for future study in a Jungian perspective would be the area of microphysics.

What Jung calls archetypes (those patterns of emotional and mental behavior coming forth from our collective unconscious) could be referred to as probabilities or tendencies in quantum physics. These archetypes tend to become manifest in a "synchronistic arrangement" (Jung) or as a *complementarity* (a term from quantum physics) that includes both matter and psyche. Von Franz maintains that the Jungian concept of meaning or purpose is an example of parallel developments in microphysics and psychology. Just as quantum physicists are looking for the connections in nature rather than for hard and fast laws, so Jung, rather than asking what causes something, asked, What did it happen for?[28]

Like Bateson's "pattern that connects" and Bohm's "folding and unfolding universe," Jung's "deeper stratum" or collective unconscious from which all has come and to which all returns offers a clue to understanding the Ultimate Mystery. For Jung, meaning and purposefulness are not the prerogatives of the mind. Rather, they operate in the whole of living nature. There is really no difference between organic and psychic growth; each will respond to its instinctual/archetypal coding. A plant will produce a flower; the psyche will create a symbol. It is the concept and experience of the archetype that engages ecofeminism. According to Jung:

> The concept of the archetype . . . is derived from the repeated observation that, for instance, the myths and fairytales of world literature contain definite motifs which crop up everywhere. We meet these same motifs in the fantasies, dreams,

deliria, and delusions of individuals living today. These typical images and associations are what I call archetypal ideas. ... They impress, influence, and fascinate us. They have their origin in the archetype, which in itself is an irrepresentable, unconscious, pre-existent form that seems to be part of the inherited structure of the psyche and can therefore manifest itself spontaneously anywhere, at any time.[29]

For Jung, psychology should focus on establishing the ways in which humans are psychologically similar rather than on the study of a seemingly infinite variety of individual differences. In other words, what are the archetypal features of human nature? Jung believed that the human psyche, like the human body, has a definable structure that shares a phylogenetic continuity with the rest of the animal kingdom. In the unconscious, Jung believed, there resided the collective wisdom of our species, the basic program enabling us to meet all the demands of life. He believed that the collective unconscious contains the entire spiritual heritage of human evolution, born anew in the brain structure of every individual. Archetypes have the capacity to initiate, control, and mediate the common behavioral characteristics and typical experiences of our kind, even though we are, for the most part, unaware of them. The archetypes transcend culture, race, and time. Thus, in Jung's view, the mental events experienced by every individual are determined not merely by his or her personal history, but by the collective history of the species as a whole, which is biologically encoded in the collective unconscious, reaching back into the primordial mists of evolutionary time.

Archetypes, then, are biological entities. Like all biological entities they are subject to the laws of evolution. Archetypes are the neuro-psychic centers responsible for coordinating the behavioral and psychic repertoires of our species in response to the environment. The archetype is an inherited mode of functioning, an innate predisposition toward something that is then responsible for patterns of behavior.[30]

The archetypal endowment of each of us presupposes the natural life cycle of our species—being mothered, exploring the environment, playing in the peer group, adolescence, being initiated, establishing a place in the social hierarchy, courting, marrying, child-rearing, hunting, gathering, fighting, participating in religious rituals, assuming the social responsibilities of advanced maturity, and preparation for death. *Ultimately every individual life is the same as the eternal life of the species.* The human is therefore a psychophysical system with a built-in biological clock; our life cycle is predetermined by the evolutionary history of our genes.

Jung believed that throughout the whole cycle of one's life the archetypal function stands behind the scenes as a kind of author-director. According to British Jungian analyst Anthony Stevens, Jung's model proposes a species-related structure composed of archetypal units, which is then filled in by individual development.[31] Jung termed this overall process of archetypal actualization and personality development "individuation." This is the biological process by which every living thing becomes what it was destined to become from the beginning. Nevertheless, for Jung, archetypes have meaning only when you take into account their relation to the living individual. Finally, Jung held that archetypal structures are fundamental to the existence of all living organisms and that they are continuous with structures controlling the behavior of inorganic matter. The archetype, then, is the bridge to matter in general. What is passed from generation to generation is a structure, a characteristic patterning of matter; it is this pattern that forms the replicable archetype of the species.[32]

Jung's concept of archetype is a useful tool to employ in the service of meaning while still respecting the unfathomable mystery of the cosmos. Jung speaks of the archetype as a formative process, more properly understood as a verb than a noun. The psyche has an apparent desire to render a raw flux of atoms intelligible and meaningful by sorting them into patterns. Archetypes create primal forms, which are then filled with the contents unique to a particular culture, a particular artist, a particular dreamer.

According to US Jungian psychologist James Hollis, although life may seem meaningless, human beings are meaning-seeking creatures who are driven to understand it and to form some meaningful relationship to it. We learn from archetypal psychology, from the core of primal religious experiences, from quantum physics, and from the artist's eye that all is energy. Matter is a dynamic, temporary arrangement of energy. Archetypal imagination seeks to connect us to this flow of energy at the heart of the universe. With such images, we have provisional access to Mystery. What is real and omnipresent is energy; what allows us to stand in relationship to that Mystery is image; and what generates the bridge is an autonomous part of our nature, the archetypal imagination. Jungians would argue that we are never more profoundly human than when we express our yearnings, or closer to the divine than when we imagine.[33]

Jung noted that psychology was the last so-called social science to be "invented" because the insights it seeks were previously the domain of tribal mythologies and institutional religions. Affective linkage to the cosmos, nature, and the community were once available through tribal creation stories, heroic legends, and transformative rituals. With the loss of these connective rites and mythic images, the problem of identity and the task of cosmic location or spiritual grounding have become individual dilemmas.

Myths are not created; they are the dramatizations of our encounter with depth, with Mystery. Myths express the divine life as they lift images from the flux of nature to serve as mediatory bridges to the cosmos. Just as there are instincts for biological survival and social interaction, there are instincts (archetypes) for spiritual connection as well.

According to Hollis, we now live in a spiritually impoverished time, what he terms "the Great In-Between," when our current gods no longer give us sufficient meaning. We live in the waning days of some larger historical period but cannot yet glimpse the rebirth that will spring forth later. But although we have lost our spiritual connection, we have not lost our spiritual desire. Hollis maintains that this is true because the images generally available to us have lost their power to point beyond themselves and thus fail to connect us to Mystery, even though we may cling to certain "image husks" with fundamental fervor. Hidden in the etymological recesses of the gods and goddesses are fundamental insights into the nature of reality. In fact, Jungians would define these divine beings as the affect-laden, highly charged, numinous images that arise out of a depth experience. Modernism diminishes the numinosity of these root metaphors and replaces them with artifacts of the intellect that no longer stir the heart.[34]

Jung held that a condition of our mortality is the fact that webs of programmed tissues and autonomous energies move us to rhythms not consciously ours. Who or what invents our dreams, our religions, our patterned choices? What powers urge us to reproduce, to build civilization, to long for meaning? These are the archetypal powers, more ancient than we can imagine. Hollis believes that this little incarnation we call our life is but the vehicle for a larger journey that divinity makes through us. We are asked to become the individual in order that our small portion of the unfolding of the divine may be achieved.[35]

Although Jung's insights into the nature and function of archetypes have been essential to the development of ecofeminist philosophy, some ecofeminists are critical of the patriarchal lens with which Jung applied his theories. Feminist Jungian analysts struggle with the concept of archetypes, attempting to adjust Jungian insights to feminist theory. No one has wrestled more with Jungian archetypes and their applicability for contemporary women than feminist psychologist and social philosopher Madonna Kolbenschlag, who has been a close collaborator of Con-spirando and a visiting lecturer as well.

Kolbenschlag has described Jung's concept of archetypes as experiences that, along with their accompanying emotions and affects, form a residual substratum in the subconscious. New experiences tend to be organized according to the preexisting pattern. Kolbenschlag found that the so-called feminine archetypes have been described primarily from the point of view of a patriarchal imagination. Today, women are deconstructing these archetypes and reconstructing them to reflect women's reality: "Archetypes of the feminine became categories to contain women—and most destructively because of their reputed origin in a transcendent and religious realm, the archetypes had acquired an irrefutable numinosity. An archetype can never be thought of as an image whose content is frozen but must be thought of as a dynamic process that forms and reforms images in relation to repeated experiences."[36]

In 1956 Toni Wolff, a protégé and lover of Jung's, proposed a typology of the feminine psyche with four archetypes: Mother, Hetaria (Lover), Amazon (Warrior), and Medium. Working with Wolff's schema, Kolbenschlag has shown how the many goddess figures of the past reflect these four archetypal yearnings.[37] She concludes:

> If we see through the patriarchal gaze to the dynamic energy fields that represent the experience of being woman, being feminine, then the archetypes and the images of them we have inherited—in our soul, as well as in the representations of human art—can be a mirror for discovering lost or repressed aspects of our own power. We can invoke them as oracles. We can question them. They can speak to us. The archetypes look backward (through evolutionary, anthropological, and cultural history). They can look forward (through dreams, creative imaginations, artistic transformations, and the real experience of women). The archetypes do not remain static. They have a dynamic aspect that only women can fully discern. In our own search for wholeness, the fragmented images of the Goddess become one again.[38]

Like ecofeminist anthropologists, Jungian ecofeminists find the discovery of the Goddess in her many forms to be deeply liberating. As Kolbenschlag writes:

> We are like orphans, descended from a Great Mother, whose teaching and values we have forgotten. We are ignorant of our true ancestry. So we must think back through Eve, rethink the "fall," the eclipse, the fragmentation, the displacement. She demands recognition and we must rediscover her. The paradigm of the future begins there. . . . The image of Eve, symbol of our lost birthright of power and our lost connection with the Mother of All, will fade as the goddesses reappear. . . . In the theophany of feminine archetypes in our time we are discovering our "original face" and a map for the future of the human community. . . . Remember, you are a goddess, and all the goddesses dwell within you.[39]

THE BODY AS A SOURCE OF WISDOM

Closely linked to the discovery of the existence of the Goddess both in history and in psychology and to the new perception of the Earth and the entire universe as one interrelated, ongoing cosmogenesis, is ecofeminism's revaluation of the wisdom residing in our bodies. Ecofeminists explicitly value the connection between women and nature to counterbalance the long patriarchal era, which denied the human species' dependence on both. In the words of Charlene Spretnak, "Earthbody and the personal body are sacred."[40]

Recovering the sacredness of the body is largely a reaction against Christianity's deeply ingrained misogyny that views the flesh, particularly that of women, as an occasion of sin and that in the Genesis myth still regards Eve as the great temptress of Adam, she who brings evil into the world. Celebrating female embodiment also attempts to cut through the dualistic split that links women with nature and men with culture. This separation sets the male apart from nature and from women in a way that allows for the development of cruel and oppressive behavior toward both. Ecofeminists remind us that we all share a universal kinship with nature and that human embeddedness in the Earth is directly related to our human embodiment. As ecofeminist Mary Mellor writes: "Ecological impacts and consequences are experienced through human bodies, in ill health, early death, congenital damage and impeded childhood development. Women disproportionately bear the consequences of those impacts within their own bodies (dioxin residues in breast milk, failed pregnancies) and in their work as nurturers and caretakers."[41] For ecofeminists, then, concern for the planet's well-being is directly related to women's embodied experiences. Revaluing that experience is key to establishing a post-patriarchal world.

Ecofeminism is in conflict with a postmodern social deconstructionist position that accords all agency to human society and culture. The physical materiality of human life is real; as a species, human beings form part of the Earth and the universe, which, as we have seen, has its own dynamics that are beyond

human "construction." Embodiment is a universal human condition. Ecofeminists point out how gender inequality has been
used to create a false division between nature and culture. Although female humans are clearly no closer to the Earth than
male humans, anthropological studies indicate that the division
that associates women with nature, the body, sexuality, mortality,
and the propensity to "sin" and men with culture, the spirit, the
mind, and the power to dominate women and nature is very ancient. According to ecofeminist theologian Rosemary Radford
Ruether, a key element in identifying women with nature is their
reproductive role. It is the woman who gives birth and then nur-
tures her offspring by producing and preparing food, clothing,
shelter, education, and so on. The man, in contrast, took on the
harder work of hunting; because it was dangerous, it also came to
be considered prestigious. Because these tasks were more occasional than continual, men had more leisure time. Ruether points
out that this leisure time was historically monopolized by men to
"make culture" as some sort of privilege of a superior order. With
time, women's work of maintaining the material basis of the home
and the well-being of the family came to be seen as inferior work,
both by men and by women themselves. The domestic work of
caring for home and children became exclusively the realm of
women. The Earth, as the birthplace of animals and plants, became associated with women's bodies, the birthplace of human
young.[42]

The ecofeminist emphasis on embodiment and on celebrating
our link with nature has rankled socialist and liberal feminists who
view women's liberation as freedom from their biological con-
straints. As feminist Cecile Jackson writes: "Ecofeminist prescrip-
tions are for women to . . . embrace the body, bond to our mothers, remain embedded in our local ecosystems, abandon the goals
of freedom and autonomy, rely on and care for our kin and community and remain in subsistence production. Such conserva-
tism can hardly claim empowerment for women."[43] Jackson's
underscoring of the feminist struggle for women's freedom and
autonomy calls attention to the contradictory aspects of
ecofeminism as it tries to bridge feminist and ecological perspectives. Ecofeminists must convince their socialist and liberal

feminist sisters to let go of their Enlightenment-based commitment to individual freedom and autonomy in favor of belonging to a larger web of life. At the same time, they must convince their mostly male deep-ecologist friends that male dominance and patriarchy are root causes of the present state of affairs.

However, radical feminists such as Adrienne Rich argue that when feminists have recoiled from their bodies, they are reflecting the patriarchal rejection of female biology. Rich calls upon women to reclaim and gain control over their bodies, to explore and understand

> our biological grounding, the miracle and paradox of the female body and its spiritual and political meanings . . . to think through the body so that every woman is the presiding genius of her own body. . . . In order to live a fully human life . . . we must touch the unity and resonance of our physicality, our bond with the natural order, the corporeal ground of our intelligence. In so far as (some) men have transcended their physicality, they have lost contact with the natural order.[44]

Failure to confront human frailty is leading humanity into a deep pathology created by the patriarchal mindset. As ecofeminists point out, human beings are the only species aware that it will die, a realization that creates a tremendous existential anxiety unless we also realize that we are finite—from the earth we have come and to the earth we will return—which is the destiny of all who form the web of earthly life. Embracing embodiment is a way out of such pathos.

Another criticism leveled at ecofeminism is that it maintains that women have "epistemic privilege" in relation to the natural world. Because women are mothers and nurturers, because our bodies are more in tune with nature's cycles, and/or because we have been oppressed, our "lived experience" makes us more "in sync" with the Earth. As Spretnak writes: "What can't be said, though, is that women are drawn to ecology simply because we are female."[45] Indian ecofeminist Vandana Shiva makes the same point when she talks about "women as knowers"—they know how to survive because they have learned to do so from nature, which is "the very basis and matrix of economic life."[46] Shiva finds that present-day development programs treat poor women as "non-knowers," despite their lived experience. Whether or not women have more knowledge of the Earth than men remains an open question. Ecofeminism invites us to remember that we are embedded and embodied human beings, male and female, who "know" the natural world because we are part of it.

Ecofeminism, then, sees all humanity as embodied, but with gendered bodies—and therein lies the contradiction. Women are materially associated with—and largely responsible for—human embodiment, whether as paid or unpaid workers. The needs of human embodiment are shared by all humanity but are disproportionately borne in the bodies and lives of women.[47] As Mellor says:

> Women do have particular bodies that do particular things, but what matters is how society takes account of sexual differences and the whole question of the materiality of human existence. Women are not closer to nature because of some elemental physiological or spiritual affinity, but because of the social circumstances in which they find themselves—that is, their material conditions. Women's disproportionate responsibility for human embodiment is partly expressed in the work that women do, but also in their availability for biological needs. . . . Whatever social lives people construct they are always delimited by bodily existence. Equally, social lives are delimited by the ecosystem.[48]

Even more to the point, Ynestra King writes:

> It is as if women were entrusted with and have kept the dirty little secret that humanity emerges from non-human nature into society in the life of the species and the person. The process of nurturing an unsocialized, undifferentiated human infant into an adult person—the socialization of the

organic—is the bridge between nature and culture. The western male bourgeois then extracts himself from the realm of the organic to become a public citizen, as if born from the head of Zeus. He puts away childish things. He disempowers and sentimentalizes his mother, sacrificing her to nature. But the key to the historic agency of women with respect to the nature/culture dualism lies in the fact that the traditional activities of women—mothering, cooking, healing, farming, foraging—are as social as they are natural.[49]

Concretely, celebrating embodiment has triggered an irruption of rituals, meditations, and other practices that engender ecofeminist spirituality. These celebrations—often linked to the Earth's cycles—are marked by embeddedness, by a remembering of our belonging to the Earth and to the universe. Inspired by a cosmovision that now offers a broader sense of self, practical ecofeminists find themselves planting gardens where they can spend time contemplating the growth cycle of their medicinal herbs, their organic vegetables, their spices. Many practice tai chi or other forms of body movement to begin or end their day, greeting the sunrise or sunset, or to feel more connected to the moon, the planets, and the stars. They engage in sacred dances both ancient and new. They celebrate their own life cycles—the arrival of a young girl's first menstruation, the croning of a post-menopausal woman. Many practice the ancient custom of walking a labyrinth.

Reconnecting with the wisdom of the body has also raised criticisms of the current "mechanistic" health system and the way contemporary society views health and disease. Ecofeminists, who know that we cannot have healthy people if the planet is sick, are committed to holistic health practices. Convinced that the mind-body split must be healed, many ecofeminists draw from the insights of the new science and connect health and well-being to the larger energy flow of the universe itself. Thus, healing bodies and healing the Earth are seen as inseparable. Many are learning and using Eastern healing practices such as acupuncture, reiki, and chakra work.

ATTEMPTS TO FORM POST-PATRIARCHAL COMMUNITIES

Just as deep ecologists hold up bioregionalism and local, community-based economies geared toward sustainability rather than growth, so also do radical and cultural feminists long for local communities where relationships are based on justice, equality, and respect for women, men, and children and where a post-patriarchal gestalt is the norm.

An ecofeminist society, as described by Mellor,

> would be egalitarian and ecologically sustainable. There would be no sexual/gender division of labor, and any necessary work would be integrated with all aspects of communal life. Relationships between humans and between humans and nature would be harmonious and co-operative. . . . Most ecofeminists are at pains to include men in these utopian dreams and hold up diversity of gender, race, age and sexual orientation as essential for a viable community.[50]

Rosemary Radford Ruether also maps out a vision for a post-patriarchal time in *Gaia and God*. She calls us to build "communities of celebration and resistance"—which she defines as local, face-to-face groups with which one lives, works, and prays. These communities have three interrelated characteristics:

> One is shaping the personal therapies, spiritualities, and corporate liturgies by which we nurture and symbolize a new biophilic consciousness. Second, there is the utilization of local institutions over which we have some control, our homes, schools, churches, farms and locally controlled businesses, as pilot projects of ecological living. Third, there is the building of organizational networks that reach out, regionally, nationally and internationally, in a struggle to change the power structures that keep the present death system in place.[51]

For Ruether, healing therapies and spiritualities need to concentrate on inner growth, on learning how to just "be," on learning how to rejoice in the goodness and beauty of life. She calls upon these communities to recover our body-psyche-spirit nexus, "to learn to breathe again, to feel our life energy . . . to get back in touch with the living earth. We can start to release the stifled intuitive and creative powers of our organism, to draw and to write poetry, and to know that we stand on holy ground."[52] These communities should create their own liturgies to mourn together and to celebrate healing and new birth. Ruether believes that such communities, if they organize in an ecologically healthy way, can become pilot projects for consciousness-raising on a larger scale, gradually affecting energy use, waste disposal, transportation, and agriculture—indeed the whole way in which a society is organized. While utopian, these communities of celebration and resistance do offer—to my way of thinking—our best hope to live justly and rightly into the future. As she concludes, "Being rooted in love for our real communities of life and for our common mother, Gaia, can teach us patient passion, a passion that is not burnt out in a season, but can be renewed season after season."[53]

Attempts to forge sustainable, post-patriarchal communities are sprouting up around the globe as more and more people realize that humanity must find alternative, sustainable ways of surviving to replace the current system of runaway capitalism. While the range of these communities is as varied as the people involved in them, amazing growth has taken place in the number of ecological learning centers, sometimes called eco-spirituality centers or even eco-monasteries, established by groups of Catholic religious sisters. While this is happening primarily in the United States, such centers are also popping up in the Third World as well as a result of the influence of US missionary sisters on their native counterparts.

Women's religious congregations seem to be most open to embracing the new cosmology. Inspired by the thought of Thomas Berry and his invitation to re-inhabit the Earth by learning from the Earth itself, nuns are becoming organic farmers and gardeners, vegetarian cooks, reiki masters, holistic health practitioners, grassroots botanists, astronomy buffs, and teachers/learners of ecology and cosmology—all within the new centers they are founding. I'm aware of three ecological learning centers in my home state of Ohio—one founded by my old community, the Sisters of the Humility of Mary; a second founded by the Akron Dominicans; and a third founded by Paula Gonzalez, a Sister of Charity of Cincinnati. Such centers are also present in Brazil, Nicaragua, and Costa Rica; there are two in Chile.[54]

Much of the inspiration for these centers comes from Genesis Farm, an ecological learning center in New Jersey that was founded in 1980 by Dominican Sister Miriam Therese MacGillis. A passionate disciple of Thomas Berry, MacGillis has a viable organic farm and has also sparked projects such as community gardens, a local elementary school that teaches the new cosmology, a university-degreed master's program in ecological sustainability, and a movement to learn about and protect the region's ecosystem. She also holds rituals to mark the changes of the seasons.

MacGillis is inspiring a generation of religious to return to rootedness. Quoting Berry, who maintains that to garden is to activate the deepest mysteries of the universe, she sees gardening "as an invitation into the journey of the cosmos as it unfolds and reveals itself in a cauliflower. To enter into the interior spaces of the natural world is to be confronted with our own arrogance. We must disarm ourselves of so many of our attitudes of inner dominance or of indifference if we are to discover the divine."[55]

MacGillis is calling for a new way of living religious life—a call to what Diarmuid O'Murchu calls "liminality":

> The task of a liminal community is to both clarify the structure of society and to be instrumental in changing it. In a sense, every society creates its own liminal groups. Usually unconsciously, a society sets aside certain individuals and groups and endows them with intensive value systems. It projects upon these liminal groups its deepest hopes, dreams and aspirations and requests the liminal person or group to embody and articulate for society at large the deepest values the society finds sacred. Put more simply, we seem to

need models that will embody for us the ideals we deeply believe in. Yet society can be very ambivalent about such persons or groups. Sometimes it dismisses them as totally irrelevant, often persecuting—even executing—them, while at the same time admiring them, however begrudgingly. We use these liminal groups to articulate our archetypal values. Society has always done this and there is good reason to believe that it always will. It is often in hindsight that a specific person, group or movement is deemed to be liminal. Liminality is not something one sets out to create. Rather, it is the product of the creative imagination, seeking to respond to the pressing needs of the contemporary world, fueled by a new vision of the future. It is a call to provide a mirror image in which people can see reflected their own searching, struggles, and hopes for a more meaningful existence.[56]

The call to liminality can be lived out in endeavors such as Genesis Farm. However, these eco-spirituality centers founded mostly by women religious are also inspired by a renewed sense of the meaning of the vows of poverty, chastity, and obedience. Poverty becomes the call to be satisfied with the community of life and the human's place within it:

> We will be content and joyful when we recognize our own place in that community. Thus, we will be able to restrain our addiction to consumption, which is eating the planet alive. From this perspective, we will be able to tap the energy necessary to create the new forms of sustainability so needed at this time. We will have the energy to bring human needs into harmony with the community of life.[57]

Chastity is seen as the human need for bonding. MacGillis notes that today there is a tremendous brokenness in the self. As a result, we often manipulate others in order to build our own self-esteem. The actual call is to be pure of heart, to be chaste. It is about *how* we bond with others, and this has nothing whatsoever to do with celibacy. For MacGillis, a lack of chastity results in sexism, racism, and militarism: "We are called to witness against the fact that the whole planet has been brought into a pornographic objectification. But now the whole planet will have to become 'chaste' to survive—will have to see all as subjects, not as objects."[58]

Finally, obedience is seen as a call to respond to the creativity at the heart of the universe. We must be obedient to that process.

MacGillis sees this understanding of poverty, chastity, and obedience as a call to all human beings. Religious vows should be seen as a covenant with the land to protect, defend, and foster the Earth's journey into the future. She advises religious communities to convert their motherhouses into bioregions and invites religious congregations to refound themselves into the larger community of life:

> We are invited to be a presence in the region. To develop the capacity to hear the voices of this sacred community. To listen to the scriptures of the natural world. To form new communities in our bioregions. We must remember that the earth is primary; the human is derivative. We must come home to our bioregions and make food a sacrament again; to sense the spirit in food lovingly nurtured. I suggest that we are coming once again to "the fullness of time." Perhaps we are not at the end of religious life. I suspect we are just beginning![59]

Although this new vision is exciting, it is a "mustard seed" that has not yet had any influence on institutional religious life. And again, it is happening primarily in the United States. Latin American religious women are rather attracted to learning about natural medicines and treatments to heal those they work with—whether victims of violence, people suffering from AIDS, malnourished children, or the indigent and elderly. A growing number of religious sisters work in the region's slums or in impoverished rural areas or with indigenous people and have been quietly training themselves as medicine women to treat specific diseases. They are also becoming experts in herbal medicine and treatments. Although they may not necessarily agree with being called such, they are assuming an ancient and revered role among Latin America's indigenous peoples—that of the *curandera* (healer), *machi* (holy woman), or *bruja* (witch/hag). Like their counterparts of old, they know that healing involves the spirit as well as the body; they use not only their skills of midwifery and herbal remedies, but also their training in psychology and counseling to offer wholeness to the people they serve.[60]

During the last twelve years of work with ecofeminist thought, especially as it applies to theology, ethics, and spirituality in Latin America, I have developed a genealogy, shown in Figure 3–1, that demonstrates the spectrum of influences described in the previous chapter and this chapter that coalesces in ecofeminism.[61]

Figure 3–1 visually describes the way in which ecofeminism combines insights coming from several different sources, including deep ecology and radical or cultural feminism. Deep ecology, in turn, has been influenced by discoveries coming from the new science and by new thinking in cybernetics. This has evolved into a new way of viewing the universe, a new cosmology. While new, this cosmology finds that it shares much with the forgotten wisdom of the Earth's original peoples (indigenous cosmologies). Deep ecologists call us toward new ways of organizing ourselves that are more sustainable and reflect the caring capacity of the Earth's bioregions.

Radical/cultural feminism looks at the patterns of culture and consciousness that sustain patriarchy. These feminist researchers have found major insights into the development of patriarchy through work being done in feminist anthropology, especially in reexamining early goddess myths and culture. They have also been influenced by concepts such as the collective unconsciousness and the archetypes as developed by psychiatrist Carl Jung. Radical/cultural feminists are rediscovering the wisdom that dwells within the body. They urge us to work toward a post-patriarchal world where equalitarian relationships exist between the sexes and between humans and the Earth community.

In summary, ecofeminism may perhaps be simply a new term for an ancient wisdom—a wisdom that still lies dormant within our genetic memories. Like that wisdom, ecofeminism's greatest insight is the dawning conviction that everything is connected.

Figure 3-1. Sources of Ecofeminism

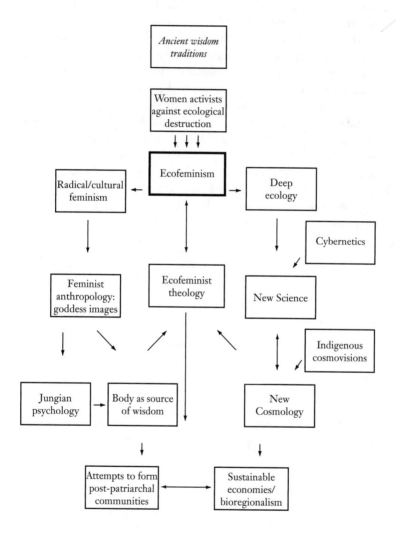

Ecofeminists make the connection that the oppression of women and of people of color by a system controlled by ruling-class males and the devastation of the planet are two forms of violence that reinforce and feed upon each other. They both come from a misguided sense of the need to control, to dominate the other. From being the source of life, both women and the Earth have become resources to be used (and abused) as the power structures see fit.

Ecofeminists join with all those searching for a more holistic world view that recognizes and celebrates the web of all life. This ecofeminist posture places those embracing it firmly in the postmodern debate as well as in the post-patriarchal quest for a more relevant and passionate understanding of who we are in relation to the entire cosmos. This is why ecofeminists are searching for a more adequate theology, the subject of the following chapters.

PART II

THE NATURE
OF ECOFEMINISM

4

Ecofeminist
Theology

You are a goddess and all the goddesses abide in thee.
—MADONNA KOLBENSCHLAG

From its beginnings, ecofeminism has had a strong link to spirituality, and many of its writers have described ecofeminist intuitions using impassioned poetic and often mystical language. Indeed, this orientation toward spirituality gives ecofeminism much of its vitality.

In general, ecofeminists can be classified—although not rigidly—on a scale running between Christian and post-Christian postures. Here, however, we walk a thin line; there is a tendency among Christian theologians to classify as post-Christian the ecofeminists who challenge key concepts of Christianity as being unredeemably patriarchal. It seems to me that unless a person actually proclaims that she is post-Christian, it is an injustice to label her as such. Re-imaging the body of Judeo-Christian theology within the new cosmology and as post-patriarchal is a daunting task. Ecofeminist theologians who do not choose to "throw in the towel" on a tradition so riddled with a patriarchal mindset must look back on their heritage and rediscover its core teachings.

POST-CHRISTIAN ECOFEMINISTS

It is not too surprising, then, to see that most of the more widely known spiritual ecofeminists are post-Christian. Included would be Starhawk, Charlene Spretnak, Carol Christ, and Susan Griffin—all drawn to an Earth-based spirituality where the figure of the Goddess as a literal divinity or a symbol is essential. Starhawk is a practitioner of Wicca, which she describes as the "old religion of Paganism."[1] Although she lifts up the Judeo-Christian heritage of social justice for the oppressed in her book *States of Grace*, Charlene Spretnak is convinced that the God of Christian revelation supports the oppression of both women and the Earth. She argues that the Christian God is thoroughly transcendent and that Christianity has a hierarchical understanding of the human as autonomous and ranking above the nonhuman.[2] Carol Christ, who calls herself a the*a*logian, finds Christianity to be male-centered and anti-body, in that it rejects the flesh, especially when it comes in the form of a woman. She argues that the Goddess legitimizes female power as beneficent and independent and that when women identify with the Goddess as symbol they find "a fierce new love of the divine in themselves."[3] Poet Susan Griffin was one of the first to hold up women's deep identification with nature: "This earth is my sister: I love her daily grace, her silent daring, and how loved I am . . . and I do not forget: what she is to me, what I am to her."[4]

Griffin, like other ecofeminists, has been deeply influenced by the writings of radical feminist philosopher and theologian Mary Daly. Daly's commitment to reclaiming women's spiritual history from patriarchal theology led her to search for an alternative mythology present in pre-patriarchal times. Her famous statement, "If God is male, then the male is God," has resonated with a whole generation of feminist theologians. In her 1973 classic, *Beyond God the Father*, Daly declared that it would be impossible to redeem Christianity from patriarchy and literally "left" the Catholic church. She called upon feminists to opt out of patriarchal cultures while at the same time documenting the evils of "the Most Holy Trinity: rape, genocide and war."[5] Daly continues to create her own symbolic language in anticipation of a post-patriarchal consciousness that will engender communities of women connected to the "elemental world" of our familiars—cats, cows, trees, the dark side of the moon—where we can touch the world of mystery that we communed with before the arrival of patriarchy.[6]

An organic vision of nature and a spirituality that affirms the sacredness of the entire Earth community are shared by both Christian and post-Christian ecofeminists. But whereas post-Christian ecofeminists such as Starhawk, Spretnak, and Christ see the Divine as totally immanent, Christian ecofeminists search the Judeo-Christian tradition for a theology of God that is compatible with an organic vision of the Earth. Christian ecofeminists whose contributions merit special attention include Sallie McFague and Rosemary Radford Ruether.

CHRISTIAN ECOFEMINISTS

Ecological theologian Sallie McFague uses the terms *mother*, *lover*, and *friend* in her search to name the experience of God in this era of anguish over the planet's devastation.[7] She is interested in the language about God in the Bible and argues that it is both metaphorical and expressive of relationship. As such, it is fluid and can evolve. McFague is also committed to a recovery of immanence in metaphors to describe the Divine. She believes that "without a sense of the nearness of God, the overwhelming sense of the way God pervades and permeates our very being, people will not find the God of Christian revelation relevant to their lives and concerns."[8] She offers the metaphor of the world as the body of God, which reflects a theological model in which all entities in the cosmos are united symbiotically in levels of interdependence but are also separated as centers of action and response.[9]

Critical of post-Christian ecofeminist insistence on the immanence of the Divine, McFague argues that God cannot be reduced to the world any more than we humans can be reduced to our bodies. She proposes a pan*en*theistic understanding of God—that is, a God-world relationship in which the world exists in God. She is careful not to equate God with the cosmos, insisting, in the classical Scholastic argument, that God is more than the sum of the parts. But while God transcends the world, nothing exists without God. At the same time, God is being "bodied forth" in the evolutionary process in an increasing complex manner. She understands creation as the continuing, dynamic, growing embodiment of God, an embodiment that counterbalances centuries of overemphasis on God's transcendence. Indeed, she describes a cosmos wherein "immanental transcendence or transcendent immanence is the model of the universe."[10] This unity between immanence and transcendence is realized in the incarnation of Jesus Christ. The Son of God is embodied in our world and becomes the sign of God's involvement with the created universe.

While McFague argues convincingly that "bodies matter" in Christian theology, her theology is, in the end, a variation of classical incarnational theology; to me, it still appears dualistic. She still images God as an external agent who directs the evolutionary unfolding of creation, thus maintaining the separation between Creator and creation. McFague has great difficulty describing a non-dualistic God. As Jennifer M. Molineaux writes, McFague "resists the ultimate, immanent identification of God with the world. She feels that pantheism would take her too far beyond Christianity. As a Christian reformist, she wants God to identify and suffer with creation, yet retain a transcendence unlimited by it."[11] As post-Christian ecofeminists point out, there is a real problem besetting religions of transcendence in that they lead us to look for the grounding of this world somewhere outside of it. Emphasis remains on a God who creates "out of nothing" *(ex nihilo)* or as the "prime mover" who is external to the created order. Even with her incarnational emphasis on God/Sophia becoming human flesh, McFague's emphasis is still on a transcendent Ultimate Source.

The struggle to overcome dualisms in describing the Divine continues to be a major stumbling block for ecofeminists who grapple with the Christian tradition.

Rosemary Radford Ruether has moved further along in this journey. Ruether, one of the "mothers" of contemporary feminist theology, has moved toward ecofeminism in the last decade. *Gaia and God: An Ecofeminist Theology of Earth Healing* is, to date, her major attempt to situate ecofeminism within classical as well as feminist theological discourse.[12]

Ruether thoroughly explores the development of the links between the subjugation of women and the rape of the Earth. She writes, "Domination of women has provided a key link, both socially and symbolically, to the domination of earth, hence the tendency in patriarchal cultures to link women with earth, matter, and nature, while identifying males with sky, intellect, and transcendent spirit."[13] Ruether says that healed relationships with one another and with the Earth call for a new consciousness, a new symbolic culture, and a new spirituality. They also call for a new vision of the source of life that is "yet more" than what presently exists, continually bringing forth both new life and new visions of how life should be more just and more caring. Ruether finds that we have constructed a concept of ourselves over against all that is not human, thus creating a sense of the natural world as both nonhuman and non-divine.

In *Gaia and God* Ruether reviews the interlocking nature of the domination of women and of the domination of nature throughout history. Her central question is how to heal the human community from both its sexism and its alienation from the rest of nature, which is the "sustaining matrix" of all life. Because she seeks to be faithful to the Christian tradition, she raises up two patterns of biblical thought—covenantal ethics and sacramental cosmology—as important resources for an emerging ecofeminist theology.

Covenantal ethics offers a vision of a community of humans—farmers and their families, other farm workers—rooted in the land, all living in a covenantal relation with a caretaking God. Ruether points out that while the patriarchal/slave-holding overlay of this local covenantal unit must be rejected, what is insightful is the sense that humans, even the farmers, do not own the land and cannot do with it what they will.

Humans are but caretakers of a land that ultimately belongs to God, and they are accountable to God for the well-being of all that dwell there—humans, animals, the very soil itself. Good caretaking demands periodic rest and restoration—every seven days, every seven years, and even after seven times seven years. The Jubilee Year will bring the great restoration, which includes the revolutionary dismantling of the systems of unjust accumulation of land and exploitation of labor that have occurred over the past two generations. Debts must be canceled, slaves must be freed, and land alienated from peasants through debt and enslavement must be restored. There must be land reform to recreate a society in which each household has the land needed for its own maintenance. Unjust social and economic relations are canceled, and animals and land are given rest to restore a just and sustainable balance among humans and among humans and the animals and soil.

Ruether maintains that covenantal ethics should be complemented by a sacramental cosmology based on the Jewish Wisdom tradition and the cosmic Christology of the New Testament. Herein she discovers a deep respect for the body as the sacramental "bodying forth" of the creative Spirit not only in the human body, but also in the whole body of the cosmos that surrounds us and sustains our life. For Ruether, the God in whom we live and move and have our being is not some detached spiritual being far away in heaven, but the one who is in and through and under the whole life process. The whole cosmos is God's body. For Christians, it is the body of Christ that overcomes our alienation and separation from God's sacramental presence in creation. We are called to commune with God, not by turning away from body, but in and through the mystery of bodies, which are sacramental presences of the divine.[14]

In these two traditions, covenantal and sacramental, we hear two voices of divinity from nature. One speaks from the mountaintops in the thunderous masculine tones of "thou shalt" and "thou shalt not." It is the voice of power and law, but speaking, at its most authentic on behalf of the weak, as a mandate to protect the powerless and to restrain the power of the mighty. There is another voice, one that speaks from the intimate heart of matter. It has long been silenced by the masculine voice, but today is finding again her own voice. This is the voice of Gaia. Her voice does not translate into laws or intellectual knowledge but beacons us into communion.

Both of these voices, of God and of Gaia, are our own voices. We need to claim them as our own, not in the sense that there is "nothing" out there, but in the sense that what is "out there" can only be experienced by us through the lenses of human existence. We are not the source of life, but are latecomers to the planet. Our minds didn't fall from the skies, but are the flowering of organic body and its capacities to know itself. We can touch our fellow beings, and intuit the source of all life and thought that lies behind the whole. This contact, though humanly imaged, can be true. Its truth lies in the test of relationships; do our metaphors bear the fruits of compassion or of enmity?[15]

Ruether does not believe that a feminist ecological culture can be recovered from past pre-patriarchal cultures. She questions the assumption that an earlier matristic, peace-loving "paradise" is possible, as suggested by Gimbutas. She finds efforts to recover such pre-patriarchal ecofeminist cultures as imaginative efforts of people in advanced industrial societies to find a more meaningful myth. "Some see the Jewish and Christian male monotheistic God as a hostile concept that rationalizes alienation from and neglect of the earth. . . . I agree with much of this critique, yet I believe that merely replacing a male transcendent deity with an immanent female one is an insufficient answer to the 'god-problem.'"[16] She calls for a more imaginative solution to these traditional oppositions than simply their reversal.

For Ruether, the weakness of such matristic societies lies in finding satisfactory roles for adult males that neither support male dominance over women nor produce demoralized males deeply resentful of women:

While the female role is built into the process of life-re-production and food gathering, the male role has to be constructed socially. Societies that fail to develop an adequately affirmative role for men, one that gives men prestige parallel to that of women but prevents their assuming aggressive dominance over women, risk developing the resentful male, who defines his masculinity in hostile negation of women.[17]

Deeply influenced by the new cosmology coming from Berry and Swimme, Ruether is firmly convinced of humanity's need to recognize our utter dependence on the life-producing matrix of the planet in order to reintegrate our system of production, consumption, and waste into the ecological feedback patterns by which nature sustains and renews itself. A transcendent God who is outside the world does not infuse human consciousness into human bodies. Rather, human consciousness is an intensification of the awareness that exists to some degree on every level of reality, from subatomic physics, to organic molecules, to photosynthesizing plants, to increasingly self-aware and communicating animals. "We might think of our particular gift of symbol-making consciousness as where all nature becomes conscious of itself in a new self-reflective way, not in the sense of separating us from other species, but in the sense of celebrating the whole cosmic creative process, as well as learning to harmonize our needs with those of the rest of the earth-community."[18]

This vision of an earth community reshapes the concept of God. A patriarchal perspective has modeled God as a male-identified mind or soul that has been thought of as prior to body, existing in an unoriginated, unembodied mental realm outside of, but dominating, the physical cosmos. By contrast, Ruether's ecofeminist theology embodies God *in and through and under the whole cosmic process*. God is imagined, therefore, as neither exclusively male nor anthropomorphic, but rather as the font from which the variety of plants and animals well up in each generation. God is the matrix that sustains and renews their life-giving interdependency.

Answering the charge that such a description of God smacks of immanentism, of a concept of God that lacks transcendence, Ruether suggests rethinking the whole concept of transcendence. She argues that transcendence-immanence has been understood for too long in dualistic terms of either-or, mind-body, and male-female splits. Ecofeminist theology sees God's transcendence not in terms of a disembodied mind outside the universe but as a renewing divine Spirit radically free from systems of domination. An ecofeminist understanding of God as divine Wisdom sustains daily life processes and also grounds the creative transformations by which we free ourselves from domination and the distortions of injustice.[19]

Like McFague, Ruether also uses the image of the universe as God's body, but Ruether seems to rise above McFague's dualism:

> We humans are the evolutionary growing edge of this imperfectly realized impulse to consciousness and kindness. But this does not separate us from the common fate we share of organisms that grow and then die. An ecological ethic must be based on acceptance of both sides of this dilemma of humanness, both the way we represent the growing edge of what is "not yet" of greater awareness and benignity, and our organic mortality, which we share with the plants and animals. We pass on our ideals to the future not by escaping personal death, but by partly reshaping "nature" to reflect these human ideals. But this reshaping is finally governed by the finite limits of the interdependence of all life in the living system that is Gaia.[20]

Nowhere is Ruether more visionary than in her short section called "Toward an Ecofeminist Theocosmology." She underlines our urgent task to convert human consciousness to the Earth in order to act as sustainers, not destroyers, of the web of life. Along with mentors such as Pierre Teilhard de Chardin, Thomas Berry, and Brian Swimme, she reminds us that we recognize our kinship with all other beings through our human self-awareness. As our sense of self is enlarged, we also become aware of the fragility of our individual self. There is a need to let go of the ego yet affirm the integrity of our personal center of being; this must always be done in mutuality with the personal centers of all other beings across species.

> Like humans, the animals and the plants are living centers of organic life that exist for a season. Then each of our roots shrivels, the organic structures that sustain our life fail, and we die. The cutting of the life center also means that our bodies disintegrate into organic matter, to enter the cycle of decomposition and re-composition as other entities. The material substances of our bodies live on in plants and animals, just as our own bodies are composed from minute to minute of substances that once were parts of other animals and plants. . . . Our kinship with all earth creatures is global, linking us to the whole living Gaia today. It also spans the ages, linking our material substance with all the beings that have gone before us on earth and even to the dust of exploding stars.[21]

Ruether calls on us to relinquish the illusion of permanence and to accept the dissolution of our physical substance into primal energy to become matter for new organisms. She reminds us that this relinquishment will fill us with a deep compassion for all living things, breaking down our illusions of otherness. And here she speaks once again of her sense of Gaia/God:

> At this moment we can encounter the matrix of energy of the universe that sustains the dissolution and re-composition of matter as also a heart that knows us even as we are known. . . . Surely, if we are kin to all things and offspring of the universe, then what has flowered in us as consciousness must also be reflected in that universe as well, in the ongoing creative Matrix of the whole. . . . But we also know this as the great Thou, the personal center of the universal process, with which all the small centers of personal being dialogue in the conversation that continually creates and

recreates the world. The small selves and the Great Self are finally one.[22]

LATIN AMERICAN ECOFEMINIST THEOLOGY

What ecofeminist theology proposes is, without a doubt, a radical—and an exciting—restructuring of ultimate meaning. Its tenets appear to make sense to a growing number of poor women in Latin America and also to ignite great passion and joy. As noted in Chapter 1, ecofeminist theology in Latin America emerged in the 1990s as part of the third stage of feminist theology. Many feminist theologians working in Latin America, including myself and other members of the Con-spirando Collective, have been deeply influenced by the work of Ivone Gebara, the region's foremost ecofeminist theologian. Gebara has been instrumental in the development of Con-spirando, which, in turn, has drawn a number of feminist theologians and other professionals, as well as women from the grassroots. The following discussion focuses on their contributions.

Ivone Gebara

Gebara, who acknowledges that ecofeminism "is not a native flower of Latin America" but takes on the region's specific tonalities and contexts,[23] has been influenced by the shift in cosmology expressed by Teilhard de Chardin, Fritjof Capra, Thomas Berry, and Brian Swimme, and from feminist theologians such as Mary Daly, Rosemary Radford Ruether, Sallie McFague, and German theologian Dorothee Soelle. Ruether, in particular, has had a strong influence on her.

Ivone Gebara is a religious sister, a member of the Canonesses of St. Augustine, a French congregation. She holds doctorates in both philosophy and religious science and is the author of many books, including her major work on ecofeminism, *Longing for Running Water: Ecofeminism and Liberation* (1999) and *Out of the*

Depths: Women's Experience of Evil and Salvation (2002).[24] Originally from São Paulo, Gebara has lived in Brazil's northeast region for the past twenty years. She taught epistemology and philosophy in the Catholic Theological Institute in Olindo/Recife for fourteen years, under the direction of Dom Hélder Câmara, one of Latin America's most famous "liberation" bishops, until Câmara's retirement. Câmara's successor was Dom José Cardoso, a conservative bishop who, acting on orders from the Vatican, closed the institute, as Câmara had conceived it, and dismissed the faculty.

Gebara has since become a self-described nomad; she travels throughout Latin America, giving courses and workshops on feminist and ecofeminist theology to grassroots communities, women's groups, religious communities, and solidarity organizations. She lives in a slum outside Recife in northeastern Brazil. Her theology has been constructed from the daily life of her neighbors, most of whom are poor women. True to feminist methodology, she always speaks from her own experience, sharing her life and her feelings with her audiences. In 1994 Gebara was "silenced" by the Vatican for her unorthodox opinions, especially with regard to abortion. Ordered "back to school" at a pontifical Catholic university in Europe, she chose Louvain and completed a second doctorate. The result is her second book in English, *Out of the Depths*.[25] Since returning from "exile," she continues to be a nomad.

In characterizing the "third phase" of Latin American feminist theology, Gebara says that it began with a suspicion about the very definition of God:

> We began to criticize the concept of God, Father Almighty, all-powerful, omnipotent, and Being-unto-himself who out of his goodness created heaven and Earth, men and women. We didn't notice that the story we were presented was a power struggle between God and humanity—and that every time humanity deviated from God's will, a "catastrophe" occurred because we had broken with God, we had gone against God's will. Our image of ourselves was of *fallen beings*. And the only way we could be saved was for God to

send His son, who was also God, to rescue us from our original sin. But who decided what was God's will, which has throughout history favored the rich, the white race, and the male? Our religious leaders, who said they were more capable of discovering what was God's will for us. Even more insidiously, we were told and came to believe that we were God's chosen people, and in God's name Christianity took on a messianic, missionary triumphalism: we were superior to all other peoples and all other religious expressions that had developed through the ages.[26]

According to Gebara, liberation theology begins with this question: How do we speak of God in the face of hunger, injustice, misery, dictatorship, and the destruction of entire peoples? Its major contribution is a more collective understanding of God as well as a sense of the social nature of sin. God becomes the God of life and of justice who has a preferential love for the poor. However, liberation theology has not challenged the patriarchal anthropology and cosmology upon which Christianity is based. Nor has it challenged the underlying patriarchal structure of Christianity itself. Gebara wonders whether Christianity will be flexible enough to change the foundations of its anthropology and cosmology to respond to what she calls "holistic ecofeminism." She maintains it must, if it is to survive.

In *Longing for Running Water*, Gebara describes holistic ecofeminism:

With ecofeminism I have begun to see more clearly how much our body—my body and the bodies of my neighbors— are affected not just by unemployment and economic hardship but also by the harmful effects the system of industrial exploitation imposes on them. I have begun to see more clearly how the exclusion of the poor is linked to the destruction of their lands, to the forces that leave them no choice but to move from place to place in a ceaseless exile, to racism, and to the growing militarization of their countries. To defend the unjust monopoly of a minority, the poor countries have become more intensely militarized: they arm themselves to kill their own poor. I have come to see how much all this fits in with the inherent logic of the patriarchal system, especially in its current form. . . . I sense that ecofeminism is born of daily life, of day-to-day sharing among people, garbage in the streets, bad smells, the absence of sewers and safe drinking water, poor nutrition, and inadequate health care. The ecofeminist issue is born of the lack of municipal garbage collection, of the multiplication of rats, cockroaches and mosquitoes, and of the sores on children's skin. . . . This is no new ideology. Rather, it is a different perception of reality that starts right from the unjust system in which we find ourselves and seeks to overcome it in order to bring happiness to everyone and everything.[27]

Through sharing their slum environments and social concerns, particularly those of health, Gebara has strongly influenced poor women throughout the region. Awareness of the relatedness of so many issues has pushed her perspective beyond that of theology to include anthropology, cosmology, and ethics.

Gebara insists that the first step is to change our understanding of men and women within the cosmos. She argues that because any image of God reflects the understanding or experience we have of ourselves, it is necessary to resituate the human within—not above—the universe. She shows this is diametrically opposed to a more classical Christian anthropology, which insists that humanity is "lord of creation" ordered by the Creator to "dominate the Earth." This lens has been used to legitimize humanity's right to dominate, control, and possess, and even to define ourselves. Gebara urges adoption of a new understanding of "relationality," which she sees as the primary reality:

[Relationality] is constitutive of all beings. It is more elementary than awareness of differences or than autonomy, individuality, or freedom. It is the foundational reality of all that is or can exist. It is the underlying fabric that is continually brought forth within the vital process in which we are immersed. Its interwoven fibers do not exist separately, but only in perfect reciprocity with one another—in space, in time; in origin and into the future.[28]

We are, then, fundamentally "relatedness." Gebara goes on to develop relatedness as a human condition, as an earthly condition, as an ethical reality, as a religious experience, and as a cosmic condition.[29] In addressing relatedness as an ethical reality, Gebara maintains that no transcendent principle or higher divinity should act as a moral grounding for our actions. Since relatedness is a constitutive experience of the very universe in which we live, ethics should be the vital foundation of our personal and collective lives as we evolve. Ethics, then, is the fruit of our humanization process, of our collective growth as we attempt to construct a world in which shared life can become a reality.

Gebara argues that an ecofeminist ethics seeks to open spaces for women and for the Earth's ecosystems to assume their rightful place in the building of new relationships based on respect and reciprocity. Patriarchy has turned both into ethical non-subjects. She is especially critical of the Catholic church with regard to its treatment of women, noting that "we are talked to; guidelines for living are imposed on us as if these guidelines were laws, of more importance than our own history."[30] This is especially true in the area of women's sexuality: a belief in the superiority of men and the need for an all-male hierarchy allows legislation of the behavior of women and their bodies. She notes: "In Catholic morality, evil and sin are defined and legislated in advance . . . producing 'guilty' persons and 'victims,' rather than citizens who seek to assume risks and responsibilities in history. In this scheme, women often are guilty parties and victims at the same time."[31] Gebara calls for an ethics of life that takes account of the diversity of humanity and the planet's ecosystems as well as the dynamic, changeable character of human relations and human-Earth relations. Ethics can never be a static system of laws but must always be attentive to the complexity of situations as they occur. Ethical decisions must be made in context, beyond pre-established universals. She insists that an ethics of life aims at creating a society in which every person and species has the right to life within a collectivity because each one has a vital need for the other. Today, she writes,

> we are presented with an invitation from the history of Life—the Life of different peoples, the Life of ecosystems, the Life of the planet. Christian tradition must join a larger movement, beyond the old frontiers, cosmologies and anthropologies. In re-encountering the Wisdom of nature, that of native peoples and marginalized groups, the Christian tradition will learn, as others have, to find a new place for itself in the Universe.[32]

Gebara's chapter on God in *Longing for Running Water* contains some of her most radical and most brilliant anthropological insights. She says that questions about God are really questions about ourselves:

> To seek God is to seek our own humanity, in an attempt to speak of ourselves beyond our own limitations and contingencies and to heal a kind of wound that we feel within us always. To seek God is to seek meaning. . . . We set up pure and perfect beings to contrast them with our own experiences of impurity and imperfection. We set up powerful beings to contrast them with our own fragility and weakness.[33]

Gebara argues that a metaphysical, anthropomorphic, and anthropocentric God became a necessity, given the psychological structure that evolved throughout the history of patriarchal culture. God was regarded as an ego of infinite excellence whose designs were inaccessible to human beings. And there was always the hope that this ego would listen and respond, offering a sense of paternal or maternal security. She writes: "The need to affirm a higher power—a power presented as being in *discontinuity* with all the powers of the cosmos, the earth, human beings, animals, plants, and even life itself—appears to be of fundamental importance in maintaining the hierarchical organization of the society in which we live."[34]

Gebara shares ecofeminists' growing conviction that human beings are part of a single sacred body; we dwell in Mystery larger than ourselves. We are part of this Mystery, which, like us, is evolving. In this body the individual is not annihilated but is instead related to a wider whole without which life would be impossible. Gebara's holistic ecofeminism, then, holds that God is in all—and therefore all is sacred. She describes this perspective with the term *pan-en-theism*.[35]

With regard to Jesus, Gebara shares her journey, noting that she was often bothered by the excessive centrality of Jesus in liberation theology, which gave so little space to other initiatives—especially those coming from women. At the same time, she finds the figure of Jesus profoundly alluring. He is the symbol of what we seek, of how we long to be. She develops the idea of symbol:

> To say that Jesus is a symbol means that, although he is Jesus of Nazareth, he is really more than Jesus of Nazareth. He becomes the possession of the community of his followers, a collective construct representing a way of life, a path to the meaning of our existence. Jesus as a symbol is in a certain sense greater than Jesus of Nazareth as an individual, because in him millions and millions of persons are encompassed.[36]

Within Gebara's ecofeminist perspective, Jesus is a symbol of the vulnerability of love; in the end he is murdered, but he rises again in those who love him.

Gebara also examines the manipulation of the Jesus symbol within our present globalized world. The power of Jesus, who triumphs over every other power, appears paradoxically as a way out for those without power. "Jesus is that power who can find a solution to all problems, but in exchange he demands conversion and submission. This Jesus becomes, then, the Great God-Man who helps all who call upon him, and with his powerful help one can stop drinking, stop smoking, stop prostituting and become a 'third-rank citizen, a little client of the system.'"[37]

Gebara rejects what she sees as a type of idolatry in relation to the figure of Jesus and seeks the salvific dimensions of other figures in biblical and Christian history. Jesus, she says, is no longer the only "way" or the "resurrection and the life" or the only one who has "the words of life" for those who hunger and thirst for justice. There are a variety of choices today.[38] She reminds us that each of us can be the "resurrection and the life" for others—resurrections experienced daily, which are provisional and continuous. She invites us to a Christology of gratitude: a capacity to contemplate gratefully the mysterious beauty that surrounds us, to feel our common belonging to the same universe. Such a Christology is understood as a pluralistic salvific effort—tenderness of humanity for humanity, tenderness of humanity for the Earth, tenderness of the Earth for humanity and the entire community of life. This Christology is present when two or three are gathered to live out this gratitude; indeed, it is in those moments that the presence of great Mystery is manifest.[39]

However, as she travels around Latin America offering workshops on ecofeminism, Ivone Gebara's overriding concern is for the oppressed—those "voiceless of history"—those who are excluded from the chance to live a full life by the very fact of where they are born. She is keenly aware that it is the poor who are the greatest consumers of patriarchal religion because of the consolation it provides, and she is determined to stay close to these voiceless ones and to do her theology from this posture.

Gebara also responds to critiques of essentialism within ecofeminist thought. Like Ruether, she says that we must stop thinking that humans are not a part of nature or that culture exists in opposition to nature. She reminds us that we are not supernatural creatures who are destined to escape our own human nature. Locating herself in the Latin American context, she calls attention to the huge numbers of Africans forced into slavery during the sixteenth and seventeenth centuries to satisfy the labor needs of the new Portuguese and Spanish colonies in the Americas. She notes that women and men were "colonized" differently, with women's bodies subject to both sexual and work-related colonization. This is not a matter of essence; it is a historical, cultural, economic, political, and religious matter:

Colonization is the occupation of others, through the dimensions of time and space, and the reduction of the identity of the colonized to that of the colonizer. . . . The worst
part of colonization is the loss of awareness of being colonized and no longer knowing one's roots, or who he or she
was or is. The worst part of colonization is losing self-con-
fidence and one's cultural values, placing oneself in the hands
of the other in a submissive and uncritical way.[40]

For Gebara, it is patriarchal society with its male division of
social labor that is essentialist. Women's bodies are viewed as pro-
ducers, both biologically and culturally, to the extent that women
give birth and nurture the young of the species. Domestic work
is not recognized as work basic to the maintenance of human
life—indeed, the rearing and feeding of children are comparable
to the activities of other mammals. Capitalism has exaggerated
this system in that the roles of procreation and nurturing are not
valued or remunerated.

At the symbolic-cultural level, Gebara notes that masculine
symbolism is dominant in all spheres. In the last twenty years,
however, women have realized that the dominance of masculine
symbolism results from an imbalance in the distribution of work
and a relegation of women to the domestic sphere. "This is why
I hold that women are colonies," she argues. "Women have been
colonized to stay home and allow men the grand flights of fancy
required for the production of culture, politics and religion. We
assist in the reproduction of a culture that makes men feel they
are the center of history, and its organizers."[41] She insists that
Christian theology must take major responsibility for the ideological colonization of women's bodies because Christianity has
taught that this is the "will of God." To change what is considered natural for women is to challenge the very construction of
Christianity itself—which, Gebara suspects, is beginning to happen. She calls for symbolism that reflects the vital web of interdependence in which we exist.

In *Out of the Depths* Gebara struggles with the way theology
understands evil in relationship to women's experience and their

lack of power. While not explicitly an ecofeminist work, her ecofeminist perspective is clearly present. By tackling evil from a radical feminist perspective, Gebara attempts to offer poor women some clues for understanding their age-old oppression. Once again she raises the nature-culture dilemma, noting that masculine evil seems somehow less evil than feminine evil. "For men, evil is an act one can undo. But for women, evil is in their very being. Being female is from the start something bad, or, at least, something limiting—so there is at bottom an anthropological question that reveals a conflict in the very way we understand what it means to be human."[42] She asks why women need a two-fold mediation to be saved—that of God and that of men—while men need only one.

Gebara also analyzes sacrifice, especially the Christian concept of Jesus' sacrifice on the cross. Here her thought can be closely identified with womanist theologian Delores Williams and Asian American feminist theologian Rita Nakashima Brock. Poor women everywhere often believe that the sacrifice of Jesus on the cross validates their own suffering and gives meaning to their lives. She notes:

> The ideology of sacrifice, imposed by patriarchal culture, has developed in women a training in renunciation. They must give up their pleasure, thoughts, dreams, desires, to put themselves at the service of others or to live as others think they should. . . . This attitude leads most women to endure and accept suffering as if it were part of God's design. . . . It is still common to hear women in great trouble say: "Jesus suffered more than this."[43]

Such attitudes hide real injustices and fail to allow women to distinguish between suffering caused by wrongdoing and the angst present in the ordinary lives of all humans.

Gebara calls attention to the deeply rooted sense among Latin American women that it is a curse to be born female. Most women will admit that they have often wished they had been born male, and they long for male children so they will not suffer the "cross" that comes with being born female. However, they also believe that as Christians they are to bear and even to welcome their crosses rather than look for ways to get rid of them.

Searching for ways to deliver women from this theological quagmire of bearing crosses willingly, Gebara reminds us that while suffering is an ever-present reality, creative forms of redemption are available. She calls these "provisional escapes in our tentative lives."[44] They are experienced in sharing a meal together, in acts of tenderness, in the straightened posture of a stooped woman, in the birth of a child, in a good harvest. To broaden the meaning of salvation and resurrection is, for Gebara, an ethical necessity: "Concretely, it means listening to the wisdom of our bodies, even with all its contradictions, because it is our bodies that point out the places of resurrection, the sites of pleasure and the paths that lead to happiness."[45] She also exhorts women to relativize the agony Jesus suffered on the cross. This suffering, though indeed great and unjust, is no greater than that of a mother whose child is wrenched from her, of women who see their children die of hunger because of the greed of those who hold economic power. Gebara cautions that the powerful of this world employ the concepts of universal salvation and an all-powerful God to consolidate their power. Salvation and resurrection are not once and for all, but instead come in small doses that remind us of who we really are. They are lived in our concrete bodies, our flesh of today.

Gebara recognizes a tendency to identify ecofeminism with New Age groups and that, for the most part, Latin American progressives feel that ecofeminism fails to offer a solid religious grounding for popular emancipation struggles to establish the reign of God here on Earth. She maintains that what critics call grounding is more often than not based on a specific sociological reading of Christianity. What they call a solid foundation is "the anthropocentrism and theocentrism that have long marked our thinking. What they call groundedness is the continuation of a theology based on a hierarchical religious system."[46] She insists that ecofeminism's invitation to love and to show mercy does not come from an external reality but from an urge that is present in our very humanness. She also insists on an ecofeminism that is based on the experience of those who have diminishing access to green things and clean water; of those who breathe an ever-greater amount of the air pollution that has spread everywhere. My ecofeminism is pregnant with health: not health as we understood it in the past, but the health of a future that promises deeper communion between human beings and all other living things. My ecofeminism is shot through with the staunch conviction that beauty is important in healing people. It might be the beauty of sounds, of colors, of words, of faces, of food and drink, or of embraces. Like my friend Rubem Alves, I too can vouch for "salvation through beauty."[47]

In the end, Ivone Gebara is a poet, a contemporary shamanistic figure who spins new visions that captivate the imagination. Her writings and her teaching are permeated with wonderings of a post-patriarchal world where salvation indeed comes through beauty.

> Beyond what is imagined by reason, there is something imagined by desire, poetry, beauty. . . . It is beautiful in its fragility, and everything beautiful has something fragile in it and something ephemeral. This eschatology commingled with earth, the cycle of life, the year's seasons, the bodies of animals, plants and flowers, this human and larger-than-human eschatology, warms the heart a great deal.[48]

CON-SPIRANDO'S CONTRIBUTION TO ECOFEMINISM

Ivone Gebara, one of Con-spirando's midwives, has greatly influenced our thinking. In the Introduction to *Longing for Running Water* she writes, "At the moment, in my view, the liveliest ecofeminist group in Latin America is the Con-spirando Collective in Santiago, Chile."[49] In her keynote speech at Con-spirando's tenth anniversary in 2002 she noted that Con-spirando is neither a purely academic organization nor is it associated with any church organization, which gives it freedom from outside control. She called attention to its structure as a collective with a non-hierarchical, multicultural team of Latin American members and members from other countries who also seek justice and tenderness. She noted that Con-spirando has become a space where the questions of many women of Latin America are echoed, including frustrations with the patriarchal society and the patriarchal church. Emphasizing that Con-spirando epitomizes a new cosmology, a new anthropology, a new epistemology, and a new ecology appropriate for our times, Gebara listed five major contributions of the Con-spirando Collective:

1. Belief in the wisdom of our bodies and the priority of knowing through our corporality in relationship. Feeling is a way of knowing.
2. Efforts to search out non-hierarchical ways of being that model "power with" rather than "power over."
3. Sharing new ways to celebrate and developing new rituals that nurture our emerging spiritualities and commitments.
4. Reexamining those foundational myths upon which Western, Christian culture is based in order to relativize them and then search for new myths that can water our emerging spiritualities, theologies, and ethics.
5. Belief in the oneness of all human beings, from the folks in the barrio to the animals, the mountains, and the rivers.

Con-spirando, a women's collective that began in 1991, works in the areas of ecofeminism, theology, and spirituality. Con-spirando publishes a quarterly journal, *Con-spirando: Revista latinoamericana de ecofeminismo, espiritualidad y teología;* holds workshops, seminars, and an annual summer school on ecofeminist theology, spirituality, and ethics; and offers a yearly cycle of rituals. The journal's first issue set out its purpose, which, more than ten years later, still defines its objectives:

In the patriarchal culture in which we live, women's contributions are not taken seriously. This is particularly true in the area of theology. Women are absent as subjects doing theology and also as a major subject matter of this theological reflection. Our lives, our everyday religious practice and our spirituality are simply not present in current theological reflection. Absent too, are our experiences of suffering, joy and solidarity—our experiences of the Sacred. Besides expressing our criticism of patriarchal culture, we also seek to contribute to the creation of a culture that allows theological reflection to flower from our bodies, our spirits—in short, our experiences as women.

We seek theologies that take account of the differences of class, race and gender that so mark Latin America. We hope to open new spaces where women can dig deeply into our own life experiences without fear. These experiences are often negative, even traumatic, in terms of the religious formation we have received. We seek spaces where women can experience new ways of being in community; where we can celebrate our faith more authentically and creatively; where we can rediscover and value our roots, our history and our traditions—in short, to engage in an interreligious dialogue that helps us to recover the essential task of theology, which is to search out and raise the questions of ultimate meaning.

We are convinced that, to bring about relationships marked by justice and equality, we must celebrate our differences and work toward a greater pluralism worldwide. To this end, we need theologies that unmask the hierarchies in which we live, theologies that, rather than seeking to mediate Mystery, celebrate and explore the Holy without reductionisms or universalisms. We call for theologies that question anthropocentrism and that promote the transformation of relationships based on dominance of one race, nationality, gender or age group over another and of the human over other forms of life. Such theologies will have profound political consequences.

Such a feminist perspective based on our diversity of class, race, age and culture must also take up our love as well as our anguish for all life on the planet that we feel is so threatened today. We call this posture ecofeminism. It is within this perspective that we seek a spirituality that will both heal and liberate, that will nourish our Christian tradition as well as take up the long-repressed roots of the native peoples of this continent. We want to explore the liberating dimensions of our experience and imagination of the Holy. To do this, we *"con-spirar juntas."*[50]

Without a doubt, Con-spirando would be located in the third stage of the development of Latin American feminist and ecofeminist theology. Our particular contributions to theology begin with the word *theology* itself. First, several of us are uncomfortable using it to define us because its patriarchal nature links us in the popular mind to religion, church, morality, doctrine, and, of course, to the science of God. Sometimes we consider dropping the term *theology* from our name altogether. However, at other moments, we renew our commitment to push the definition of theology past its patriarchal confines by broadening the term to grapple with constructs of meaning as concretely experienced by women. We are dedicated to bringing forth the insights of anthropology, psychology, literature, and gender analysis to our understanding of theology.

Con-spirando has made significant theological contributions in the following four areas: (1) unmasking some aspects of theological violence toward women; (2) renaming and connecting with the Sacred; (3) offering an embodied theology; and (4) bringing an ecofeminist perspective to theology. These areas are interconnected and relate to our work in developing ecofeminism from a Latin American perspective.

Unmasking Theological Violence toward Women

Influenced by feminist/womanist theologians such as Delores Williams, Rita Nakashima Brock, Joanne Carlson Brown, and Rebecca Parker, we have been working toward a non-sacrificial reading of redemption in order to liberate Christianity from patriarchy.[51] Along with these theologians we have been challenging Christianity's core doctrine that Jesus' death on the cross was essential to redeem humanity from sin. Indeed, helped by their analyses, we sense that the theme of atonement and redemption in Christ may be directly related to "allowing" violence and child abuse. According to Delores Williams, "If we as Christians understand that our redemption happened through a violent act and that God in some sense intended this to happen, is that not giving a sacred status to violence?"[52] According to Rita Nakashima Brock: "The father allows, or even inflicts, the death of his only perfect son. The emphasis is on the goodness and power of the father and the unworthiness and powerlessness of his children, so that the father's punishment is just, and the children are to blame."[53] The women of Con-spirando have translated the essay "For God So Loved the World?" by Joanne Carlson Brown and Rebecca Parker into Spanish for use in our workshops. It argues that the central image of Christ on the cross as the savior of the world communicates the message that suffering is redemptive—a message that is further complicated by a theology that holds that Christ suffered in obedience to his Father's will. The authors criticize Christianity's central belief of Christ's suffering and dying for us as accepting and even encouraging suffering; they ask if it is really so strange that there is so much abuse in society when the predominant theological image of our culture is what they term "divine child abuse."

In 1994 Con-spirando dedicated an issue to the underpinnings of violence, paying particular attention to theological violence.[54] In the June 1996 issue two members grappled with the theme of child abuse and of images of God related to the concept of power. Their reflections grew out of a workshop on images of the Sacred in our understanding of power. Participants discovered that the patriarchal image of an all-powerful God who rules over humans had impeded them from understanding that "all of us form part of each other and we co-create each other in the depths of our being."[55]

Violence and beyond violence was also the theme of a program of theological education held in 1997–98. This was a cooperative educational effort with the Women's Alliance for Theology, Ethics, and Religion, based in Washington, DC, and co-founded by feminist theologian Mary Hunt and feminist liturgist Diann Neu, Ivone Gebara and her team in Recife, Brazil, and the Con-spirando Collective in Chile. In three separate sessions centered on the theme of gardens, participants worked with Ivone Gebara on unmasking the myth of Adam and Eve's "fall" from paradise, and they were exposed to Elisabeth Schüssler Fiorenza's concept of kyriarchy to describe the system of hierarchical power relationships that impinge upon Christians at every level. At each stage women were encouraged to untie the knots of violence embedded in the memory of their individual bodies as well as in the "bodies" of church, society, and theology. At the same time they were encouraged to move "beyond violence" to nurture new theologies based on women's experience that would offset kyriarchical theologies that permit "contexts of violence."[56]

Renaming and Celebrating the Sacred

Con-spirando feels that naming and reflecting upon one's own experience of the Holy is essential in the process of speaking one's own theological word. Offering new images of the Sacred—out of which evolve both new ethical demands as well as new spiritual practices—has been part of Con-spirando's work since its beginning. Its journal, workshops, and rituals try to empower women to rename the Sacred according to their own experience and insights. New images that have surfaced include, among others, a pregnant woman giving birth, a great uterus as the body of God, a nest, a tree, a mountain, a flowing river, the ocean, a gentle breeze and a wild wind, a web, a hungry child, an elderly invalid, a circle of laughing children, and the sunset. Con-spirando workshops encourage women to draw, mold, and dance their sense of the Sacred.

The March 1997 issue of *Con-spirando* focused on the creation and evolution of symbols.[57] The lead article describes how symbols of the Sacred reflect the belief system of an entire people and an entire historical period and, as such, contain tremendous power over those people and their historical context. However, the author, Con-spirando member Josefina Hurtado, stresses that symbols of the Sacred are created by human beings in response to our experiences; they can and should evolve.[58]

Yeta Ramírez of Nicaragua described that evolution quite clearly:

Ever since I was eight years old, I was surrounded by images of the saints and of the Virgin in the homes of my aunts. I remember one aunt in particular who lived in the country and every afternoon she would sit in front of her altar with all of her statues and pray the rosary and other prayers. We kids used to laugh at her because she was always interrupting her prayers to give orders about domestic matters, etc. At that same time, every Saturday I had to go to catechism classes to receive instructions for making my First Communion. What symbols of the Sacred did I receive then? The image of Christ on the Cross, Christ in his casket that was paraded through the streets every Holy Week. The Sorrowful Virgin was also very present; she was dressed in black and was crying at the foot of the cross. Later on, as an adolescent, I began to work with the Catholic Action movement. At that time, I was very impressed by colors—the white of the Virgin and of the Resurrection. In the 1960 liturgical reform, I began to discover the Risen Jesus who was with us, and the historical Mary, the *campesina* woman who baked bread. Work became a sacred symbol as well as the tools we used for work. We also began to integrate the struggle for liberation into our symbol system. The color green was important—giving a green light for Latin America to take over the land, for agrarian reform. Green was present in our liturgies as a symbol of commitment, hope, and the struggle for land.

Then, in the 1980s, I began to go deeper into nature and incorporate this in liturgy. In my time with Catholic Action, a symbolism of God in nature was present as well as a certain contemplative dimension. More recently, I have taken up an ecological perspective as if I was finally remembering something that I had somehow forgotten. Also, in this past decade, there has been a renewed interest in rediscovering our own cultural roots that have been repressed.

Now we no longer speak of father god, but also of mother-god and of the goddesses.

All this symbolism comes out when I work in the area of ritual and liturgical celebration. In the women's group that I belong to (which is a group committed to stopping violence in all its forms), we have celebrated rituals of healing where we use oils and plants, water, flowers, candles, food, etc. We are now at a stage where we are reclaiming our bodies as sacred in order to combat all the physical and psychological violence we have been subjected to. We have come to see that the concept of "god" is very closed and that really the divinity is much, much broader. We have come to understand that the churches do not have the power to name sacred symbols—power is in the people and so it is we ourselves who must discover those symbols that speak of the divinity for us. This allows us to build spirituality from our own conception of what is divine. The religious symbols of my childhood were all given to me from outside; now, however, I mold them and give them meaning based on my own experience.[59]

Embodied Theology

Con-spirando's third theological contribution is in the area of methodology. We espouse an embodied theology holding up women's bodies as "sacred text." This method developed from years of working with the conscientization methodology of Brazilian educator Paulo Freire, by which oppressed groups, concentrating on their own experience, engage in social analysis for change (praxis).[60] Con-spirando members have learned that our women's bodies are social and cultural constructs, that our history of violence and pain and of joy and pleasure is stored in our bodies' memories. The body, then, becomes our theological starting point to counteract the patriarchal mindset that a woman's body is the source of evil, to heal the dualistic split between body and spirit, and to learn to love our bodies as embodied temples of the Holy.

Much of Con-spirando's pastoral work involves healing. Workshops introduce simple practices such as tai chi, deep breathing exercises, and massage techniques. Real transformation does take place, and healing touch more often than not awakens new life and insights. Participants tell of feeling loved, cared for, safe, and protected. We also promote learning and returning to some of the age-old healing practices of our indigenous ancestors who did not separate physical and psychological illness and whose concept of health was based on a power to heal that comes from within.

This methodology has opened our eyes to the intrinsic connection between our bodies and our spirituality. Since the beginning we have celebrated the link between wholeness and holiness, and we have developed rituals to pray through body movement, dance, and chant. We see this embodied methodology as a more holistic, intuitive way of learning that makes us more aware of the interconnectedness of all matter. An issue of *Con-spirando* also focuses on the theme of embodiment as a method for both personal and cultural transformation.[61]

Ecofeminist Perspective

A fourth contribution of Con-spirando to theology is its growing commitment to an ecofeminist perspective. This is true of all articles in the Con-spirando journal[62] as well Con-spirando's many workshops dealing with ecofeminist theology and spirituality. The annual summer school on ecofeminist spirituality and ethics also has a strong ecofeminist component in its content and methodology. And equally significant are rituals, in a myriad of creative forms, that convey that we are one sacred body, with all its welcome diversity.

Perhaps a description of Con-spirando's summer school, which is a microcosm of the larger program, will clarify the group's strong emphasis on an ecofeminist perspective. Since 2000 Con-spirando has organized an annual summer program entitled "Ecofeminist Spirituality and Ethics," which brings together around forty activist women leaders from Latin America. This initiative grew from an earlier project called the Shared Garden, which first surfaced for us the theme of myths and their power over us. Participants first enacted and then analyzed the creation story of Adam and Eve found in Genesis 2, the foundational myth that undergirds our current patriarchal Christian culture. We began to realize how much we have internalized this myth, which sustains both our cultures and our cosmologies and continues to operate within us at a very deep, although frequently unconscious level.

Con-spirando members felt the need to delve more deeply into how myths originate and how they operate to uphold patriarchy as "normal" or "God-given." This led to Con-spirando's commitment to hold an annual summer school of ten days that would offer a contained space where women could ask their theological questions without fear. It would be a safe space, allowing participants to search together for more life-giving theologies, cosmologies, and ways to celebrate their emerging spiritualities. It would be a space for Latin American women engaged in the religious debates of our region to search together and to formulate a body of thought, study, and reflection.

We were convinced that it was absolutely key for women in Latin America to deepen their analysis and theoretical deconstruction of the Genesis myth and myths in general in order to see how they act in the subconsciousness and to determine how they affect the way we relate to one another. At the same time, we recognized the need to build new practices and power relations in order to sustain ourselves as we search for new constructs of meaning individually and communally. In the end, we felt the need for new stories of meaning, new myths, and new rituals.

The first school program in January 2000, "Myths and Their Power over Us," began with the important process of deconstruction. Participants developed understandings of myth based on their own experiences, examining in particular those myths that deal with women's bodies, how myths evolve in the human psyche, and how they develop in an individual woman's life cycle. The analysis included the cultural and psychological need for myths and how they can be transformed from using their power over us to myths that empower us. We identified four basic archetypes that shape us as women—mother/life-giver, lover/companion, Amazon/warrior, and wise woman/medium—and saw these archetypes reflected in the many goddesses who have appeared throughout the ages.

Because both participants and the leader team found these themes to be so gripping, it was decided that the second school program in January 2001 would continue this theme, building on the previous year. The second session concentrated on the four feminine archetypes, as developed by Toni Wolff, a close collaborator of Carl Jung. The mother/life-giver archetype helped us trace the lineage of women in our lives, and it honored those who gave us life, whether physically, intellectually, or spiritually. We discovered the strength of the overriding image of the Virgin Mary, Mother of God, throughout Latin America. We began to look behind the Mary image to older, more indigenous images of the mother. This, we recognized, was a major area for further research.[63] In the companion/lover archetype, we looked at the evolution of sexual pleasure and puzzled over how the separation, or even opposition, between pleasure/eroticism and spirituality came about. The Amazon/warrior archetype brought participants face to face with the whole issue of power: how women's power has been symbolized in different periods of history and in different cultures, and how, from a gender analysis, "man" and "woman" are social constructs. The discussion also looked at how power can be used in new ways to move beyond the stereotypes from the past of women "warriors" sacrificing their lives for their people. Finally, the wise woman/medium/witch archetype invited us to meet our shadow side—that part of us we often repress or ignore. It became evident that what has been kept in the shadows or repressed can become a deep source of wisdom for us.

Based on evaluations of the participants and facilitators, the Con-spirando team pursued this theme in its third year but decided to concentrate on the shadow side of each of the archetypes and to examine how ethical norms that relate to women and their bodies developed over time, with patriarchy becoming more entrenched.

With regard to the shadow side, the mother/life-giver archetype presentation asked participants to look at their own history of being contained—by mother, church, political party, and various movements—to determine how they were nurtured as well as "devoured." Specific attention was given to the Virgin Mary in Latin America and how she might be a domesticated form of earlier, more sexual, "dark" goddesses. The shadow side of the companion/lover archetype surfaced in the patriarchal need to control eroticism, placing it safely within the confines of marriage or the "bad woman," or prostitute. To touch our erotic powers and feelings, two women from the feminist collective Newen Kuche in Concepción, Chile, gave a workshop on belly dancing, a dance among women to the goddess and often a dance to help women at the time of childbirth, to demonstrate that sensual movement can be liberating. To connect with the shadow side of the warrior archetype, participants chose to be a certain animal and enacted a battle for territory. Most participants did not choose to attack, but they all were aroused to defend their territory. It is worth noting that most participants recognized that they were indeed warriors, that is, leaders within their different communities, and that they were tired of always having to lead the charge to fight for their rights. Many participants discovered that they had overdeveloped their warrior energies at the expense of their erotic and wise woman energy fields. The group concluded that the wise woman/medium archetype has been relegated to the shadow side by patriarchy. Although elderly women appear to be invisible and irrelevant in modern society, it is precisely in times of crisis that the vision of the wise woman would be useful.

As noted above, ritual is a key ingredient of the summer programs. One of the most powerful is the reenactment of part of the Sumerian myth of Inanna, the queen who descends to the underworld to meet her dark sister Ereshkigal.[64] On the descent to the underworld each participant left a sign of her power at each of seven gates marking the descent. Once below, each saw her essence—now stripped of all powers—reflected back as she gazed into a mirror; behind her appeared her dark sister, a masked figure clothed in black. The task of the participants was to integrate this dark sister into their psyche. After some time participants began their ascent, donning again the seven powers, now transformed by contact with Ereshkigal. This ritual had a powerful effect on everyone.

Another powerful ritual is walking the labyrinth, an ancient practice that has been rediscovered in recent times. The invitation is to walk slowly in silence to the center, which symbolizes journeying to one's own center. This is an exercise in integration that formally concludes the summer school program. At the end, participants and leaders form a circle to thank the spirits for their accompaniment.

From "learnings" from the three summer sessions, participants gained new perspectives on the Christian tradition that situated it within a broader framework. Most can be grouped as new insights, ethical implications, or calls to action.

New Insights

A significant new insight was that it is possible to situate the Christian myth within the broader sweep of our evolution as a species and to gain a much larger sense of the history of the universe and of the antiquity of our roots. Part of this process is to rediscover the feminine image of the Divine. When the feminine is not present, honored in ritual or in a culture's sacred image of the Divine, the entire social fabric is affected, and violence against women becomes commonplace.

Although women may examine their roots in antiquity, they do not want to return to some ancient past; rather, ecofeminist women are concerned with synthesizing and moving toward a post-patriarchal future. This process may bring moments of chaos and uncertainty, but this space is essential for bringing about a new ordering of thoughts and beliefs.

The starting point of ecofeminist methodology is listening to our bodies. This includes staying profoundly connected to dreams, intuitions, emotions, sensations, and the wisdom found in women's rituals. Our indigenous ancestors are another source of wisdom that help us to examine critically our own *mestiza* roots.

Ethical Implications

It takes courage to look critically at the Christian myth and reinterpret it, knowing full well that others may look askance at our efforts or even label them heretical. Ecofeminists require "safe spaces" in which to do the work of deconstruction.

Participants are committed to accepting their differences, remaining flexible, and refusing rigid postures. They take seriously the responsibility to continue educating themselves in their acceptance of diversity. They work toward solidarity, sisterhood, and compassion among women as they journey together toward wholeness. Empowering each other is part of the process. Ethical decisions should be grounded in the bodily experiences of ordinary daily life, but always in communion with other women.

The United Nations Universal Declaration of Human Rights, which includes a gender perspective, is a key framework for a universal ethic. Ethical postures, however, are always evolving, and women must make their own ethical decisions in their daily lives and be responsible for the consequences.

Calls to Action

Ecofeminists work from the micro toward the macro. Priority should be given to small groups and to promoting networks among these groups. A pertinent image is that of a spider web; it is strong but flexible, containing many junctures. Working toward deeper cultural change must begin at the local level. Such nurture can begin with ancestral wisdom and through ritual dance and music, small-scale organic gardening, bartering, and local experiments of economic sustainability. Participants are committed to developing the use of natural medicines and herbs and to eating lower on the food chain.

Work at the micro level means a commitment to work for small changes without taking on patriarchy in a confrontational way. By building and strengthening links with other women's groups, ecofeminists can find spaces for renewal and in which to discover new methodological tools to promote cultural transformation.[65]

IN CONCLUSION

Although members of Con-spirando are proud of its accomplishments, it is clear that ecofeminist thought is only beginning to have an impact on theology and feminist theory in the region. Mainline patriarchal theologians, as well as some liberation theologians, are threatened by ecofeminism because of its moves beyond more orthodox definitions of God and of the human in relation to the Divine. Some feminists criticize ecofeminism as being too "eco" and not sufficiently "feminist." They also warn against identifying women with nature, which is falling into an essentialist trap that, in the end, would unwittingly support patriarchal dualistic constructs.

A major tool for transformation is a commitment to embodied learning. Body prayer, ritual, intuition, and healing practices all offer new ways of learning—not only for women, but for all humanity. Rituals give flesh to the commitment to empower women to celebrate the Sacred as they see fit.

There are voices that caution us to water our Latin American ecofeminism with the streams coming from the lives of the region's poor majorities. In addition to the danger of essentialism, we must avoid the label of being New Age with an individualist, "make me feel good" spirituality. And Latin American ecofeminists must respond with visible actions to the accusation that an ecofeminist posture avoids justice and human rights issues.

While our numbers are small and our resources limited, we must commit to being seeds. The metaphor of the seed suggests "power within" rather than "power over." The seed lies dormant until it breaks open, sprouts, blossoms, and bears fruit. Then it matures, withers, and falls to the ground again. It will be what it is meant to be. Thus is Con-spirando a seed—what it is meant to be, nothing more, nothing less.

5

Charting the Change

Reflections of Latin American Women

People do not change because of intellectual convictions or ethical inclinations, but rather through transformed imaginations.
—MADONNA KOLBENSCHLAG

Although Ivone Gebara and the Con-spirando Collective have been working in ecofeminist theology, spirituality, and ethics for the past decade, ecofeminist thought is still quite new to Latin America. While the term may not be familiar to most Latin Americans, it seems that the vision and perspectives described in the previous chapters are being embraced by an increasing number of Latin American women. A growing number of activist, faith-based women who had been historically aligned with liberation theology now describe themselves as ecofeminists. This is evident in the way they perceive themselves in relation to the rest of the Earth community and to the universe, in the way they are reimaging and renaming the Ultimate Mystery, in their beliefs about death and life after death, and in their spiritual and ethical practices.

This shift in perspective is documented in transcripts of interviews with twelve Latin American women who have been engaged in the field of feminist theology for a number of years. The majority of these women have been activists in liberation theology and in other liberation movements in their countries.

They share a commitment to the poor and oppressed based on their Christian faith. The majority identify with ecofeminist thought, although not in its entirety or without some reservations and questions. The twelve women represent a number of countries, with several reflecting the region's pattern of internal migration, moving from their country of birth to another. They also represent a variety of ages and religious traditions. While there is a wide range of diversity among these women in terms of their experience, temperaments, and points of view, all work with poor and disadvantaged women and all of them recognize the influence of Ivone Gebara on their own theology and spirituality. These women are not strangers to me; they are friends and colleagues in the small but lively circles of feminist theology in Latin America.

I am a journalist by profession. During my doctoral research in 2000 and 2001 I tried to elicit from these colleagues and friends those "dearest, deep down" intuitions of the soul in five different areas: their self-understanding, their understanding of the Divine, their understanding of life and death, the implications of these three areas for ethics, and the nature of their spirituality.

These themes, which form the theological quest of all ages, namely, the definition of the human (anthropology), of the divine (cosmology), of "how" we know (epistemology), and the implications for ethics and spirituality, seemed to form a likely barometer of these women's changing perspectives. Because feminist theology usually starts from lived experience, each woman was asked to describe at the outset her own journey within the larger political, social, and theological context of her country. The interviews were designed to determine (1) if, and why, liberation theology might no longer appeal to faith-based women activists as it had during the 1970s and 1980s, and (2) why these same women were now attracted to ecofeminism. I often abandoned a rigorous question/answer methodology in favor of pursuing a living story with personal reflections. The complete interviews, published in Spanish under the title *Lluvia para florecer*, tell of the inspiring journeys of twelve remarkable women searching to be faithful to themselves and to their deepest yearnings and intuitions.[1]

THE LATIN AMERICAN WOMEN

The brief introductions that follow describe the women's origins and their experience.

- *Agamedilza Sales de Oliveira* (b. 1950) is from Manaus, a frontier town deep within Brazil's Amazon jungle. From the Catholic tradition and a teacher by profession, she has extensive training as a biblicist and calls herself a grassroots feminist biblicist. She is the founder of María Sem Vergonha (Shameless Maria), a grassroots women's organization dedicated to the empowerment of women.
- *Marcia Moya* (b. 1965) is from Quito, Ecuador. Also Catholic, she is a dentist by profession, although she has done graduate work in theology and teaches feminist theology and biblical studies at the university level. She also works with grassroots women and religious congregations. She is the author of *Propuesta pedagógica de Jesús* (Ediciones Abya Yala, 1999).
- *Coca Trillini* (b. 1951) is from Buenos Aires, Argentina. From the Catholic tradition, Coca is a teacher by profession and a feminist theologian and biblicist by choice. She is currently part of the coordination team for Católicas por el Derecho de Decidir in Latin America. She is the author of *¿Qué son las Comunidades Eclesiales de Base en la Argentina?* (Ediciones Paulinas, 1993) and *De la pirámide al arco iris: Cuaderno de Trabajo sobre Mujer y Biblia* (Ediciones Paulinas, 1995).
- *Sandra Duarte* (b. 1966) is from São Paulo, Brazil. A Methodist, she recently completed her doctoral studies in ecofeminist theology, spirituality, and ethics, focusing on an analysis of ecofeminism from a biosocial as well as from a social-constructivist perspective. She is currently a member of the religious studies faculty at the Methodist University in São Paulo.
- *Fanny Geymonat-Pantelís* (b. 1940) is originally from Uruguay, where she was raised in the Waldensian tradition, but she has been living and working in La Paz, Bolivia, for many

years. Now a Methodist, she is a religious educator with advanced degrees in religious education and ecumenism and is currently working on her doctorate in feminist theology with a thesis titled "Naming God in the Andes." She has represented the Latin American Council of Churches in the Southern Cone and has written Christian educational materials. She has published a book of poetry, *De Cipotes y Guerra*, and a series of testimonies by Central American exiles living in Washington, DC, entitled *Entre el Obelisco y la Cruz*.

- *Sandra Raquew* (b. 1973) is from Brazil's Northeast. Born in the interior, she lives now in João Pessoa, where she earned a degree in journalism. She is currently studying for a master's degree in popular education, communication, and culture. She is from the evangelical tradition and is a member of the feminist theology collective Chimalman, initially mentored by Ivone Gebara.
- *Graciela Pujol* (b. 1950) is from Montevideo, Uruguay. From the Catholic tradition and an architect by profession, she has also studied social psychology and feminist theology. She is the past editor of *Conciencia*, the Spanish publication of Catholics for a Free Choice and now runs her own publishing house. She is also the founder of the ecofeminist organization Caleiscopio.
- *Alcira Agreda* (b. 1955) is from Santa Cruz, Bolivia. A Catholic and a nurse by profession, she now has her licentiate in biblical studies and teaches theology and biblical studies at the university level in Bolivia and also gives classes to grassroots groups. Currently she is the academic dean and a professor at the Instituto Superior de Teología Andina in Santa Cruz.
- *Clara Luz Ajo* (b. 1949) is from Matanzas, Cuba. An Anglican, she is a religious educator with a doctorate in feminist theology from the Methodist University in São Paulo, Brazil. Her thesis is on how the body is seen in the divinities, symbols, myths, and rituals of Santería in Cuba. She is currently a member of the faculty at the Evangelical Theological Seminary in Matanzas. She and her partner Pedro composed the well-known *Misa cubana*.

- *Doris Muñoz* (b. 1958) is from Santiago, Chile, and the Catholic tradition. A popular educator, she has a licentiate in Catholic theology. A teacher of holistic health and spirituality through understanding the body, she is co-founder and co-coordinator of Capacitar-Chile, a grassroots health and education project. She teaches theology and biblical studies from a feminist perspective to grassroots communities as a member of the Diego de Medellín Ecumenical Center in Santiago.
- *Gladys Parentelli* (b. 1935) is originally from Uruguay but has been living in Caracas, Venezuela, for the past thirty years. A grassroots organizer and journalist, she has a long history of working with ecumenical and UN-related organizations in the Third World. A long-time feminist, she has fostered a number of local and regional feminist organizations and feminist periodicals. Now retired, she tells her remarkable theological journey as an activist Latin American Catholic in the 1950s through the 1980s in her autobiography *Mujer, Iglesia, Liberación* (Biblioteca Nacional, 1990).
- *Silvia Regina de Lima Silva* (b. 1962), originally from Rio de Janeiro, Brazil, now lives in San José, Costa Rica. A Catholic, a teacher, and a social activist in Latin America's Afro movement, she has a master's degree in biblical studies. She defines herself as a black feminist theologian and is presently the dean of studies and a member of the faculty at the Universidad Bíblica Latinoamericana in San José. She is the author of *En Territorio de Frontera: Una Lectura de Marcos 7:24–30* (DEI, 2001).

These short descriptions only hint of the richness of these women's lives. For instance, Gladys Parentelli comes from *campesina* stock. A local priest in her small town in Uruguay spotted her leadership talents when she was a teenager. Gladys rose in the Young Catholic Agrarian Movement to become a national leader, then a regional leader, and finally was elected as one of the international coordinators of the movement and sent to its headquarters in Belgium. There she was one of three Catholic lay women invited to be an observer at the sessions of the Second Vatican Council. The story of her dawning feminist consciousness within the Catholic church in the 1960s and 1970s is one of both anger and courage. Her countrywoman Fanny Geymonat-Pantelís (from the same small town in rural Uruguay) also rose to national leadership within the Latin American Council of Churches but because of her outspoken feminist views was refused ordination in the Methodist Church. She and her family were forced into exile in the 1980s by the Bolivian dictatorship, only to return to a church run by native Aymara pastors who ruled with an iron hand. She then faced discrimination for being non-indigenous and a woman.

Both Coca Trillini and Graciela Pujol were active in the leftist insurgency movements in their countries in the 1970s. Influenced by the work of Brazilian educator Paulo Freire, as were many of these women, Coca tells about her work in consciousness-raising among the rural poor. She describes the rise of the Montoneros, the guerilla movement in Argentina, and how many were motivated by a revolutionary understanding of Christianity to take up arms to create a more equitable Argentina. Coca recounts her years of mentoring of the Christian base community movement and her increasing knowledge of scripture and theology—and how she was never "taken seriously" by her male clerical colleagues. Graciela, a contemporary of Coca, tells of her ultra-conservative Catholic upbringing—and how she rose to become a leader in the Tupamaro National Liberation Movement and the national director of its student cadre. As the Tupamaros were targeted by the Uruguayan dictatorship, Graciela went underground to avoid arrest and certain torture. Forced into exile in neighboring Argentina, she raised her family while remaining faithful to the option for the poor and active in her Christian base community. Her battles with her rigid Catholic sexual upbringing and her gradual liberation parallel her rise in feminist and ecofeminist consciousness.

Agamedilza Sales de Oliveira's story of an abrupt switch from her childhood relationship to God as a kind father to God as an all-powerful, punishing judge, as taught by the nuns during her school years, is unfortunately all too common. Fortunately, a priest friend empowered her to see through the patriarchal veil of biblical texts to bring a feminist perspective to each text. Agamedilza brings great enthusiasm to re-creating myth and ritual in a feminist key.

Several of the women come from backgrounds of extreme poverty. Alcira Agreda was an indigenous *campesina* from the jungle region of Bolivia. At the age of thirteen she was beaten by her father and ran away from home, promising herself that she would never again suffer such abuse from a man. Hers is a story of determination to assert her selfhood while at the same time serving her impoverished people. Her search for wholeness in the Catholic Charismatic movement, and then in liberation theology, especially in the life and example of Jesuit priest Luis Espinal, who was assassinated by the Bolivian dictatorship in 1980, tells the moving story of a contemporary "saint." She also describes her experience in forming a new kind of religious community of women who would live and work among the poor, her efforts as a poor woman to study theology and scripture, and finally, how she discovered the healing effects of an ecology of the body while struggling against cancer.

Sandra Raquew, born and raised in a small village in the interior of Brazil's impoverished, drought-ridden Northeast, describes the conservative mores and the close-knit ties of the region. As Sandra's father had left the family when she was ten, and her mother had at one time had to become a sex worker to survive, the family worked extra hard to win the approval of the town. Sandra tells of her conversion to the Baptist church and how good it felt to "belong," to have a personal relationship with Jesus, and to express that relationship creatively through art, dance, and song. However, church members did not encourage her when she decided to study journalism, predicting that she would lose her faith. Today, Sandra is a professional journalist, an active member of the PT (Workers' Party), a mother, and a firm believer in both roots and the impossibility of belonging to a religious institution. She is nourished by a small community of feminist theologians.

Doris Muñoz also comes from *campesina* roots and has never minded proclaiming that she is a *pobladora* (a shantytown dweller).

A missionary priest from Maryknoll saw that she had remarkable leadership talent and was able to capture liberation theology's most sophisticated points and translate them into language that the poor could understand. At an early age Doris became a "popular educator" of liberation theology, social analysis, and biblical history. However, it was not until the arrival of Capacitar founder Pat Cane and of Ivone Gebara, both in 1993, that a new way of doing theology and of teaching emerged. In language filled with images, Doris tells how she discovered the centrality of the body and taking care of the body—one's own, that of one's neighbor, and that of the Earth itself—as key to any feminist or ecofeminist understanding of theology and spirituality.

Silvia Regina de Lima is from a working-class family that lives in a small suburb of Rio. Her African roots mark her entire experience of being Catholic. At a young age she entered a Franciscan congregation, a German teaching order of nuns. She recounts the joys of serving the people in those years but also her growing discontent with the congregation's lack of commitment to the poor. She eventually left the congregation and founded a small religious community—three blacks, two young men, and Silvia—to live and work among the poor. One of the greatest joys of her life was living in that community of solidarity and love. However, her desire to study led to a scholarship at the Universidad Bíblica Latinoamericana in Costa Rica, where she fell in love with a young Mennonite professor whom she married. Silvia has also had a struggle against cancer and wants to live at all costs in order to be with their small son and to continue her work and study.

Clara Luz Ajo tells what it was like to live in Cuba in the early years of Castro's overthrow of the Batista government. Clara, coming from a Quaker background, describes the uneasy relationship the churches had with the new revolutionary government and how, at each step, she and her partner, an Anglican priest, had to prove that they were not reactionaries. She also describes her decision to go to Brazil to study feminist theology and Brazil's Condomblé religion. Her study and eventual "initiation" into Santería is an enlightening snapshot of a cosmology that is still deeply embedded in today's Cuba.

Sandra Duarte and Marcia Moya, who, along with Sandra Raquew, are the youngest of the interviewees, have formally studied feminist theology. Sandra recently obtained her doctorate, writing a thesis on ecofeminist theology, and Marcia is also on an academic track. However, both women have strong connections to their countries' indigenous peoples. Sandra has spent long segments of time living and working with the Guarani tribes in Brazil, observing gender relationships and participating in their rituals and ordinary lives, and has been given a "name," a sign of belonging. Marcia is engaged with her *mestiza* identity, and her research focuses on pre-Christian myths and cosmovisions that can once again empower women. Both Sandra and Marcia combine feminist theological insights with anthropological and psychological tools to reconstruct Latin American identities. Sandra is also researching the phenomenon of religious "shopping around." She finds that many Brazilians, especially women, say they are Catholic, but at the same time, they consult tarot cards, astrology charts, crystals, and runes to know the future; they might also practice an Oriental spiritual discipline such as yoga, reiki, or tai chi, or study Buddhism, Hinduism, or Sufism. Sandra points out that no one feels guilty about putting together her own "package" of sources of meaning. Marcia, on the other hand, must battle conservative waves in Ecuador that find her classes in feminist theology too "unorthodox."

So these women telling their stories based on their own experience include an observer at the Second Vatican Council; two founders of religious congregations; two women with doctorates in feminist theology and a third nearly finished; women who have founded grassroots feminist organizations, written books, held and then lost positions of authority in their churches because of their feminist views; women who compose their own liturgies and rituals; women who are poets, artists, dancers, and body therapists. While their experiences have been different, to some extent they have all shared a radical shifting of perceptions. Their worlds have grown wider, including their anthropologies, their cosmologies, and their theologies. Indeed, this shift or evolution of perception describes the major themes of ecofeminism.[2]

SELF-UNDERSTANDING

One of ecofeminism's key insights is the shift from a sense of the human as an individual to a larger sense of self that is linked to the energy of the Earth community and to the cosmos itself. Most of the women interviewed have acknowledged this shift, noting that a change in thinking has often come about through very personal experiences.

Many Options

Sandra Duarte, fascinated with Brazilians' ability continually to construct a new synthesis in their belief systems, reflects on this:

> We humans are always inventing and reinventing ourselves. I think we are persons who are constantly changing, which is why I believe that we cannot limit ourselves to any single thing—be it a religion, a tradition, or even a paradigm. We are beings in transition: at each moment we are building our affective relationships and our relationship with the Sacred, with our work, with our thought—we are continually changing our ideas. There is no final product, because we are always looking for "the final product." In my study of how Brazilians are constantly "in transit" as they look for religious experiences that satisfy them, I have heard it said that we are more individualistic than ever before and that religion is more and more individualistic. This is simply not true! There is a growing process of religious individualization (in the Jungian sense), but not of individualism. There is a collective process taking place, but while before it was the priest or the pastor or another religious leader who told us what our religious symbol system should be, now we ourselves decide. We live this collectively; it is not just an individual thing.
>
> I've also observed that people are looking for symbolic anchors of the most diverse kind. From the outside, it might

seem very puzzling that a person has faith in Catholic saints and at the same time faith in the Orixas of the Afro-Brazilian religion Condomblé, while also participating in a ritual to the Pachamama. But it is precisely through these devotions that a person constructs a particular symbol system. Our religious institutions have problems with this because they are in charge of offering a specific "package" of symbols. If people begin to take what they want from the package and leave the rest, it clearly weakens these institutions. Today we have a veritable market of symbolic goods from which to choose. I don't see this as negative. People have more options and are therefore less able to be manipulated.

The Influence of Cosmologies

Based on her long experience working with the indigenous peoples of the Bolivian Andes, Fanny Geymonat-Pantelís opines that we humans construct definitions of ourselves from our own contexts. She finds that within the Andean context there are two ways to define who we are as humans:

The first, present in both the Aymara and Quechua cultures, sees the human couple as the center of cosmology and anthropology. Andean cosmology is cosmos-centered, while that of the Christian tradition is anthropocentric. In the Andean culture everything has its sex and everything is dialectically symmetrical, with balance found in the complementarity of opposites. Thus man and woman complement each other and establish equilibrium in their coming together, which engenders new life. Those who remain single never really become a person in this cosmology; they are considered immature. One becomes a person only when one marries.

However, in this complementarity of opposites, the masculine, the right side of things, is the stronger and dominates the other pole, which is feminine, weak, and docile.

Even the images of the Sacred reflect this dichotomy. The Pachamama (Earth Mother), which represents the feminine pole, is dependent on superior powers (such as the Sun God). This form of cosmology and anthropology is hierarchical and androcentric—in short, patriarchal. Nevertheless, the Pachamama is a powerful force and over time has gained ascendancy over the far away Sun God. The Pachamama provides rich support for ecological awareness, and devotion to the Pachamama implies love and reverence for the Earth as the sustainer of human life.

Sandra Raquew's origin defines who she is:

I am a flower of Brazil's Northeast, from a tiny village in the interior. I am deeply marked by being a woman born in this small place. We have a very strong sense of the presence of the Sacred, a profound respect for the forces of nature—and this defines my sense of ancestral belonging. This sacred space strengthens you, finds you, and affirms you. I think of myself as a space of both corporality and eternity, part of the same material of the cosmos. Understood in this way, my body has incredible value and can do the most incredible things. This means that my life has eternity in that it is connected with the lives of my mother, my father, and my village where I lived for many years, and I am also connected to those who will come after me. What will I offer them? Nothing perfect—I don't seek perfection. I am what I am: woman, worker, journalist, militant feminist who belongs to a great feminist theological group. I am many things at the same time!

Human Beings as Part of the Cosmos, Not Apart from the Cosmos

Fanny describes her new feeling of connectedness:

As human beings we are incomplete. We form part of a process of ongoing creation by a wise and ever-present transcendent energy. In its human form, this energy always seeks life that is more abundant, full, harmonious, and just. We form part of a planetary ecosystem that is dynamically interrelated. The natural world is a gift of infinite variety of loveliness and bounty for life itself, which graces and heals the human spirit. When everything seems hopeless at the human level, the green fields, the majestic mountains, the glorious colors of the sky, the movement of the clouds, the variety of texture and scent of the flowers speak of a vital energy that struggles to augment the weave of life at all times—often despite human beings.

To plant a rose bush or a tree, to place seeds in a pot are creative acts that form and nourish both human life and the life of the planet, our only home. We humans need to assume responsibility for life itself and augment the creative process that is ours to carry out. Unfortunately we have divided and compartmentalized life into peoples, institutions, classes, churches, and genders with some forced to submit to the domination of others, thus violating the primordial equilibrium of that energy that we call God.

Alcira, who acknowledges her peasant and indigenous roots, describes her evolution in self-understanding:

For a long time I could not describe who I was. . . . I could describe my existence with clarity only when I began to reconstruct my roots as a woman and as a *campesina*. I discovered that I am unique and whole, both for myself and for others. I have abilities and limitations, but also innate value as a person, and thus can engage in the process of learning and unlearning all that life offers in its intimacy and everyday-ness. I am in relationship and solidarity with others, with the Earth, and with Divine Energy. . . . Who I am has to do with the quality of life in all its dimensions, with my spirituality, with my dreams, and my work. In the end, it is the full realization of myself as a person.

At the same time, I find that the cosmology of indigenous peoples offers a more holistic, integral vision of what it means to be a person. The indigenous speak of the physical body, the emotional body, the mental body, and vital Energy—and all are interrelated. This is a very ancient vision. I have also discovered that I live within an ecosystem and that I am not in any way superior to other beings. Of course I was taught that humanity was the center of creation and superior to other beings. This vision has generated domination, violence, and destruction both of the planet's ecosystems and of human beings.

Marcia, a poet and a biblical scholar, describes her understanding this way:

I have always felt close to the Earth—mostly through my poetry where I could identify with the sea, the mountains, with the flight of the birds, with the dawn, the moon, and so on. But this identification was primarily intellectual. Only later was I able to actually feel the Earth through my body. These sensations and vibrations appeared when I began to locate myself as part of the larger cosmic body. I now realize that I am the culmination of both created energy and reciprocal energy. I was conceived through the exchange of my parents' energy—energy that we call love, affection, desire, and passion. Throughout my life, I have continually felt an energy that has sustained me and those who surround me. This experience provides my support.

However, it took a long time to discover that the human person is not superior to other species. Because we have the ability to talk and to reason we feel superior, but in fact we are quite limited compared with other animals. The human is as different from a bird as a bird is from a tiger; each has its place in the cosmos and each must live in harmony with other species. The abuse of the Earth by huge sectors of humanity enslaved by power and greed is based on the mistaken belief that we are superior. We must remember that we are one of a great diversity of species, and that there is great diversity even within our own species. We must respect that diversity while assuring that our own diversity is respected.

Embodiment and Healing

Doris's self-understanding broadened when she began working as a healer:

> When I discovered that I was an embodied human being, my world changed. It was a revolution for me, daughter of rationality that I am. Previously my body simply had no value for me. I now understand that my body is who I am and what I have. My body contains my spirit, my conscience, my affections, and my memories. Reclaiming my body was the first great step in the process of healing myself and in helping others to heal.
>
> I discovered the sense of body as energy, and that everything that came through my senses, my thoughts, and my relationships affected my body. I realized that I became sick when I was not able to channel my emotions in a holistic way, when I was blocking the normal flow of energy in my body. Everything that happens to the Earth also happens to me, it passes through my body. All the elements affect me: water, air, soil, and fire. That is why clean air is so important and why I am deeply anguished by the menacing cloud of smog that sits over Santiago.

Alcira experienced these interconnections in much the same way:

> I have also discovered my own internal ecosystem, which is in communion with the ecosystem that surrounds me externally. I became more aware of this connection when I began to pay attention to what I was eating. [In order to heal herself of cancer, Alcira decided to make a radical change in her diet, which she attributes to her recovery.] By caring for, nourishing, and protecting my internal ecology, I was also able to care for, nourish, and protect the external ecosystem. This confirmed for me that we must realize that our essence is both internal and external. It is as if we persons depend on creation and creation depends on

us. Thus the potato, rice, vegetables depend on me and I on them. We live in a relation of constant reciprocity.

For Silvia, who, like Alcira, is recovering from cancer, the struggle to live changed her understanding of who she is:

The experience I have lived through with my cancer forced me to review my whole life. The experience was one of being born again. In the hospital, where I was going through chemotherapy, I met people who were going through the same treatment—people who each month got worse. I began to ask myself, what is life? Why do I live while others don't? I find it is because I want to live, and have discovered this source of life within myself. And I continue to be nourished by that source. It seems that some people overcome cancer simply because they want to live, because they decide to activate all the healthy cells in their body and because these cells are capable of eliminating or healing those cells that are diseased.

Since I love symbols and believe in them, I asked myself how I could relate to my cancer at a symbolic level. I don't believe that cancer is the devil's work, as some churches teach. I realized that I had to activate all those healthy cells within my body to be in solidarity with my sick cells and help the part that is sick to heal. At many moments before the cancer struck, my body told me that all was not well, that I needed to change my rhythm of life, to do things in another way, but I didn't listen. This cancer was a huge internal outcry to reorient my way of dealing with my body. I think this happens when we are in such disequilibrium not only with our individual bodies, but also with the entire cosmos. The level of violence in the world is the proof of this. It is as if evil is the fruit of disharmony, of a lack of growth in communion. Our bodies are part of this. Pollution in the environment is another major cause of cancer. My sick body is related to the Earth's devastation, and this experience has committed me to care for the Earth. My recovery is related to the reduction in the number of buses polluting the atmosphere in San José. That is why, for me, one human being must be in communion with other human beings and with the entire universe. We form this totality of energy and power; to the degree that we are in communion with other powers in the universe we will renew our own lives and the life of the rest of the ecosystem.

These testimonies all underline an emerging sense of a broader understanding of the human person. The interviewees speak of feeling the Earth through their bodies, of understanding reality as energy, of the interconnectedness of all. They speak of belonging to both internal and external ecosystems; they believe that "everything that happens to the Earth happens to me." This appears to reflect a systematic change in their anthropological understanding of what constitutes the human person.

UNDERSTANDING THE DIVINE

Nowhere is the shift toward an ecofeminist posture more evident than in the women's understanding of the Divine. Their God-images are clearly shifting from a deity somehow outside and above the created universe to a sense of something within yet beyond. Most of these women use images to describe their evolving understandings of the Divine, and they talk of *experiencing* this energy rather than defining it.

Moving beyond God the Father

Agamedilza's story is especially poignant:

In my childhood we always prayed to the kind father in heaven to protect us, but when I went to study with the nuns, I encountered a very severe God the father who punished, who sent his daughters to hell. I found such an image repugnant and never accepted it. Instead, I continued to search for the God my mother taught me about, which included the strong presence of Mary. When I reached puberty, I especially needed a mothering divinity to pray to, to confide in about my desires, my changing body, my fears, my conflicts, and my first sexual relationships. God was male; what would he know about my life as a woman? The only possibility was through Mary. But Mary was Jesus' mother, a virgin, pure, who did not know man. How could I talk to her about my sexual desires? And so, little by little, I became a woman who discovered the Sacred in other persons and in nature. Later, when I discovered images of the Goddess, it was like rediscovering that lost feminine presence of my childhood.

Gladys Parentelli makes a similar point:

The God I was introduced to as a child—an old man with a beard—strikes me as an aberration. I imagined God to be superior, indefinable, and powerful! And yet, as well we know, most world cosmologies speak of the Creatrix of the world as feminine, or as masculine and feminine combined. Defining God in only masculine form has subordinated and devalued the feminine.

Doris describes the evolution of her own images of the Divine in a similar manner:

My first image was of a Father God who was a magician. Then I learned of a militant Jesus whose kingdom would be established in justice. My idea of God also had to do with the humble, the small, the insignificant: the widow's mite, the bread crumbs under the table. God was never associated with the powerful. A second moment in my development of God-images came when I began to relate God to the marvels of nature: the majestic mountains, the stars, the cycles of the seasons, and giving birth.

My cosmology changed when I became familiar with physicist Brian Swimme's understanding of the cosmos as a sacred experience. This was my first hunch that the images we had of God might be only one dimension of that great sacred mystery we call God. Today, I cannot speak of my experience of God, of the Sacred, without talking about my own human experience, my experiences of affection, of sexuality, of my spirituality in relation to the cosmos. I think my experience of the Sacred has broadened to include everything from the most intimate feelings of my body to the farthest outreaches of the cosmos. I am also discovering that all is related.

Today I feel comfortable with the idea of pan-en-theism, that all is in God, all is sacred, and that all our experiences of God are partial and within a specific context. I have also been greatly influenced by Ivone Gebara. She has helped me understand that we are not the owners of God and that the Sacred is not imprisoned in a church or a book, no matter how sacred they are thought to be. No reality is outside sacred space. There is no outside/inside or up/down—all is part of the Sacred. All of life is sacred, including our bodies, and that is why we must struggle to end torture, violence against women and children, and hunger and cold for the millions of marginalized people. The rivers are the Earth's bloodstream, and if they are contaminated, death will circulate throughout the whole body. I don't believe that there is any divine reality above or outside.

It seem to me that Jesus was the first to question that God dwelt in the Temple. He preferred to pray in the garden and on the mountainside, and called the Temple a den of thieves. Jesus changed the sense of the Sacred because he called for compassion for bodies that were sick and rejected. That was the beginning of the reign of God. Today, for me, God still exists, but my understanding of God has changed. God doesn't exist as a magician Father. What does exist is a Force, an Energy, and a Spirit that develops and evolves with perfect precision. This is visible in the perfection of the flowers, our bodies, and the cosmos. Although this is only what we humans can observe, God is much, much more than this; God is the great Mystery. My descriptions are mere sputterings that reflect my limited understanding. We have no certainty but that we know we live and move in this great Mystery, which we can never know totally, but do indeed experience.

Clara Luz admits that her involvement in the religious expressions of African origin have opened her to a whole new perception of the Sacred:

My studies and experiences with Cuban Santería and Brazil's Condomblé have led me away from rigid definitions and to connect with the Sacred in nature. At the same time, though, I realize that I can't reduce holy Mystery to static concepts or images. I think that what we call the Sacred or the Divine is in all of us and at the same time is in all that is; the Sacred surrounds us, penetrates us, and envelops us as a loving mother. We are part of this sacred, divine envelopment that also dwells within us.

The Sacred as Energy

Reflecting on the evolution of her images of God, Alcira says:

Before, it was easy for me to speak of God as Father or as Lord. Then to name God as Mother, Friend, or Lover seemed even more intimate and real. But I am most comfortable and honest when I name the Sacred as Fountain of life, energy, wisdom, tenderness, that which is within and breaks forth from each person. All this is experienced in friendship, in sharing, in giving service in solidarity, in celebrations, in the trees, in water, in food, in the daily struggles for justice. I like to understand and feel the Sacred as an experience of energy, which is a very open image. It is an energy that is here, in me, in the trees, the animals, in relationship, in the ways we love, the way we live out our commitments. This energy is Sacred; you find it and experience it through many symbols and names, rituals and myths, in relationship with others. This divine or sacred Energy is circular. It is like a current that flows and infuses life. It makes all life blossom forth and grow, not just human life but the entire ecosystem.

Marcia's images of God echo those of Alcira:

God is not all-powerful, but rather something that goes beyond the imaginable, something that needs to be discovered at every moment of our existence; it is there where the human-divine mystery is found, because both are, in the end, *mystery*. God is the impulse for my body, the strength of my thoughts, the container for my feelings, and the energy behind all that I am creating. God is the vitality I find in both people and in nature.

Silvia struggles with images coming from Christianity and those coming from her Afro-Brazilian heritage:

God is life, goodness, and positive energy that is present in others, in nature, and in history. I don't intend to contradict Christianity, which is a history of God's manifestation. But there can be more than one history of salvation. I have discovered a multifaceted God; in difficult moments God is crying with me, feels with me, laments with me. And my experience with Afro-Brazilian religions has taught me to contemplate and celebrate God in nature. In these religions the Orixas manifest themselves in nature; the river is not simply a river but is also where energy and strength are stored. I recognize that this terminology may be considered dangerous within the Christian world. Even so, I firmly believe in God's presence in these other religions.

Other Sacred Images

Coca, a biblical scholar and writer living and working in Buenos Aires, finds it difficult to describe what she believes:

I don't know if I would describe it as energy, God, goddess, or a star. I notice that when I write articles on these themes, I'm forever using more and more names to describe this relationship. Contact with nature, contact with other people, contact with tenderness as well as with pain—these all speak to me of a superior Existence, of a different Existence, of an Existence that encircles us and at the same time has something to do with fluidity. As yet I haven't been able to write about this, because it is not yet clear for me. Despite the ability I have to work with images, I have not yet been able to give shape to the Sacred. At the moment I am most likely pantheistic, experiencing God in many places, in the sunset, at a moment in a relationship, in the confidence someone has in me, or in someone in pain.

Sandra Duarte, influenced by her mother's recent death, describes the Divine as memory:

I believe that what I end up with is memory. Memory is very powerful to me because of the link with my mother. What is in me of her is the memory of a happy childhood, and this is very important for me, something that is sacred. It goes beyond a simple remembering. How do we arrive at the Sacred? Through our questions and our desires. When I sit down here in my small living room, drink a glass of wine, light candles, and listen to music, I feel immersed in a truly sacred moment because I am with my memories and find what I am looking for. It is a moment when I feel whole—not only in the present, but in the fullness of all time.

Fanny describes additional images:

Many times, in key moments, something happens that speaks to me once again of a wise presence, a protecting spirit and counselor who nourishes and augments life, showing that the horizon is always broad and wide. It is centered in energy and is always open and transforming. I find security and confidence in being part of this spiral of energy.

Another metaphor for God that I love is that of matrix or womb, because that is where life is gestating, taking form, being nourished, developing and maturing, where there is protection and warmth but where one cannot linger too long. The moment arrives when you must be born and free yourself to continue on your own journey. Both Andean cosmology and biblical texts present God as the great matrix, the fountain of compassion.

Understandings of Jesus

Tangential to a changing understanding of the Divine is the role the person of Jesus plays in the lives of these women. What appears clear is that Jesus continues to be a major historical figure, a prophet, and a wisdom figure. He is seen as counter-cultural and authentically human. He is with those who have died. He is a heroic figure who has inspired a whole civilization with his message. Agamedilza, Marcia, Graciela, and Doris, four women who continue to work as biblical scholars and teachers, enlarge on the significance of the biblical Jesus.

Agamedilza see Jesus as

> a very special person who, like many others, lived and fought against the Temple laws that excluded the poor, the sick, and women. I admire the courage he showed in his time— a time when women were forbidden to read the Torah. Yet he founded a movement in which women were allowed to assume leadership. I believe that Jesus is with those who have died. He is in that great energy that forms the essence of the web of life.

For Marcia,

> Jesus wanted to raise up humanity to our most authentic dimension, free of political, economic, or religious interests. His ancestors, who tried to live in harmony with the Earth, inspired him. That is why Jesus was different from

most humans of his time. He had another goal, which was to assess power and religion critically. He became conscious of this gradually and began to act responsibly, but not as a great leader or as one sent by God. I don't think Jesus ever thought of himself as having certain "Godlike" traits. It was only after his death that his followers discovered that his way of being human was so authentic that it revealed the Divine. In his life's project Jesus offered three proposals to humans: first, each of us can relate directly to God as son or daughter; second, this means that a relationship of equality and solidarity exists among us; and third, the first two proposals demand that we live a relationship of respect and harmony between our species and the Earth.

For Uruguayan Graciela Pujol, "Jesus of Nazareth is a reference point, but not because he is or isn't the only Son of God." At this point Graciela turns to Italian philosopher and writer Umberto Eco. "Eco, an atheist, says that the miracle of Jesus consists in that humanity had arrived at a moment in its history where we could take up the values Jesus proposed—love without exclusions, giving one's life for another. These are manifestations of the presence of God."

Finally, for Doris,

Jesus is an extraordinary person who has deeply marked my own journey. His experiences have helped me in my search for meaning and also many others who have grown up in the Christian tradition that so marks Latin America. However, now I see Jesus as only one reference point toward understanding the Sacred. I believe that his experience enlightens me because it was a counter-cultural experience so immense that the patriarchal culture in which he lived could no longer tolerate him. Jesus' own way of acting and being was not based on power structures, which helps my work with women, teaching them how to reread scripture from this counter-cultural perspective. What does anger me is how the churches and the hierarchies have appropriated the experience of Jesus as their own.

These many reflections on the nature of the Divine, and Jesus, represent a major change in perception: the Divine—or holy Mystery—is more immanent and more enveloping than in traditional Christian cosmologies. In all cases, however, varied understandings of the Divine are both rooted in and incorporated into experience and belief systems. These changes challenge Latin American theology to move toward more nuturing images, suggesting terms such as Energy, Wisdom, Matrix, Memory, Swaddling, Fountain of Life.

THE MEANING OF LIFE AND DEATH

The women's shifting cosmology is revealed in their reflections on death. The majority view life and death as part of the same cycle. They speak of death as returning to that primal energy, that original goodness from which they have come. Some speak of going into a different dimension, of being transformed. Others speak of memory—how loved ones are present in the memories we have of them and how they will be present in those who remember them. For some, the concept of ancestors, a concept shared with indigenous and African communities, is key. Several spoke of a fear of death that disappeared when they experienced the death of a loved one or when their images of God saw all as interconnected.

The Absence of Fear of Death

Agamedilza describes how she lost her fear of death through discovering the Sacred in her own body, in the bodies of others, and in the universe itself.

Sometimes I am captivated by the thought of my own death because I feel it will fulfill some great desire of mine. Those who have died are with us still and circulate among us; this is a connection I feel at times. Perhaps that is why I am not anxious about death. I always invoke those great women who have gone before us to accompany us by sending us their energy and wisdom. I'm not sure what will happen to me when I die, but I hope to form part of that energy and to somehow be present to those women and men who will come after me.

Gladys also speaks about death and fear:

Most people don't talk much about death because they fear it. I have never been afraid of death, however. Perhaps it might seem strange, but death seems as natural to me as life. Nor do I worry about the future, because I have always believed that my future is created in each of my actions. Death is part of the future and the only thing we can be sure of. Just as my life is the result of how I live, so too will be my death. I believe that all is Sacred and all is energy, which is why I have such great respect for all life on Earth. When I die, my spirit will return to its place of origin and I have confidence in that original goodness.

Death as Transformation

Marcia's understanding of death is marked by the death of her father:

Before the death of my father, I feared death, but that fear no longer exists. I was able to experience that death is not the end. My father's existence is transformed into a different dimension where I too will be someday. I experienced his resurrection in my life because I remember all those events and positive experiences that I shared with him. I also overcame my fear of death when I understood that while my father lived I was part of his very essence and both of us came from that essence "that is God." Death, then, is a transition of time, space, and place. More than a physical place, it is living intensely in a dimension without limits or borders, without laws and rules. We will be in those persons with whom we have experienced God. I will live on in the memory of those who have known and loved me, just as my father lives on in me. Death, then, is not the end. We are transformed, we become part of the energy of the cosmos.

Coca believes that

with death we return to where we have come from and are transformed into something else. A long discussion about the meaning of death and resurrection with a dear priest friend helped me immensely, particularly when he reminded me, "Resurrection isn't resuscitation, always remember that!" How did we develop such a fear of death? We must find a reason for this fear. And while I still fear death, I am now totally certain that it is a process of ongoing transformation.

Sandra Duarte is perhaps most vocal about what she does *not* believe:

I know what the feminist theologians say, I know what the ecofeminists say, I know what Christian theology says, I know what Condomblé says, and what the indigenous say about death—but I don't identify with any of them. I am not interested in knowing if my mother is in heaven, or part of a tree, or whatever. I feel her presence through my memories. I don't have a theological position on death, perhaps because the death of my mother was so hard and the pain so strong that I refused to think about it. Nevertheless, my memories are sacred, and this allows my mother to come to life every day in my dreams. Someone recently suggested that I had better go for some therapy. But this is no aberration; it is quite marvelous. I am very content.

Life after Death

Fanny has been influenced by many years of working with people in the Andean highlands:

In front of me are a collection of photos of my family, many of whom are dead. In them I see my children and myself. Yes, we die, at least physically. Indeed, our earthly lives are but a sigh, a second in universal time, despite the fact that some moments seem to last an eternity and others will never be forgotten because of their intensity, tenderness, beauty, or pain. After death our bodies can still feed life on Earth, both animal and plant life. Our bodies consist of life that decomposes. These concepts of the continuity of life and death and time and space are also present in Andean cosmology. Even after someone dies, he or she lives on in the memories of the family, the community, in the hills, and in the Pachamama herself. I believe that life and death are intimately connected. Although death is a specific individual event, it is also a communitarian and global event. My ancestors rise in me, as I will in my descendants. Life and death are interactive, continuous parts of the great matrix of *oikoumene*, where individual life is a cell in the universe.

Graciela holds on to a belief in transcendence. She admits that one of her strongest foundational beliefs has always been life after death:

If you ask me what sort of life, I cannot say, but I have always believed in a transcendence, an integration into the whole, into this greater reality. I think our mistake lies in always thinking that life after death is something individual. I continue to believe in some kind of fullness of life after death. I have no images, nor the ability to think how this integration into wholeness comes about, but I do believe in transcendence. I like thinking about life after death using the image of God as relationality, a concept of Ivone Gebara that describes a God who weaves relationship among all the beings of the universe.

Alcira, like Sandra, is very marked by her mother's death, which led her back to earlier indigenous beliefs about life after death:

I look at death from the experience of my mother's death. When she died, I found that traditional theology didn't nourish my faith. So I returned to the beliefs of our indigenous people that life and death are not separate. Those who die continue to live among us. They live on in their teachings, their examples, their counsel and witness—and in the very atmosphere that surrounds us. They remain in the things they liked: music, food, plants, candles, flowers, and in their gestures of kindness.

At the same time, we know that they are not with us physically; they have gone and are now enveloped in divine Energy. So the experience I have had with my mother is that while she is no longer here physically, she continues to be my companion and confidant. She is alive in all those kind ways in which she influenced my life. Based on this experience I can say that I feel resurrection in life. Our loved ones live on and accompany us. They are present in their words, in advice given, in a garden they planted. I feel that the dead give us strength to go on living. I do not like to think that the bodies of the dead stay in the cemetery while their souls go off to heaven. No, the dead stay with us. That is one reason why rituals surrounding death are so important for indigenous peoples.

Clara Luz would be content to return to the Earth:

I like the idea of becoming part of the Earth, a seed that flowers in another form, that can give life to others, that might become a tree or a flower. I love the natural world and if I eventually form part of the cycles of this marvelous Earth that produces so much life, I will be very happy indeed.

Silvia's beliefs about life after death are influenced by those of her African ancestors:

The Brazilian-Afro religions have a greatly enhanced sense of community. These ancient belief systems tell us that, after death, we are more than what we are now. Those of us who are here form a community, but those who have gone on before us are also members of this community. We are not speaking of reincarnation, but of bodies that are now enjoying themselves, who enjoy ways of being that are not the same as what we experience here. When they are here, they enjoy our world. This is another way of explaining the ancestors, and it gives me much joy. Those who die communicate energy to us.

Ancestrality means the continuation of life, of a mission. These ancestors continue in nature, perhaps as rocks or rivers. For Afro religions those who die really do become immortal in that they become a permanent presence in nature and are symbolic of the life of the person. Their histories stay with us forever. Indeed, the person is more present than absent. Nonetheless, I am still afraid to talk about my death, but that is because I am just recovering from cancer. I love to hug and kiss people and the thought of losing the ability to enjoy my body frightens me. I also fear the suffering one has to endure in order to journey to the other side. I need to reflect more on the physicality of death.

These reflections are filled with beauty, hope, and longing. They also reflect vulnerability, uncertainty, and fear. But in the end, hope prevails that nothing that comes into existence is ever lost, and this is key to ecofeminism.

THE BODY AS THE LOCUS FOR ETHICS

All twelve women interviewed addressed the topic of ethics from their own experience with great passion, calling for a major shift. Alcira's statement summarizes many of their major concerns:

Ethics has to do with life in all its dimensions, the ways we relate to each other, the way we are, the way we act, our attitudes; our stance on justice, on ecology; and the way we live at home, in our communities, and in society. I feel that

I am capable of making my own decisions, according to my conscience, my abilities, my commitments, my options, my creativity, and my feelings of solidarity with all of humanity, and then I take responsibility for those decisions. Ethics lived from this perspective makes me more human, more dignified, more honest, more coherent, more whole.

I feel that ethics should not be static but always dynamic and subject to rethinking and revisioning according to the new circumstances in which we are living and feeling and acting. We should be free to question those norms and any institutions of societies that advocate an ethics that is not connected to the lived reality of the majority or that makes the body a prison of guilt.

Until recently, official ethics, whether of society or religious institutions, has defined the way women must behave. Women have been confronted with an androcentric and patriarchal ethical code that has exercised strict control over our bodies. This is an ethics that punishes and imposes; it represses our sexuality, our affectivity, and our ability to control our own bodies and feelings. It has not allowed us to make our own decisions. To live by an ethical code that flows from our bodies will allow us once again to value our bodies as sacred. The ethics imposed by our institutions has often battered women's bodies with a morality based on guilt, leveled from on high, that determines what is good or bad, pure or impure. But we are the owners of our own bodies, of our sexuality, of our decisions, of our options. As dignified adults, we should be able to orient our lives according to our own conscience and experience of the Sacred.

The Importance of the Body

All twelve women maintain that ethics must begin with the experience of one's body, one's history, and one's longings. Starting with the body is essential. This is particularly true if women are going to challenge the patriarchal mindset that has long considered women's bodies to be sources of sin and evil. Agamedilza is very straightforward:

> I believe that we must always start from the body, from respect for each person, for her right to decide how she wants to live—always with the understanding that human rights must be secured for all. I don't much like laws and rules, but we do need norms with which to guide our daily lives. It is through my daily living with people, with the Earth, and with my own body that I construct my ethics.

Gladys, the eldest of the women interviewed, agrees about the importance of women's bodies:

> Clearly the human body is sacred. That is the main reason why we must take care of ourselves and respect and love ourselves. This is a source of my anguish, which is shared by all feminists, when I experience the violence that patriarchal cultures level against the female body. It is usually a violence that sees women only as reproducers of the species, as wombs, and that never sees us in our fullness with our hands that create, our minds that think, and our spirits that soar. The quality of the body's sacredness is directly related to how we respect, love, and commune with others.

The Responsibility of Women Themselves

As a Latin American coordinator for Las Católicas por el derecho de decidir, Coca deals with ethical questions from women on a daily basis. She points to two key concepts in the construction of an appropriate ethics:

> The first has to do with the body, which for me is fundamental. A starting point for any ethics must be from the experience of the body and the memories stored there. The second is that we must make ethical decisions based on the

experiences of our *own* bodies. Often a decision that might be a good one for me might be the worst possible decision for someone else. Unfortunately, this position is often labeled relativism. I am convinced, however, that we women are capable of making our own ethical decisions about our lives and that we have the right to make these ethical decisions. We cannot universalize laws; we cannot establish, once and for all, absolute norms that apply to every person. One of the problems in trying to systematize ecofeminist ethics is that most expect us to come up with definitive, justifiable definitions and scales of values—and that is just what we don't want to do.

Graciela, one of the region's foremost ecofeminist ethicists, maintains that

ethics is fundamental because it touches the key point in traditional theology, which is freedom. Dogmatic religiosity has been key in maintaining oppression—especially in the case of women—by denying our ability to make ethical decisions. I underline the importance of an ethics that breaks with a theology of guilt and sin. We see the need to create a new ethics from the experience of women, for it is women who have experienced this oppression for centuries and therefore it is women who must elaborate something new. Resituating freedom involves the creation of new relationships in which humans are now seen as autonomous subjects. Within this new view of freedom we can embrace pluralism and diversity—always based on experience. Ethics, then, is built from our contextualized experience. Each person is a different expression of freedom.

A Concern of the Community

Clara Luz focuses on the importance of human persons in relationship:

I believe that ethics are part of a process whereby we must open ourselves to a new understanding of who we are as humans, who we are as women, and how we understand ourselves in relation to our world, to those people who surround us, to the animals and the plants, to the whole with which we share an intimate relationship. For me, ethics consists of a relational attitude toward life, in the measure that we manage to understand ourselves as part of a relationship of communion, of respect, of justice and love. To the degree to which we feel part of a greater body, we can become ever more "humanized" by deeper and deeper relationships. It is from there that we can build a viable ethics that liberates. Relationships based on mutual respect and reciprocity with all the life community can transform power relationships that dominate and harm to those that engage, defend, and empower the weakest.

Sandra Raquew also values community:

The first topic we considered in my feminist theology group was abortion. Looking back, I realize that the only way to understand this issue is by listening to the experience and the wisdom of the group. I couldn't discuss abortion honestly and openly in my school or church or university or work place. I am sure now that ethics must be built in a common space as a collective exercise. While I want to hold on to the liberating ethics of Jesus and incorporate the values I learned from my home, my mother, my grandmother, my father, my brothers and sisters, my group can help me to see some errors in my family's approach to decision-making. Together we study cases and weigh social factors. We also consider the particular situation of each woman, including her past and her context, so that we have a more mature understanding of how we make our choices.

Doris, a theologian with much experience teaching and counseling women, calls for an ethics based on "power with":

The challenge is to recover power and autonomy for women and for all people so that we can make our own decisions, and make them in a more integrated context. More and more we are realizing that everything is related—and that decisions made at every level affect everyone and everything else. The challenge of ecofeminism is precisely to promote a more integrated view of life. Each decision made should promote more equitable relations while curtailing domination over the weak and voiceless, including the entire life community and the Earth itself. We need to be able to pay attention to what our bodies are saying and to hold conversations with those we trust to get advice. The question of power is key. I am talking about "power with," not "power over" or from outside me. If I am going to make a decision or share my deepest experiences, I'm not going to seek out persons who might condemn me a priori. No, I'm going out to friends who will listen and ask questions to help me clarify my thinking. In the end, though, I am the one who will make the decision. We must create spaces where we women can share our power and help each other to make decisions, but not make them for the other.

Silvia calls for an ethics based on joy, not just individual happiness, but happiness for the community:

I am guided by happiness. I believe that humans were created to be happy, to be fulfilled. But I must place the happiness and fullness of life of others on the same scale with my own happiness. That is why my criterion is to search for happiness, but my happiness can never, ever mean the death or the unhappiness of others. We are to create happiness for all. When we say "Thou shall not kill," we should mean it in the fullest sense: we are not to kill dreams, we are not to kill through hunger or through violence, we are not to create the unhappiness of others. This is how we can create an ethics for life. Happiness is a right to life that all people have, that all life, nature, and the universe have.

Ethics vs. Morality

Marcia insists that we differentiate between morality and ethics:

Morality establishes an ideology of correct and incorrect ways of acting that respond to preestablished codes, nearly always established by a patriarchal, capitalistic society. A characteristic of morality is that it judges what is right and prohibits what is judged wrong; it usually does not allow a person to grow in responsibility. Women's bodies—especially in the areas of sexuality and genitality—have always been seen as immoral, sinful, and negative. Our modern societies consider those who follow accepted moral codes good, even if their behavior reveals conformity, hypocrisy, or an inability to establish their own moral principles.

Ethics, on the other hand, holds that life itself demands respect for and from all and responsibility by and for all. Ethics should be accompanied by a spirituality that expresses these attitudes daily. This has everything to do with our vision of the cosmos and the way in which we perceive all of life. In the end, ethics does not depend on ideologies or religions or codes of law, but rather on how we responsibly assume our location in the cosmos—a stance that is prior to both ethics and morality. Ecofeminists do not perceive humanity as separate from the rest of the cosmos; nor is the human person superior to other species or the male superior to the female or the white race superior to other races. It is this kind of thinking that has caused our current crisis.

While morality tends to make us passive beings, ecofeminism is searching for, defending, and trying to create new alternatives to enhance life's evolution. Ecofeminist ethics calls us to try new possibilities and to recreate ourselves in a new spirituality that invites each to contribute from its own diversity to the whole, instead of providing a list of "shoulds" and "should nots."

The Goals of Ethics

As a sociologist of religion, Sandra Duarte observes that "to-day people are looking for meaning and not for an ethics. They are seeking those symbolic elements that will respond to their immediate questions or needs." She notes that ethical questions always come later or not at all:

> I sense that we are at a moment when we need new ethical constructions—a new global ethics. We need to search for ways to build an ethics that evolves with people's aspira-tions. For instance, I am here with my experiences and sym-bols of meaning, but what can I offer that is more than just my own ecstatic experience of, say, the goddess? This ec-static experience may be important for me and it may offer me key symbolic meaning, but I must also bring something else to the table, something that conveys how I am com-mitted to act within the world.

An ecofeminist ethics involves calling forth respect and re-sponsibility from each and for all—and it involves seeing the human in relation to the rest of the living community and the unfolding universe. As part of a greater body, ecofeminists try to take into account the whole when making ethical decisions. Such a system of ethics is always contextualized, and it is pluralistic and respectful of diversity. It does not attempt to legislate uni-versal laws. It is based on an expanded meaning of the human person and of the Divine. It is aimed at the happiness of the com-munity and draws from the wisdom and experience of the com-munity to benefit individuals but always in relation to the entire cosmos.

AN ECOFEMINIST SPIRITUALITY

Latin American women drawn to ecofeminism nurture their spirituality in many different ways. Most involve their bodies, either through movement or quiet meditation or by connecting their bodies with the natural world about them. It is this strong sense of the importance of the body and of the senses that both penetrates and characterizes ecofeminist spirituality.

Women and Community

Agamedilza admits that she no longer finds nourishment celebrating in her traditional church community. "The celebrations don't relate to me. In our gatherings of women, on the other hand, we celebrate our bodies and everything that surrounds us—we celebrate the elements, the lives of other women; we celebrate life with our women's bodies."

Graciela also finds security and solidarity in gatherings of women:

I find myself celebrating in small groups where new expressions of spirituality are being born. First, we are breaking with being disassociated from our bodies. This is a fundamental change for us women who have been socialized as beings-for-others; in the past our sexuality and our bodies have been expropriated for the service of others. Women's transformation must include this dimension of consciousness-raising. Mind-body spiritual practices, while pleasurable and liberating, may also be painful because we must deal with the many hurts stored in our memories. Now, at last, we are beginning to weave new relationships and experience solidarity among ourselves as women, counting on tenderness to help empower each other.

Silvia, a liturgist from Brazil, greatly enjoys encouraging people to celebrate, bringing the liturgy alive. She has dedicated much of her life to making liturgies real celebrations of life:

I am Brazilian, and in Brazil we celebrate everything. It is a way to circulate energy, to radiate more life. However, during the last few years, removed from my black community that has always been a real source of energy for me, I sometimes feel as if I am drying up. At the same time, I am discovering I can recharge by participating in the liturgies of the Mennonites or in a Catholic Mass, in a celebration of Condomblé in Brazil, or with the gay community here in Costa Rica. I seem to be able to find spaces to water my spirituality wherever I look.

Marcia expresses a deep longing to celebrate with like-minded people:

I have come to realize that life must be lived intensely at every moment. I must live each moment intensely because it is not repeatable and it is an opportunity to find deeper meaning in my everyday life. I am sustained by sharing what I know with those with whom I share dreams or small achievements. Contemplating the natural world also sustains me and I never tire of discovering its hidden mysteries. My family and friends also fulfill me, and the women I work with support me, because with them I can express who I am, what I feel and think, what I am learning and discovering. Together we try to create new possibilities to better our lives. All this is a profound expression of life and God. Right now, I am also delighting in the potential in Ecuador's *mestiza* cultures, where spirituality is found in dance, music, colors, rituals, myths, and community celebrations.

Sandra Raquew shares a deep sense of community with her feminist theology collective, Chimalman, and finds it a fundamental source of sustenance: "Together we cultivate seeds of new beliefs and values for ourselves. This is our space, the place where we can feel accepted, where we can think, share, and celebrate together. The Sacred for me takes place in sharing experiences with others. In these moments, I know I am not alone." She notes, though, that "spirituality also has to do with contact with color, art, poetry, photography. These are powerful moments of interiority."

Other Resources

Coca describes her search:

At this time in my life, three practices are profoundly spiritual. First, I engage in mind-body spiritual practices, which help me to move into a different time and space. I also love the rituals and celebrations we create with women, which are powerful moments that connect me with the depths and heights of life. And I love being alone in nature.

Fanny relates a mystical experience with nature:

A heron and I were one, in our brief time together, breathing the same air. We both, in our own way, seemed to feel the beauty and peace of the moment. She came close to me, as if to seal our relationship. Then my heron moved away, but we continued to look at each other. We formed some sort of sisterhood, a friendship. We were silent partners in a scene that rang out God's glory.

Clara Luz also speaks eloquently of her connection with what she calls "the deep":

I connect with the deep in many different ways: through strong feelings related to friendship, love, passion, joy, anger, and impotence; through pleasurable movements of my body when I dance, when I hug someone, when I make love; through contact with nature—the perfume of the flowers, the smell of the sea, the sound of the rain on my windowpane, the sound of the breeze at sunset. When I do tai chi, when I swim in the sea, when I meditate in my favorite corner surrounded by trees and flowers, when I contemplate the sea or the river from afar. I also connect with the deep in the warmth of the company of my children, through the laughter and pure gaze of my granddaughter, through the love of my husband and of my parents. Through the friendship and warmth of friends, or when I hear a lovely melody or taste a rich cup of chocolate or enjoy a tasty meal;

when I can extend a helping hand to someone in need, or when someone gives me a hand in tough moments; when I experience deeply the sufferings of others as a result of injustice; when I hurt with the cry of the children and all victims of the disorders of our world; when I am able to perceive the pain of others as my own pain.

Gladys also finds spirituality resources in "how I relate to all I meet along my path—with those I love, with friends, with those I meet for the first time, a little girl, a little boy, a dirty beggar who asks me for food. My spirituality, my peace, rests in how I relate to all of life." Gladys also draws on mind-body spiritual practices and nature: "I also meditate each day, which is a practice I engage in to clear my mind of all thought and center myself. I also climb Mount Alba every day. To walk for a few hours in the midst of such beauty, to enjoy the harmony of the forest, the birds, the butterflies—all this gives me a great sense of harmony."

Mind-body spiritual practices also sustain Doris, who insists that her spiritual practices have to do with remembering to be in contact with herself:

For a long time, my spirituality was centered on external practices—marches, protests, *via cruces*—that had to do with the context in which we were living. But today my practices always begin within me. They are a response to my own core, my own need for contemplation. I practice tai chi; I love to meditate in nature and to participate in women's rituals. Thoughtful conversations with friends, sharing dreams, dancing, singing, and chanting give meaning to my life. The spirituality I live today has to do with movement and sacred dance, with being in community. It is my whole being that celebrates now, not just my spirit.

An Integrated Spirituality

The development of Alcira's spirituality mirrors the development of feminist theology in Latin America. Her spirituality began to develop in alternative spaces such as women's reflection groups, local Christian base communities, and in indigenous and black organizations. She also credits the witness of many theologians and biblical teachers who dared to present alternative readings of theology and biblical texts that offered integrity and honesty. She was helped greatly by the hermeneutics of suspicion and feminist research that "passed through my own skin, my body, and my feelings as a woman."

Alcira's spirituality is also sustained by contemplation, meditation, and concrete reflection on her surroundings: "I live next to a *campesino* market where I have the opportunity to study life through the faces of so many people from all social strata." She also draws on women's rituals and mind-body spiritual practices: "I am watered by the rituals we do as women that are connected in some way to the Earth, and to healing rites for women, the Earth, and our ecosystem. I love to dance and to express through my body my dreams, hopes, and desires."

Community is also important for her: "I try to keep contact with other women throughout Latin America who think as I do, so I don't feel alone and to remind me that there are many who dare to 'suspect,' intuit, and search for new ways of living." Alcira's teaching includes biblical texts, alternative health approaches, self-esteem building, gender studies, reflexology, and aromatherapy. She admits that she no longer participates in the eucharist because she finds it an empty, patriarchal, androcentric ritual that gives her little opportunity to express what she thinks or feels. Instead, she says,

> I visit the trees. One of my favorite personal rituals before taking a trip is to go to the park in Santa Cruz to sit for a while under the trees. I greet each tree and ask it to orient me and accompany me with its wisdom and strength so that I may do what I am meant to do. I feel a deep bond with these trees, a communion and solidarity. When I return, I go to thank them. This ritual fills me with energy. Through it I find the Sacred. The trees become part of me and I part of them. I follow their cycles throughout the year and their

closeness inspires me to be creative and more sensitive to people.

In summary, the spirituality of many Latin American women drawn to ecofeminism is based on a wide variety of spiritual practices. It is noteworthy that while these women actively seek out moments to connect with the Sacred, they no longer rely on churches or religious institutions. Instead, they often turn to women's groups that offer friendship and understanding and that create rituals and celebrate embodiment. As individuals, they also turn to a variety of mind-body spiritual practices, including movement, meditation, and the contemplation of nature. The sensuality and richness of poetry, color, and music as well as an awareness of the pain and suffering of their fellow human beings add depth and breadth to their engagement with the Sacred.

WOMEN AS FEMALE, SEXUAL BEINGS

Another characteristic of ecofeminism is a clear recognition of the sexual nature of women. This came to the fore particularly in an extended session in 2002 when the twelve women met in Santiago, Chile, to reflect on their theological journeys. Ivone Gebara, who was present, played a key role in raising questions and offering input.

The women found the courage to discuss a category rarely spoken of. They reviewed the history of God and female genitality—subjects usually not considered together—as both places of oppression and places of social power. Early on, some participants were uneasy about speaking of such an intimate and taboo subject and wondered if they were not being irresponsible in their commitment to the poor of their continent and to their task of transforming structures of oppression. Were they not diverting the locus of theology? Were they not reflecting on their own intimate experiences without giving thought to larger, supposedly more urgent, political and social contexts? However, as they continued to reflect, they discovered that they were breaking one of patriarchy's most entrenched rules—they were speaking truthfully about what had either been slandered by pornography or described only in medical or academic circles using "rational" or "objective" terms.

Their reflections concentrated on the "shadow side" of genitality: that which has been labeled by patriarchy as unclean, sinful, the result of temptation, the door of concupiscence, and a curse for the pains of childbirth. The women did not focus on the marvels of sexuality or on sexuality as part of their identity—aspects very well known to them. The shadow side, dominated by the world of patriarchy, has been portrayed historically as the source of sin; never has it been seen as a space of freedom. The women noted that within Christianity, freedom has never been a part of these "lower areas." On the contrary, the patriarchal nature of Christianity has controlled and denied this site of our instincts and being, perhaps because it is a reminder that we too are part and parcel of the flesh of all living things and of the very womb of the Earth itself. Female genitality has been darkly construed as subject to cycles and secretions and associated with the darkness of caves and with secrets of a hidden and feared mystery.

The women observed that for millennia a patriarchal God has controlled the political world of empires and the bodies of those who built the empires. The bodies were divided into classes, colors, and genders, and also into nobler and lesser parts. The head dominated, as did masculine gender and male genitality. Patriarchal tradition lifted up the grandeur of rational (male) thought and frowned on the sordidness of genitality—especially female genitality. The more that rational thought was elevated and the spirit hailed as supreme, the more the female body became an object of forbidden desire, an object of lust, war, and rape. In its attempts to deny and hide genitality, patriarchy labeled it sin and punished it with rigor.

Reflecting together, the women concluded that a result of—and perhaps the motivation for—patriarchy's system of dualism, dividing body from spirit, was the domination, injury, brokenness, and violation of women's bodies. While this system of dualism repressed freedom, the Age of Reason held sway and civilizations were founded and flourished. This was at the cost of a dominated "eros" that became the foundation for a culture of repression. Meanwhile, we accepted the illusion that we lived in freedom.

Extended discussions together awakened the women's collective corporal memory in a very real way. Many women said that their grandmothers, mothers, and friends were also present. Tears from the past watered their memories as they recalled that the oppression their ancestors experienced in their bodies would have been much worse than what these feminist theologians knew. (Silvia wondered if her cancer wasn't in some real way an ancestral illness that witnessed to the pain her grandmothers and great-grandmothers had suffered as slaves.)

Together they asked what could be learned from such suffering. What could be salvaged from it? The women concluded, as a group, that sexuality—and explicitly genitality—has always been present in patriarchal religious discourse but in the form of silence. They agreed that the denial of genitality as a human attribute of beauty and freedom is linked to an asexual image of the Divine and is grounded in a dualistic understanding of life. As scripture was interpreted, the patriarchal God seemed to take a stand against genitality, especially feminine genitality. He exerts power over women, condemning their genitality as a place of transgression and disobedience, even a source of competition.

Female genitality was never viewed as a place of dwelling of the Christian God. Christ was conceived in the womb of a virgin and born of her in a totally miraculous way. In Christian symbolism, Ivone Gebara reminded the women, sexuality appeared mysteriously by the power of a patriarchal God capable of "birthing sons of Abraham from the rocks" and by sending his all-powerful Holy Spirit to engender his only Son. She noted that even after many centuries women have still not been able to understand and assimilate the transcendent sexuality of Mary. Women continue to be condemned and continue to feel guilty when experiencing the "sinful" behavior of sexual pleasure.

The women were somewhat stunned by the audacity of these theological reflections and their own audacity in giving voice to them. They committed themselves to continue theological reflection on women's genitality with their local communities as a major step in the process of healing and moving beyond the current patriarchal culture. This would be essential to redeem women's own value systems and self-esteem.

ECOFEMINISM AND LIBERATION THEOLOGY

While most ecofeminists recognize their debt to liberation theology, they also express a certain frustration with it at present. Some think liberation theology is still too situated in constructs of traditional theology that are both androcentric and anthropocentric. Doris notes this is true particularly of its symbolism, spirituality, its concept of God, and its sacred images.

Their reflections on liberation theology also mirror the evolution of feminist theology in Latin America (discussed in Chapter 2). For example, while Agamedilza drew close to liberation theology through analyzing biblical texts with a priest friend, she says: "But I missed women's participation as active subjects; women were in the texts only as helpers or those who listened. I also became aware that women are not often included in the lectionary, nor are we included in liberation theology, which tends to lump us together with the generic poor. This does not help liberate women from the burdens of patriarchy and machismo." She adds that she misses women "inside" liberation theology, she misses the feminine "inside" scripture, she misses the feminine in the Divine, and the mother in the Creator. "Never have I accepted the fact that a man, a male, even if God, can give birth." She concludes: "However, reading feminist theologians I discovered the Great Mother, the Goddess. I found peace and since have never felt alone."

Feminist biblical teacher Marcia is more upbeat about the contributions of liberation theology:

> Initially, the poor were spoken about in very general, theoretical terms by a certain elite, without bringing about deep changes. However, with the help of a grassroots reading of the Bible, the poor really began to feel subjects of their own process. They discovered their own faces in the struggle for liberation, which opened a new stage of liberation theology.

Over time the proposals of liberation theology have become more concrete and more identified with those people now beginning to raise their own voices of liberation. The theological task that we must face will be undertaken by this great web of men and women of different cultures, races, and ethnic backgrounds.

Marcia notes that half of all Christians are women. She continues:

I'm convinced that we women can find elements for our liberation through studying the Bible. At the same time, I recognize that although the Bible was written by those responsible for patriarchy, it still contains many traditions of poor people, men and women in search of dignity, equality, and justice. To live out these values, we must deconstruct stereotypes to bring good news to all. For us women, this process must begin with healing our bodies. If we say that the gospel is generosity, love, and service, then first of all we must heal ourselves.

Sandra Duarte is even more emphatic about her debt to liberation theology:

It was because of liberation theology that I became deeply involved in politics. In fact, I think it would be correct to say that it also was the reason why I later became involved in feminism. It was through liberation theology that I realized that classical theology wasn't the only possible theology. Although liberation theology has received much criticism from feminists and others in recent years, I know that for many feminist theologians in Brazil liberation theology was key in their evolution toward feminist theology. So, although I too have my criticisms of liberation theology, I think that these criticisms often neglect to mention the importance that liberation theology has had in our lives. More work must be done in the area of gender, but this does not mean that we are no longer liberation theologians.

I want to be a feminist theologian of liberation. That's why I'm uncomfortable with denying liberation theology; it was our "cradle." When we write the history of feminist theology, we must begin with liberation theology.

On the other hand, Graciela believes that today it is women who are moving liberation theology forward. She says, "One of the limitations of liberation theology is that it has made an absolute out of one dimension of oppression—economic oppression—while ignoring others that are just as fundamental, such as gender and sexual oppression."

It is Alcira who, after years of involvement with the liberation movements in Bolivia, levels the harshest criticism:

> In my opinion, liberation theology is in a period of stagnation and institutionalization. Many of the theologians once in the vanguard are now silent. Liberation theology was born out of the cry of the poor as a response to the excluded of history. It confirmed many of my own theological intuitions and for a long time I identified with liberation theology.
>
> Today phrases like "the preferential option for the poor" are just slogans, emptied of what they once contained. I feel more and more uncomfortable with this theology, without denying its prophetic voice. It is the liberation theologians who are defining the poor. I miss the presence of other actors—women, blacks, the indigenous people, and those who speak from daily life for the environment and for gender equality. I feel more at home with ecofeminist theology and with biblical studies from the perspective of women, blacks, and indigenous people. I feel it is time for a radical revision of the basic constructs of liberation theology.

LATIN AMERICAN COMMITMENT TO ECOFEMINISM

While all twelve women reflected seriously on these concerns of ecofeminist theology, some would not choose the label of ecofeminist. Others would be sympathetic with its goals and methodologies; some would embrace ecofeminism wholeheartedly, while others would perhaps redefine it within the Latin American context.

Sandra Duarte expresses her support but also some reservations:

> Because I was very involved with Brazil's feminist movement, I began to notice the importance of rituals for women. I began to study ecofeminism in the university in order to see why so many women in Brazil were participating in ecofeminist rituals, often without understanding what ecofeminism entailed. I am convinced that ecofeminism contains some very dangerous positions, one of which is its essentialism. There are many different tendencies in ecofeminist thought, but one central idea is that women will save the planet. I think this is very dangerous because it puts an immense responsibility on the shoulders of women.
>
> I began to read ecofeminist theory, especially what is being written in Brazil and in other Latin American countries. The ecofeminist rituals I have witnessed include many elements related to nature and similar to shamanism. Originally I intended to concentrate on these ritual practices, but I discovered that I must first understand the theory behind ecofeminism. That is why my thesis concentrates on ecofeminist discourse. In my study I could distinguish between those ecofeminists who were essentialist and those who were more social-constructionists. But in actual practice, it is not so clear. When I participate in a ritual, I don't hear the discourse; I only see a women who is constructing her own symbol system. Today she might have one question and tomorrow another. However, one constant in all of my research is the need to enter into greater contact with nature.[3]

This feeling is shared by Marcia, whose perspective is colored by her work with Ecuadorian indigenous women. Marcia says:

Healing of women's bodies is totally connected to the healing of the Earth. Today women's bodies as well as Earth's body are fragmented by the idea of male superiority. The two processes of healing go hand in hand. In my biblical work within the Andean culture, I have learned that this indigenous cosmology has a clear ecological focus. Ecofeminism offers a real possibility for recovering women's cultural and religious values and for re-creating and re-dimensioning our own symbolism, rituals, celebrations, life cycles—as well as the whole dimension of the Divine revealed in nature.

Alcira, who was most critical of liberation theology, is also the most concrete about her emerging ecofeminist convictions:

When I lived in the mining areas of Bolivia I reconnected with the Earth and was anguished by the erosion, the poisoning, and the violence leveled on that land. It was there in the Siglo XX mine that I made the connection between the body of women and the body of the Earth and how both have been subjected to abuse of every sort. For me, to speak of the Earth as body is to speak of my own woman's body. The Earth and we humans are one; I am part of her and she is part of me. The damage she receives, I receive; what I suffer, she also suffers. A deep, inseparable bond exists between us both.

At the same time, my experience with cancer gave me another way to see and experience life. I discovered how the internal ecosystem of each person is as important, and as violated, as our external ecosystems. As a woman, I cannot continue to reinforce the ideology of the patriarchal, androcentric system that is present in church and society. I am convinced that there must be another way of being human.

Alcira notes that it was Ivone Gebara who helped her express many of her latent suspicions and intuitions: "What she said gave

form to many of my questions. I had observed and suffered in my
own flesh the violence leveled against the ecosystems and against
women, but I didn't know how to talk about this violence. Ivone
gave my suspicions and intuitions a name: ecofeminism."

Coca's reaction to ecofeminism is quite different:

> I must admit that I am totally urban. I was born into a world
> of concrete, and I'm petrified of bugs. I think any strong
> wind is an earthquake. But I experience ecofeminism in my
> body by connecting with its rhythms, and I see other women
> doing the same. Ecofeminist theologies have put more
> meaning in my life. My ecological commitment is still small
> and must be developed. I do plant my herbs and try to be
> more in harmony with the seasons, and I try to use the car
> only for more than two people, and I try to teach these
> values to my grandson. I don't have a systematic statement
> of reasons why I am an ecofeminist, but I am convinced
> that ecofeminism is absolutely inclusive of both men and
> women, of the diversity of culture, class, race, age, and many
> other variables. We must always retain a critical posture,
> and we must leave behind the mechanistic paradigm in
> which we usually operate. Ecofeminism allows me to dia-
> logue with theology from a new perspective.

Graciela likes to call herself an ecofeminist because it gives
her a wider perspective on issues of justice:

> Feminism has given me the ability to recognize that there
> are different ways of engaging in the struggle for justice.
> I'm now working against gender oppression, but without
> losing sight of class, race, and other oppressions. These
> struggles are not mutually exclusive. For me, ecofeminism
> is all embracing. It offers a feminist and an ecological per-
> spective that is very broad. Ecofeminism has provided me
> with tools to deconstruct all the dogmatic precepts that were
> oppressing me and to reconstruct what is important to me
> now.

Doris also acknowledges the broad influence of ecofeminism, which has laid bare the anthropocentric mindset that has resulted in the domination of women and the Earth:

> It is much deeper than either neoliberalism or capitalism; it has to do with patriarchy, which bases political parties, the church, the family, the university, every kind of construction of knowledge, and every kind of institutionalism on hierarchies and dualisms. In this same dualistic structure we have God and humans, heaven and Earth, the sacred and the profane, the spirit and the body. As an ecofeminist I can understand my experience as a woman and I can also understand myself as part of this expanding cosmos, part of this fifteen-billion-year-old history.

6

Challenges for the Future

The continent of the Unconscious
turned upside down
And out flew spirits of the dreamtime
A rainbow serpent coiled itself
into a brain
(The color of dried blood)
We are children of the rock
       —MADONNA KOLBENSCHLAG[1]

I feel myself and those who have shared their lives with me on the threshold of a new venture. We seem at the beginning of a new common creation as we embark on the journey of ridding ourselves and our world of a patriarchal mindset. This mindset has become so embedded in us that it seems as normal as the air we breathe, and it becomes hard to imagine what a post-patriarchal world might look like. But we have our intuitions, dreams, and hunches. *And* there is a growing circle of like-minded seekers, each now knowing that she is not alone in her search.

SHIFT IN CONSCIOUSNESS

That we are leaving behind patriarchal constructs and pushing toward something new—something that we only intuit and cannot yet define—is evident in the testimonies of the twelve

Latin American women theologians reported in the previous chapter. At this point in their history few of the women would insist that their evolving theological, spiritual, and ethical insights be labeled ecofeminist. But they would not dispute that there is a paradigm shift, that their intuitions are changing, and that their insights mark a whole new way of understanding the human and the Divine. *Ecofeminism* is only one term to describe the constructs of meaning they are feeling and giving voice to; some long for a more adequate metaphor, a more poetic, authentic term that would also reflect the region's earlier indigenous cosmologies. At the same time, what Ivone Gebara describes as holistic ecofeminism has struck a deep chord in the hearts of these women. Over and over they have told me: "She was able to give words to what I was feeling. She helped me put the pieces of the puzzle together."

In any case, the term *ecofeminism* is not as important as the actual shift in consciousness that is taking place. The shift is manifested in the evolution of these twelve women's anthropology (the way they define the human), cosmology (their understanding of origins, which in turn has altered their images of the Sacred), and their epistemology (the sources for their knowledge, *how* they know things). And, not surprisingly, this shift in consciousness has affected their ethical postures and their spiritual practices.

Shifting Anthropology

These Latin American women express, in a variety of ways, a shift in understanding of who they are as human beings, as *anthropos*. Their sense of themselves as individual, separate egos is evolving toward a larger sense of self—what Joanna Macy would call the ecological self. This shift in identity from an isolated entity or being to identification with a large cosmic body is evident in all their accounts. We humans are not superior to or apart from the rest of the life community; we are part of the natural world, part of the materiality of the universe, or, as Agamedilza reminds us, "We are brothers and sisters of nature." Because of our particular kind of intelligence, we are meant to be the Earth's caretakers and to ensure its well-being. "Everything that happens to the Earth, happens to me," reflects Silvia, paraphrasing Chief Seattle's well-known prophecy, "What happens to the Earth will also happen to the children of the Earth." Silvia feels her own recent breast cancer is "related to the Earth's devastation."

Some women spoke of themselves as beings in process, incomplete in themselves yet linked to all who have gone before them and to all who will come after. This is especially true of the women who have been deeply influenced by Latin America's indigenous cultures. We are, it seems, the collective memory of all that has gone before—the very elements in our bodies were present in the primordial fireball—and it is probable that in some recycled form we will be present in the future generations of the community of life.

The anthropologies of these women support what deep ecologists describe as a remembering of who we are. This recalls David Bohm's "implicit order," which sees everything linked to the universal reservoir of life; past, present and future are all one in a space-time continuum. And it echoes Brian Swimme's definition of human beings as "geological formations" as much as the rocks and the seas and the mountain ranges—a mode in the universal dynamics of evolution that is wondrous to behold but is still only one manifestation of cosmic creativity among trillions of others. It also fits with Jungian psychologist James Hollis's thought that "this little incarnation we call our life is but the vehicle for a larger journey which Divinity makes through us." This perspective sees the world as an intrinsically dynamic web of relations in which no absolute dividing lines separate the living and the non-living, the animate and the inanimate, the human and the non-human. Instead, recalling the images of Bateson, there are minds within minds in a myriad of interlacing networks.

More than anything else, most "ecofeminist" sojourners seem to experience a deep sense of belonging and of intimacy and participation with the Earth and the entire cosmos. This is a remarkable shift. *We sense we belong to a larger, greater self than our current flesh and bones configuration*, something that most indigenous peoples have known intuitively, but which is now being demonstrated empirically by the new science. Everything is related to everything else; nothing is truly independent. We are one inter-connected web with all and in all.

Shifting Cosmology and Sense of the Sacred

One obvious conclusion of most ecofeminist Latin Americans is that the all-powerful, omnipotent God the Father of yester-year is no longer a valid God-image. Indeed, such an image is considered a major cause of our current ecological crisis and an obstacle to appropriate care for the Earth. Ecofeminists see the essential flaw in our Judeo-Christian heritage to be its unques-tioning belief in a monotheistic, personal, male deity who cre-ated a universe clearly distinct and apart from him. The tradition holds that the entire human community is being led to fulfill-ment in a divine kingdom, a kingdom with a millennial fulfill-ment here on Earth in historical time and a post-historical ful-fillment in an eternal transcendental mode of being (heaven). Thomas Berry argues that because we see ourselves as transcen-dent beings, we have a hard time believing that we really belong to the Earth, that we are indeed "earthlings." This, he stresses, is a deeply ingrained pathology that has led to an understanding of ourselves as having a destiny beyond that of the Earth and that has given us permission to use the Earth as we see fit while we are here.[2]

Ivone Gebara echoes Berry's critique of Christianity's mono-lithic, all-powerful God-image. She maintains that an anthropo-morphic and anthropocentric God became a necessity within the psychological structure that evolved throughout the history of patriarchal culture. Affirming a higher power in discontinuity with, apart from, and superior to all the powers of the cosmos, the Earth, human beings, animals, plants, and even life itself has been and is of fundamental importance to maintaining the hier-archical organization of the society in which we live. Gebara also reminds us that questions about God are really questions about ourselves. We continually construct pure and perfect beings and contrast them with our own experiences of impurity and imper-fection, of fragility and weakness.[3]

Because our understanding of ourselves is changing, we are also changing our intuitions about our origins and our destiny (cosmology). Cosmology is both a metaphysical term dealing with theories surrounding the nature of the universe and a scientific term that addresses the origin, structure, and space-time relationships of the universe. Many of us look for a religious meaning of life that leads us toward a sacred meaning in our cosmologies. As Gebara reminds us:

> A cosmology has to do with our collective representations regarding the origin of the world and of the human. It is larger than the sacred. The sacred comes into play as something that gives a construct of meaning to a specific group in a specific historical moment. It is we who define the cosmos as sacred, but not everyone is comfortable with the word "sacred."[4]

However, at this point in history Latin American women theologians and a growing number of ecofeminists *are* defining the cosmos as sacred. The older, patriarchal images defining or describing the sacred are swiftly becoming outworn vestiges of another time. For many women, God-images are shifting from a deity somehow outside and above the created universe to a sense of something within yet beyond, a relationship that holds everything together. To describe this changing view of God-images, they use words such as *Energy, Presence, Wisdom, Matrix, Complementarity, Memory, Intuitive Space, Greater Reality, Envelopment, Fountain of Life*. And they talk of *experiencing* this Energy rather than being able to define it.

Although several women used the image of the Goddess, they see the feminine principle in Ultimate Mystery as a corrective rather than seeking a literal return to Goddess worship. However, Latin American ecofeminists are comfortable invoking the Pachamama, Gaia, or Madre Tierra as root images for the deity. Many speak of finding divinity in the natural world, of feeling part of the web of life that pulsates at the heart of the cosmos. For some, Afro-Brazilian and Afro-Cuban religions appeal because of their close link with nature. Some of these women theologians are clearly pantheistic or pan-en-theistic, while at least one still holds out for a superior being and is comfortable with parental images.

I am more and more convinced that the debate between immanence and transcendence reflects the dualist thinking of patriarchy. This may be why women theologians and most ecofeminists embrace immanence as the understanding that we are *part of* the Earth, which is part of an ever-expanding universe. There is no "outside." Many would undoubtedly agree with Rosemary Radford Ruether, who imagines God as the font from which plants and animals well up in each generation, the Matrix that sustains and renews their life-giving interdependency. Ruether argues that transcendence-immanence has been understood for too long in dualistic terms of either/or, mind/body, and male/female splits. She sees transcendence not as a concept that implies a God who is a male, disembodied mind outside the universe, but as a renewing divine Spirit radically free from our systems of domination, yet closer to us than we are to ourselves.[5]

The shift taking place in cosmology is nowhere more evident than in the women's beliefs about death and resurrection. The majority view death and life as part of the same cycle. They speak of death as returning to that primal energy, that original goodness from which they came. Most reflect a peacefulness about returning to this matrix, to being dissolved into the Earth; they refer to death as "coming home." Women who have lost parents recently speak of how the deaths of loved ones have convinced them that a deep connection continues. They speak of memory—how those dearly loved are present in the memories we have of them. This seems to be the sense of "ancestrality, a connectedness to those who have gone before. These loved ones live on in the collective unconscious of the species, in our gene pool, in the very characteristics that make us kin—a certain laugh, a way of walking, a gesture." Alcira describes the continuing presence of her mother: "She is alive in all those kind ways she marked my life. Based on this experience I can say I feel resurrection in life. She is present in the music she liked, the food she cooked, all the advice she gave me over the years, in the garden she planted."

Ivone Gebara, the region's leading ecofeminist, also speaks of returning to the Earth, "to a Living Body in transformation, which is mortal and yet open to endless possibilities." She tells us that she prefers "for my last sigh and my last repose, the arms of the earth—which, according to the book of Genesis, is the place where God walks. Beyond what is imagined by reason, there is something imagined by desire, poetry, beauty."[6]

An expanding definition of the self as part of a larger whole is integral to this emerging cosmology. The body doesn't decay while the soul soars off to some eternal abode that patriarchy has told us is our "true home." Our very innards tell us that we share the same fate as all earthlings; we also return to the Earth. The shift in cosmology is that *our individual ego disappears and merges again with the Great Self from which it came.* We return to what Bohm calls the "folding and unfolding universe," to Bateson's "pattern that connects," to Berry's "dream of the earth," to Jung's "collective unconscious," to the indigenous peoples' "Great Spirit," to what I call "sustaining wisdom," and to what many ecofeminists would call "primal energy."

Shifting Epistemology

Nowhere is the shift to a post-patriarchal way of being more notable than in the way the women theologians perceive or know (epistemology). *The body and bodily experience become the locus for understanding, for feeling both pleasure and pain, and for judging right and wrong.* The body—not in the abstract but in women's bodies that are sexual, sensual, and sometimes abused and wounded—is where these women construct their cosmologies and theologies, their ethics, and their spiritual practices. This emphasis on the body is a reaction to millennia of patriarchal oppression when women's bodies were seen as property to be dominated and used as receptacles to reproduce the species. It is also a reaction to centuries of Judeo-Christian teaching that women were the cause of humanity's fall from grace and thus a font of evil, temptation, and concupiscence. Feminist and ecofeminist insistence that we do theology from the body is also a protest against the many dualisms that separate the mind, the spirit, and the soul from the body. Multitudes of women throughout Latin America are reclaiming their bodies as sacred, as a source of holiness, righting a long-overdue imbalance in which men/mind/spirit was considered superior to women/body/materiality.

A major contribution to how we know came during the gathering in Santiago when *genital embodiedness* was used as a theological category to unmask patriarchy. All present recognized how patriarchy has emphasized the grandeur of rational thought and contrasted it with the sordidness of female genitality. The denial of genitality as a human attribute of beauty and freedom is grounded in a dualistic understanding of life and clearly linked to an asexual image of the Divine. Given the standard patriarchal perspective, the God of the Bible appears to exert power over women and to condemn female genitality as a source of transgression and disobedience, a space that draws men away from God. As a result, women's genitality has also become a source of guilt, burdened by the weight of sin. Retrieving a healthy sense of genitality can be a major step in the process of healing and a first step toward redeeming women's self-esteem.

This bold, new affirmation in the evolution of feminist and ecofeminist theology in Latin America may be the most original contribution of this movement. *It is precisely this "lower" side—our menstruating, nursing, secreting woman self—that patriarchy and patriarchal religion have sought to control and repress because it reminded humans of our true nature, our earthiness, our materiality.*

A return to the body as a locus for theology does not, however, concentrate exclusively on *our* bodies. As ecofeminists move to a larger understanding of who we are as human beings, our sense of the borders of our own bodies fades. As the intuition of being "earthlings" begins to seep in, many women begin to understand themselves as clusters of energy bound for a moment in a particular body. They often experience a sense of great communion with those of our own species and with other members of the Earth community, entering for fleeting moments, or for a lifetime, into their pain, their pleasure, their anguish, and their joy. Then the individual ego becomes part of a fifteen-billion-year-old cosmogenesis.

ECOFEMINIST INSIGHTS: IMPLICATIONS

The implications of this shift in anthropology, cosmology, and epistemology influence both ethical and spiritual practices, often going beyond what was previously considered orthodox into new and sometimes uncharted waters.

Implications for Ethics

The hallmark of patriarchy is its ability to establish what is right and wrong and to punish wrongdoers. Normative behavior is established by outside authorities, usually male, who decide what is orthodox and legitimate, what is allowed or forbidden. The women in my study who have chosen to move beyond patriarchy all call for a new ethics based on the experiences of their own bodies, with their accumulated history, wisdom, and longings. Starting from the body is essential. Because ethical decisions will be based on one's own experience, they will be contextualized, pluralistic, and respectful of diversity. It is impossible to base such ethical decisions exclusively on universal, unchanging laws.

So how do we establish limits in moving toward a post-patriarchal ethics? What criteria should govern actions and desires? The twelve women realized that they could not deny the heritage of the past or turn a blind eye to the many efforts toward justice and compassion present throughout patriarchal history. They were emphatic about not pretending to be more ethical or moral than individuals in other periods of history.

They agreed that an ecofeminist ethics must call forth respect and responsibility from each and every person and must see human beings in relation to the rest of the Earth community and the unfolding universe. We are part of a greater body, and we must take account of repercussions to the whole. This becomes a major guideline. Emphasis is placed on those community spaces where listening to the experience and wisdom of the group becomes important as decisions are freely made.

The challenge is precisely to promote a more integrated view of life, so that every decision is made with a focus on promoting more equitable relations that do not continue domination over the weak and voiceless. Although women theologians and ecofeminists in particular are groping toward ways of living and being that are healthier for the planet and for humankind, they have no given set of blueprints. But ethical postures flow from utopian visions. They are the concrete ways, incorporating the disciplines and practices that we suspect will lead us toward those visions and dreams. As such, they are always derivative. When self-understanding changes (anthropology) as well as understandings of the Divine (cosmology), ethical practices must also be transformed.

It is here that ecofeminists find relevance in the life of Jesus of Nazareth and his project for a different world. Christian ecofeminists find value in the Christian experience, particularly in the values of the Jesus movement, although they are critical of the patriarchal way in which these values have been communicated throughout history. None of the twelve women interviewed identified herself as post-Christian. Jesus continues to be a major historical figure, a prophet and wisdom figure to whom women turn for inspiration. Some view Jesus as the archetype of the good and just man, which is why he remains relevant and attractive as a human being. Others are drawn to the totally counter-cultural side of Jesus. An authentic earthling, he exemplified "power within" and "power with" in an extraordinary way. In the end he was felled by the same "power over" system that has entrapped so many of us in its snare. The figure of Jesus will continue to be a major reference point as we grope toward a post-patriarchal time. But he will be one of several reference points.

Implications for Spirituality

A radical shift has taken place in the way women are nurturing their evolving intuitions about the meaning of life and who they are. First, the twelve women seem to be no longer nourished by the liturgies and worship services offered by their churches. Although some women, such as Silvia and Graciela, can find a communal connection in a Mennonite liturgy, a Catholic Mass, or a small Christian community, the majority have simply stopped participating in the worship services of their traditions because of the patriarchal language and content of those services.

While participation in official church worship wanes, a veritable boom in women's rituals and celebrations is taking place all over Latin America, and most of the women in this study are actively involved in creating, convoking, and participating in these celebrations. *A hallmark of these rituals is celebrating with one's whole body—through movement and dance*. And it is life that is being celebrated: their own lives, the lives of loved ones, of other women, of those suffering, and the lives of their ancestors. They also celebrate connections: to each other, to their bioregion, to the seasonal cycles, to the elements, to the Earth itself, and to the entire cosmos. They celebrate dreams and hopes: their own, those of the community, and those of the planet. Many of these rituals are inspired by indigenous cosmologies, and most demonstrate a remarkable creativity in which the gathered women celebrate wholly and freely with their entire bodies.

Spirituality is also nurtured through the mind-body practices such as contemplation, meditation, and tai chi. Although some women continue to be nourished by reflection on biblical passages, more turn to the natural world to find peace and to renew their being. They climb mountains; they commune with trees; they garden; they paint. All twelve women speak of the natural world as the font of their spirituality. Poetry, color, and music, as well as sharing the pain of others, are also essential elements of this evolving spirituality.

Another vital source of spirituality lies in the friendship and community of spaces for sharing joys and sorrows. Circles of women sprouting up everywhere have become spaces of freedom and healing. Such a group is described by Sandra Raquew:

> My feminist theology collective, Chimalman, is a fundamental source of sustenance for me. Together we cultivate seeds of new beliefs and values for ourselves. This is our space, the place where we can feel accepted, where we can think, share, and celebrate together. The Sacred for me takes place in sharing, in sharing our experiences with others who

also share their life journeys. In these moments, I know I am not alone.

This echoes Ivone Gebara's description of the Sacred as not "something" in itself, but a situation, a relation, a happening that takes us beyond ourselves, an experience of "going deep."[7]

IMPLICATIONS FOR LIBERATION THEOLOGY

I recently participated in a workshop in Santiago on gender and liberation theology. Doris Muñoz and I were invited to challenge liberation theology from the perspective of Latin American feminist and ecofeminist theology. We presented the three stages of feminist theology, and then we concentrated on the third phase, where ecofeminism comes to center stage. Other sessions included talks on patriarchy and on masculinity. In the workshop's opening session Diego Irarrázaval, one of Latin America's leading liberation theologians, spoke frankly about the "black holes" present in liberation theology, especially in the area of sexuality. He admitted that Finnish feminist theologian Elina Vuola is right when she says that liberation theologians simply have not given sufficient consideration to the sufferings of poor women with regard to their sexual and reproductive rights. He also talked openly about liberation theology's fear of sexuality and his own dawning realization of the link between sexuality and spirituality. Irarrázaval said that few Latin American liberation theologians share such concerns, with occasional exceptions, such as Brazilian theologian Leonardo Boff. (I suspect that Irarrázaval and Boff might represent one side of a growing debate within Latin American liberation theology, which would be welcomed by the region's ecofeminist theologians.)

Dialoguing with liberation theology was not a priority for the women involved in my study. I had originally hoped that my work might trigger a more serious dialogue between liberation theology and emerging ecofeminist thought in Latin America. But there was simply no interest or energy for such a dialogue on the part of the women theologians. While all admit their origins in liberation theology, they do not see a need to debate liberation theology—either point by point or in general.

However, neither is liberation theology seen as "the enemy" as they move into the future. Indeed, the women expressed their gratitude to liberation theologians for uncovering the region's structures of oppression and for reflecting on them theologically. Although liberation theology appears to be stagnating somewhat at this point, as José Comblin has acknowledged, having lost its utopian vision with the fall of historical socialism, it does not seem to have found a dream (except that of "resistance") to warm our hearts and kindle our spirits, as once it did. Perhaps if liberation theologians explore new understandings of anthropology and cosmology, they too might develop post-patriarchal yearnings.

CHALLENGES TO MINISTRY

What does all this mean? After all, I am a Catholic missionary and a Catholic theologian who struggles daily to insist that I am not post-Christian but only post-patriarchal. I am no psychologist, but with age I have grown, I believe, in both wisdom and grace. Our great trauma at this stage of our evolution seems to be our narrow sense of understanding who we are. Our identity within patriarchy has been so limited to the individual ego that we may have lost our sense of resting in the security of a much larger and grander self.

This narrow understanding of who we are has led us to gauge everything in terms of "power over." Where do I fit on the totem pole? Who holds the power and how can I get my share of it? Within patriarchy, it is often power that gives the individual a sense of security and worth. And, yet, it wasn't always so. At an earlier time our identity was that of the tribe, the clan. We were kin to all and saw our individual selves only in relation to the larger group. This was our sense of belonging. As Paleolithic and Neolithic women and men, we were part of and communed deeply with the entire Earth community. The patriarchal "interlude" of the past five thousand years has skewed that sense of kinship.

As we move toward the uncharted waters of a post-patriarchal world, an expanded sense of self is key. Cultivation of a sense of belonging to an amazing process of what Bohm calls "folding and unfolding" is essential if we are to find a new yet ancient sense of security as humankind. Our value does not lie in the power we hold or in our possessions. Our value, our worth, our ecstasy lies in the overwhelming realization that we form part of the dream of the universe, which has been present from the beginning of time. Pierre Teilhard de Chardin once said that the greatest discovery of the modern period has been the discovery of evolution. Evolution can be understood as a continual awakening, an ever more complex process of transformation, a groping toward a future horizon of possibility that was present from the beginning of the universe.

Laying bare the aberration of patriarchy will not necessarily move us forward to something different. It takes a dream, a vision, an intimation of what could be to captivate the imagination and energize us to look for new ways of being and becoming. This can bring about change in our earthling selves, the Earth, and the universe. Thus, my ministry, my pastoral call, my vocation is to tell the new story coming from quantum physics; to invite us to reconnect with our collective unconscious and to discover that in a very real way we always were and always will be. My strategy is to foster new relations based on "power within" and "power with" that flow out of the realization that we belong to a greater self and that the underlying net that holds us all is woven of relationships.

I want to convince everyone of the wisdom of the seed, the primary metaphor of ecofeminism. The seed sprouts, grows to fruition, flowers, bears fruit, withers, dies, and returns to the soil to begin the process once again. The seed will be what it is meant to be, nothing more, nothing less, enriching the entire Earth community. We also must be what we are meant to be. We should take on new mindsets so we understand ourselves as each having a unique contribution in our time—and that each of us will blossom forth fully only when others also sprout and bear fruit as they were meant to do. This shift in consciousness will move us toward complementarity and diversity.

As I conclude this work, the Twin Towers of Manhattan, a symbol of mighty US capitalism, have been gone for several years. Stock markets around the world are jittery as the price of oil soars. The US occupation of Iraq continues, despite the fact that a growing number of US citizens no longer support their leaders' position on the war. The forces of globalism reach into every country, affecting people on all continents. Warnings of climate change and global warming increase, while steadily accumulating scientific evidence says this is indeed happening, and at a faster rate than earlier predicted. Argentina, the most developed Latin American country, continues to reel because of large-scale corruption. The Catholic church is wracked by scandals: pedophilia in the United States, Italy, Ireland; and the sexual abuse of nuns by priests here in Chile and in Africa. It seems that the patriarchal constructs of centuries may have started to tremble, like an unsteady house of cards.

We have been mistaken before about the tenacity of capitalism, the latest manifestation of patriarchy. However, our task, futile though it may seem at times, is to push forward with new alternatives, so that there will always be islands of possibility and seeds of hope sprouting forth. May our seeds, our concerns, our rituals, and our hopes point to a better way in the future.

Epilogue

Surprise without End

The universe is full of surprises. Indeed, it is continuous creativity, surprise without end. And you and I form part of it all.

You were there and I was there when the universe burst forth some fifteen billion years ago in one great flaring forth. Energy, fire, light, and heat radiated in every direction, creating the universe, time, and space. All that one day would come into existence was present in that first flaring forth—the galaxies, stars, planets, oceans, mountains, trees, ants, and elephants. Buddha, Jesus, Teresa of Avila, Montezuma, Sor Juana Inéz de la Cruz, you, and I—all were present in the energy of that first unimaginable first moment.

You were there and I was there during the following billions of years of fecund night when atoms joined together to become first hydrogen and then helium.

You were there and I was there when in an instant during that fecund night the universe in another great burst of creativity birthed more than a hundred billion galaxies—among them our own relatively insignificant Milky Way. Each galaxy has its own inner dynamics, and each in its turn has created millions and millions of stars.

You were there and I was there five billion years ago when in a corner of the Milky Way, our own star was born from the stardust of the explosion of a supernova. Once born, our sun demonstrated the same self-organizing principles present in the entire universe and created its own system of planets, including our own dear planet Earth.

You were there and I was there when the Earth mixed within its womb minerals, gases, and liquids from which was brought to birth, some four billion years later, the first tiny cell. With the passage of time, these cells learned to remember, to join together, and to adapt. And in a great leap of creativity, they learned to "eat" the sun's energy! To reproduce themselves, they invented sex, and by learning to eat one another, they invented death.

You were there and I was there when, some six hundred million years ago, a fantastic array of multi-cellular organisms was born: worms, corals, insects, crabs, starfish, sponges, spiders, and vertebrates of every sort. Worms learned to crawl; other beings developed wings. Some invented teeth; others invented shells.

You were there and I was there during the following millennium when ocean waves washed up some sea plants among the rocks. These plants learned to live along the seacoasts. Little by little, some of these plants became trees, and soon the continents were roaring with green life.

You were there and I was there when the sea creatures followed the plants onto the land. During the next several millennia, amphibians, reptiles, and insects of all kinds inhabited the continents.

And you were there and I was there some sixty-seven million years ago when a great astronomic collision changed the Earth's atmosphere to such a degree that almost all the forms of animal life had to reinvent themselves or disappear. This destruction also opened new possibilities; the birds and the mammals that were not able to develop in the presence of the dinosaurs now flourished as a result of this so-called disaster.

You were there and I was there sixty million years ago when the mammals, now a permanent presence on Earth, began to develop emotional sensitivity—a new ability of the nervous system to feel the universe in a new way. Beauty as well as terror of the world became deeply encrusted in the mammalian psyche, including that of the human. In some rare occasions, especially among the primates, this emotional sensitivity combined with the neural ability of consciousness to be conscious of itself—which was the case with the human animal.

You were there and I was there four million years ago when our ancestors stood up on two feet; some two million years ago when we began to use our hands to mold tools from the Earth and to harness fire; some thirty-five thousand years ago when we arrived at a new level of consciousness that we expressed in dance and music, in celebrating the changing seasons of the year, in burying our loved ones who died; some twenty thousand years ago when we began a cycle of domestication of plants and animals, which also domesticated us. We slowly abandoned the hunting and gathering lifestyle of our tribes and clans and began to settle down and grow food.

You were there and I was there when, with our food supply more secure, we began to live in villages. In this new context we were able to develop ceramics, weaving, architecture. We could build temples and perform rites to the Great Mother. Between ten thousand and five thousand years ago, we created the structures of language, religion, cosmology, and art that define human civilization until the present time.

You were there and I was there some five thousand years ago when we began establishing the great urban civilizations as humanity's new centers of power: Babylon, Paris, Rome, Jerusalem, Athens, Cairo, Mecca, Delhi, Teotihuacán, Cuzco. These great cities were characterized by their hierarchical relationships and their emphasis on specialization and the division of labor. This was an era of many transformations: rivers and seas would now be navigated and used as trade routes; forests and minerals could be exploited as natural resources. In this stage human civilization increased in number and in wealth; we built great cathedrals, palaces, and temples. To defend this wealth, we developed military force with arms that became ever more sophisticated. War became chronic. The Great Mother of Neolithic times, who was so identified with agriculture, was replaced by a Father God who, like the king, ruled from on high.

You were there and I was there during the nineteenth and twentieth centuries when we evolved the nation-state with its mystique of nationalism, progress, democratic freedoms, and individual rights to private property and economic gain; when we developed tremendous power in the areas of science, technology, and economics to the point that—as a species—we can control the very process of the Earth itself and use it for our own good.

You were there and I was there when, in the last few years, we began to discover that the universe is not a "place," a backdrop for the stage upon which the human acts, but an evolutionary community continually birthing ever more complex life forms.

You are here and I am here when life itself is forcing us to remember what is stored in our body's memory, what our genes have always known: *nothing exists, or has existed, or will exist for its own sake.* Nothing exists without the rest. We are a link in a chain of DNA that is at every moment reshaping and transforming itself.

Let us remember well: you were there and I was there in the fireball at the beginning of the universe; then in the galaxies, then in the planets, then in the wiggle of the worm, in the flight of the bird, in the broad-reaching branches of the araucaria tree, in the first human who stood up on two feet and used her hands to start a fire, then as a member of the tribe collecting fruit in the forest, then in the village taking part in the fertility rites to the Great Mother, and then in the city dominated by the cathedral where we went to pray to God the Father.

And finally, if the Earth's journey continues—and, oh, how we pray that it will!—you will be there and I will be there in those beings who will come after us and reach out their hands and touch the stars. We will be in those forms of life that come after us, who, without a doubt, will be more complex than the human species and will discover ways of being more intimately in communion than we have known. New surprises in this cosmic dance of surprise without end.

Notes

1. The Development of Feminist Theology in Latin America

1. María Pilar Aquino, *Our Cry for Life: Feminist Theology from Latin America* (Maryknoll, NY: Orbis Books, 1993). Aquino's work is particularly insightful for the first two stages of Latin American feminist theology.

2. Elsa Tamez, "Latin American Feminist Hermeneutics: A Retrospective," in *Women's Visions: Theological Reflection, Celebration, Action*, ed. Ofelia Ortega (Geneva: WCC Publications, 1995).

3. Mary Judith Ress, "Ecofeminism and Panentheism: Interview with Ivone Gebara," in *Readings in Ecology and Feminist Theology*, ed. Mary Heather MacKinnon and Moni McIntyre (Kansas City: Sheed and Ward, 1995).

4. Tamez, "Latin American Feminist Hermeneutics," 89.

5. Elsa Tamez, "Descubriendo rostros distintos de Dios," in *Panorama de la Teología Latinoamericana*, ed. Juan-José Tamayo and Juan Bosch (Navarra, Spain: Editorial Verbo Divino, 2001), 647–60.

6. Tamez, "Latin American Feminist Hermeneutics," 78.

7. For an excellent analysis of the current state of CEBs in Latin America, see Barbara Fraser and Paul Jeffry, "Base Communities, Once Hope of Church, Now in Disarray," *National Catholic Reporter*, November 12, 2004, 12–16.

8. Tamez, "Latin American Feminist Hermeneutics," 86.

9. Ibid., 77–89. I have basically summarized Tamez's article, adding reflections from my experience of the development of feminist theology in the region.

10. This interview was originally published in Spanish in *Con-spirando: Revista latinoamericana de ecofeminismo, espiritualidad y teología* 4 (1993): 44–49, under the title "Entrevista con Ivone Gebara: Ecofeminismo holístico." It has since been translated into English and reproduced in several feminist anthologies.

11. Tamez, "Latin American Feminist Hermeneutics," 85.

12. Gustavo Gutiérrez, "Situación y Tareas de la Teología de la Liberación," *Teología Latinoamericana: Evaluación, Retos y Perspectivas. Alternativas* 18/19 (Managua: Editorial Lascasiana, 2001): 54.

13. Ibid., 62–66.

14. Juan-José Tamayo, "Cambio de paradigma teológico en América Latina," in Tamayo and Bosch, *Panorama de la Teología Latinoamericana*, 18–19.

15. Ibid., 30–35.

16. "Presentación," *Alternativas* 18/19 (2001): 7. This issue of *Alternativas* contains many of the papers given at the Congress.

17. Leonardo Boff, "El Pobre, la nueva cosmología y liberación: Cómo enriquecer la Teología de la Liberación," *Alternativas* 18/19 (2001): 76.

18. Ibid., 79–80.

19. Ibid., 86.

20. Márcio Fabri Dos Anjos, "Teología en América Latina: Cambios y Alternativas," *Alternativas* 18/19 (2001): 40. Another telling example of this tension is present in the following quotation from the same documents: "But there were resistances and questioning, among them: the revelation in our thought of a universe of millions of light years—won't this be a form of making us fly away from the grounding of an economic and political reality in which the poor suffer? In this paradigm, eminently holistic, won't complexity and fluidity become so enlarged to the point of giving us over to a type of 'pantheistic fixation with the cosmos,' congealing our commitments and responsibilities?" (cited in Luiz Carlos Susin, "Teología y nuevos paradigmas," *Alternativas* 18/19 [2001]: 28.

21. José Comblin, *Called for Freedom: The Changing Context of Liberation Theology* (Maryknoll, NY: Orbis Books, 1998), 203.

22. Ibid., ix.

23. Ibid., 55.

24. Ibid., 57.

25. Ibid., 78.

26. Ibid., 80.

27. Ibid., 181–82.

28. Ibid., 214–15.

29. David Molineaux, "Notes on the Current Status of Latin American Liberation Theology," talk given at the Call to Action Conference, Los Angeles, July 2002, 2–4, 5.

30. Elsa Tamez, ed., *La sociedad que las mujeres soñamos* (San José, Costa Rica: DEI, 2001), 13. This work contains lectures and the final document from the EATWOT meeting of women theologians from Latin America and the Caribbean held in Bogota, Colombia, in August 1999.

31. María Arcelia González Butrón, "Efectos de la globalización neoliberal en algunos aspectos de la vida de las mujeres: Una mirada desde América Latina y el Caribe," in Tamez, *La sociedad que las mujeres soñamos*, 17–38.

32. Elina Vuola, *Limits of Liberation: Praxis as Method in Latin American Liberation Theology and Feminist Theology* (Helsinki: Suomalainen Tiedeakatemia, 1997), 18.

33. This development can be traced in *Mysterium Liberationis: Fundamental Concepts in Liberation Theology*, ed. Ignacio Ellacuría and Jon Sobrino (Maryknoll, NY: Orbis Books, 1993).

34. Vuola, *Limits of Liberation*, 88.

35. Ibid., 183.

36. Ibid., 218.

37. María Pilar Aquino, quoted in ibid., 146.

38. Ivone Gebara, "Ecofeminismo: Algunos desafíos teológicos," *Teología con rostro de mujer. Alternativas* 16/17 (Managua: Editorial Lascasina, 2000): 174–75.

39. Ivone Gebara, *Longing for Running Water: Ecofeminism and Liberation (Biblical Reflections for Ministry)* (Minneapolis: Fortress Press, 1999), 46–47.

40. Carmiña Navia Velasco, "Teología desde la mujer, un paradigma fértil," *Alternativas* 16/17 (2000): 134.

41. Ibid., 134.

42. Ibid., 135.

2. Sources of Ecofeminism

1. Thomas S. Kuhn, *The Structure of Scientific Revolutions* (Chicago: Univ. of Chicago Press, 1962), 5.

2. Mary Mellor, *Feminism and Ecology* (New York: New York Univ. Press, 1997), 15.

3. Françoise d'Eaubonne, quoted in ibid., 44.

4. Vandana Shiva, *Staying Alive* (London: Zed Press, 1989), xvi.

5. Mellor, *Feminism and Ecology*, 21.

6. Ibid.

7. Fritjof Capra, *The Web of Life: A New Scientific Understanding of Living Systems* (New York: Doubleday, 1996), 7.

8. Mellor, *Feminism and Ecology*, 132.

9. Michael E. Zimmerman, "Deep Ecology and Ecofeminism," in *Reweaving the World: The Emergence of Ecofeminism*, ed. Irene Diamond and Gloria F. Orenstein (San Francisco: Sierra Club Books, 1990), 141.

10. Capra, *The Web of Life*, 7.

11. Michael Dowd, "The Big Picture" (Earth Day, 1992). Available online.

12. For a description of this ritual, see John Seed, Pat Flemming, Joanna Macy, and Arne Naess, *Thinking Like a Mountain: Toward a Council of All Beings* (Philadelphia: New Society Publishers, 1988).

13. Joanna Macy, *World as Lover, World as Self* (Berkeley, CA: Parallax Press, 1991), 15–27.

14. Ibid., 5–11.

15. Ibid., 14.

16. Ibid., 192, italics added.

17. Mellor, *Feminism and Ecology*, 140

18. Ibid., 139.

19. Ibid., 141.

20. Marti Kheel, "Ecofeminism and Deep Ecology: Reflections on Identity and Difference," in *Reweaving the World: The Emergence of Ecofeminism*, ed. Irene Diamond and Gloria Orenstein (San Francisco, Sierra Club Books, 1990), 129.

21. Brian Swimme and Thomas Berry, *The Universe Story* (San Francisco: HarperSanFrancisco: 1992); Thomas Berry, *The Dream of the Earth* (San Francisco: Sierra Club Books, 1988); Brian Swimme, *Canticle to the Cosmos*, twelve-part video series (Livermore, CA: Newstory Project, 1990); Diarmuid O'Murchu, *Quantum Theology* (New York: Crossoad, 1998).

22. Capra, *The Web of Life*, 27.

23. Ibid., 30.

24. Werner Heisenberg, quoted in Capra, *The Web of Life*, 30.

25. Quoted in O'Murchu, *Quantum Theology*, 66–69.

26. Ibid., 28.

27. David Bohm, quoted in Moni McIntyre, "Toward a Theological Perspective on the Implicate Order of David Bohm," in *Readings in Ecology and Feminist Theology*, ed. Mary Heather MacKinnon and Moni McIntyre (Kansas City: Sheed and Ward, 1995), 382–83.

28. O'Murchu, *Quantum Theology*, 58.

29. Elisabet Sahtouris, *Gaia: The Human Journey from Chaos to Cosmos* (New York: Pocket Books, 1989), 9. This excellent text, written by an involved biologist who is also a feminist, describes with passion the evolution of the planet.

30. I have found Bateson's works difficult to read and have relied largely on the detailed summary of his thought found in Morris Berman, *The Reenchantment of the World* (Ithaca, NY: Cornell Univ. Press, 1981), esp. chaps. 7–9. Berman relies on Gregory Bateson, *Steps to an Ecology of Mind* (New York: Ballantine, 1972).

31. Berman, *The Reenchantment of the World*, 238.

32. Ibid., 244–45.

33. Ibid., 259.

34. Ibid., 257.

35. Humberto Maturana and Francisco Varela, *The Tree of Knowledge* (Boston: Shambhala, 1987).

36. For a summary of the Gaia hypothesis, see Capra, *The Web of Life*, 100–110.

37. Paul Davies, *The Mind of God: The Scientific Basis for a Rational World* (New York: Simon and Schuster, 1992), 50.

38. O'Murchu, *Quantum Theology*, 197.

39. Berry, *The Dream of the Earth*, 13–14.

40. Ibid., 21.

41. Ibid., 132–33.

42. Thomas Berry, *The Great Work: Our Way into the Future* (New York: Bell Tower, 1999).

43. Ibid., 165.

44. Berry, *The Dream of the Earth*, 81.

45. Berry, *The Great Work*, 201.

46. See Swimme, *Canticle to the Cosmos*. For more of Swimme's thought, see also Brian Swimme, *The Hidden Heart of the Cosmos: Humanity and the New Story* (Maryknoll, NY: Orbis Books, 1996).

47. Swimme, *Canticle to the Cosmos*. Each segment is dedicated to developing one of these twelve principles.

48. Brian Swimme, *The Earth's Imagination*, eight-part video series (Mill Valley, CA: Center for the Story of the Universe, 1998).

49. Ibid.

50. Berry, *The Dream of the Earth*, 4.

51. "Platform for Action," Fourth UN Conference on the Status of Women, Beijing, China, 1995.

52. Andy Smith, "For All Those Who Were Indian in a Former Life," in *Ecofeminism and the Sacred*, ed. Carol J. Adams (New York: Continuum, 1993), 168, 171.

53. Berry, *The Dream of the Earth*, 184.

54. Berry, *The Great Work*, 177.

55. Diego Irarrázaval, *Inculturation: New Dawn of the Church in Latin America* (Maryknoll, NY: Orbis Books, 2000), 20.

56. Ibid., 90.

57. Mary Judith Ress, "After Five Centuries of Mixings, Who Are We? Walking with Our Dark Grandmothers' Feet," in *Women Healing Earth: Third World Women on Ecology, Feminism, and Religion*, ed. Rosemary Radford Ruether (Maryknoll, NY: Orbis Books, 1996). What follows is a summary of that article.

58. Elena Aguila, "Mestiza, champurria, revoltijeada," *Revista Con-spirando* 2 (October 1992): 2–5.

59. Ibid., 5.

60. Berry, *The Dream of the Earth*, 166.

61. Judith Plant, "Searching for Common Ground: Ecofeminism and Bioregionalism," in Diamond and Orenstein, *Reweaving the World*, 156.

62. David Korten, *When Corporations Rule the World* (West Hartford, CT: Kumarian Press; San Francisco: Berrett-Koehler Publishers, 1995), 11.

63. Ibid., 261–62.

64. Herman Daly, quoted in ibid., 272.

3. Ecofeminism's Roots
in Other Feminist Movements

1. I should stress that cultural or radical feminism is deeply marked by US feminist history, which is also my own experience. The history is not the same for Latin America.

2. These four categories were mapped by feminist theologian Maria Riley, cited by Anne M. Clifford, *Introducing Feminist Theology* (Maryknoll, NY: Orbis Books, 2001), 23.

3. Ynestra King, "Healing the Wounds: Feminism, Ecology, and the Nature/Cultural Dualism," in *Reweaving the World: The Emergence of Ecofeminism*, ed. Irene Diamond and Gloria F. Orenstein (San Francisco: Sierra Club Books, 1990), 106.

4. Charlene Spretnak, "Ecofeminism: Our Roots and Flowering," in Diamond and Orenstein, *Reweaving the World*.

5. Ibid., 6.

6. Ibid., 6

7. King, "Healing the Wounds," 117–18.

8. Letty M. Russell, "Patriarchy," handout, Yale Divinity School, 1996.

9. David Molineaux, unpublished notes.

10. My summary shows the influence of the works of Thomas Berry and Brian Swimme as well as that of feminist anthropologist Marija Gimbutas, described in Riane Eisler, *Sacred Pleasure: Sex, Myth, and the Politics of the Body—New Paths to Power and Love* (San Francisco: HarperSanFrancisco, 1995). For an earlier summary on the development of patriarchy, see Mary Judith Ress, "La historia del *homo economicus*: una version ecofeminista en cuatro actos," in *Revista Con-spirando* 11 (1995): 6–12.

11. See Mary Judith Ress, "Redescubriendo quienes somos: En memoria de Marija Gimbutas (1921–1994)," *Revista Con-spirando* 19 (1997): 10–15.

This article was based on an issue of the *Journal of Feminist Studies in Religion* 12:2 (Fall 1996) dedicated to the work of Gimbutas.

12. Carol Christ, "Introduction: The Legacy of Marija Gimbutas," *Journal of Feminist Studies in Religion* 12:2 (Fall 1996): 33.

13. Marija Gimbutas, *The Civilization of the Goddess: The World of Old Europe*, ed. Joan Marler (San Francisco: HarperSanFrancisco, 1991).

14. Ibid., 324.

15. Ibid., viii

16. Ibid., 321.

17. Ibid., xxi.

18. Mara Lynn Keller, "The Theory of Early European Origins and the Contemporary Transformation of Western Culture," *Journal of Feminist Studies in Religion* 12:2 (Fall 1996): 83.

19. Carol Christ, "A Different World," *Journal of Feminist Studies in Religion* 12:2 (Fall 1996): 57–58.

20. Ibid., 53–54.

21. Gimbutas, *The Civilization of the Goddess*, vii.

22. Leonard Shlain, *The Alphabet versus the Goddess* (New York: Penguin Books, 1998), 7.

23. Ibid.

24. Spretnak, "Ecofeminism," 5.

25. Carol Christ, quoted in Mary Mellor, *Feminism and Ecology* (New York: New York University Press, 1997), 53.

26. Carol Christ, "Rethinking Theology and Nature," in *Reweaving the World: The Emergence of Ecofeminism*, ed. Irene Diamond and Gloria Orenstein (San Francisco: Sierra Club Books, 1990), 65.

27. Carl Jung, *Memories, Dreams, Reflections*, ed. Aniéla Jaffé (New York: Vintage Books, 1965), 402.

28. M. L. von Franz, "Science and the Unconscious," in *Man and His Symbols*, ed. Carl Jung et al. (New York: Doubleday, 1964), 306-9.

29. Jung, *Memories, Dreams, Reflections*, 392.

30. Anthony Stevens, *Archetypes: A Natural History of the Self* (New York: Quill, 1983), 29–47.

31. Ibid., 14.

32. See ibid., 21–62.

33. See ibid., 4–12.

34. See ibid., 18–25.

35. Ibid., 24.

36. Madonna Kolbenschlag, unpublished notes.

37. Colectivo Con-spirando, *Diosas y Arquetipos* (Santiago, 2000). This publication contains Kolbenschlag's last lecture summarizing her work on Toni Wolff's typology.

38. Ibid., 14–15.

39. Madonna Kolbenschlag, *Eastward toward Eve: A Geography of Soul* (New York: Crossroad, 1996), 134–35.

40. Charlene Spretnak, "Earthbody and Personal Body as Sacred," in *Ecofeminism and the Sacred*, ed. Carol Adams (New York: Continuum, 1993).

41. Mellor, *Feminism and Ecology*, 2.

42. Rosemary Radford Ruether, in Mary Judith Ress, "Una critica al ecofeminismo: el esencialismo," *Revista Con-spirando* 23 (1998): 40–44.

43. Cecile Jackson, quoted in Mellor, *Feminism and Ecology*, 73.

44. Adrienne Rich, as quoted in Mellor, *Feminism and Ecology*, 87–88.

45. Spretnak, "Ecofeminism," 4.

46. Vandana Shiva, as quoted in Mellor, *Feminism and Ecology*, 104.

47. Mellor, *Feminism and Ecology*, 188–83.

48. Ibid., 184.

49. King, "Healing the Wounds," 116.

50. Mellor, *Feminism and Ecology*, 69–70.

51. Rosemary Radford Ruether, *Gaia and God: An Ecofeminist Theology of Earth Healing* (San Francisco: HarperSanFrancisco, 1992), 269.

52. Ibid., 270.

53. Ibid., 273.

54. My own Maryknoll community has begun an eco-spirituality center in cooperation with the St. Joseph Sisters of Corondelete in Vilches in southern Chile, and with my team, Capacitar, I helped found a holistic health and eco-spirituality center in the Cajon de Maipo, outside Santiago.

55. Miriam Therese MacGillis, "Genesis Farm Links Holistic Living with Envisioning a New World Order," *IDOC Internazionale* (Rome: July-August, 1990), 39.

56. Diarmuid O'Murchu, *Religious Life: A Prophetic Vision* (Notre Dame, IN: Ave Maria Press, 1991), 36–37.

57. Miriam Therese MacGillis, taped reflections on religious life.

58. Ibid.

59. Ibid.

60. It was Ivone Gebara who, after reading this section of my thesis, pointed out this phenomenon to me.

61. Mary Judith Ress, "Las Fuentes del ecofeminismo: una genealogía," *Ecofeminismo: Hallazgos, preguntas, provocaciones (Revista Con-spirando* 23 [1998]). The discussion that follows is based on this article.

4. Ecofeminist Theology

1. Starhawk, "Power, Authority, and Mystery: Ecofeminism and Earth-based Spirituality," in *Reweaving the World: The Emergence of Ecofeminism,*

ed. Irene Diamond and Gloria F. Orenstein (San Francisco: Sierra Club Books, 1990).

2. Charlene Spretnak, *States of Grace: The Recovery of Meaning in the Postmodern Age* (San Francisco: HarperCollins, 1991), 114–54.

3. Carol Christ, "Repensando la teología y la naturaleza," *Revista Conspirando* 4 (June 1993): 28–29.

4. Susan Griffin, *Woman and Nature: The Roaring inside Her,* quoted in Mary Mellor, *Feminism and Ecology* (New York: New York Univ. Press, 1997), 49.

5. Mary Daly, *Beyond God the Father: Toward a Philosophy of Women's Liberation* (Boston: Beacon Press, 1973).

6. Mary Daly, *Outercourse: The Be-dazzling Voyage* (San Francisco: HarperSanFrancisco, 1992). In her autobiography Daly tells the story of her evolution and her contributions to radical feminist thought.

7. Sallie McFague, *Models of God: Theology for an Ecological, Nuclear Age* (Philadelphia: Fortress Press, 1987); idem, *The Body of God: An Ecological Theology* (Minneapolis: Fortress Press, 1993).

8. Sallie McFague, quoted in Anne M. Clifford, *Introducing Feminist Theology* (Maryknoll, NY: Orbis Books, 2001), 236–37.

9. McFague, *Models of God*, 11.

10. Clifford, *Introducing Feminist Theology*, 238.

11. Jennifer M. Molineaux, "God's Living Body: A Pantheist Reading of Sallie McFague," thesis, Graduate Theological Union, Berkeley, California, February 1997, 12.

12. Rosemary Radford Ruether, *Gaia and God: An Ecofeminist Theology of Earth Healing* (San Francisco: HarperSanFrancisco, 1992). The Conspirando Collective spent a semester studying the Spanish-language edition of *Gaia and God* in 1995.

13. Ruether, *Gaia and God*, 3.

14. Rosemary Radford Ruether, "Ecofeminism and Healing Ourselves, Healing the Earth," a lecture in the series Keeping the Spirit Alive, presented by St. Stephen's College and given in Edmonton and Calgary, Alberta, June 2–3, 1998.

15. Ruether, *Gaia and God*, 254.

16. Ibid., 4.

17. Ibid., 167.

18. Ruether, "Ecofeminism and Healing Ourselves, Healing the Earth."

19. Ibid.

20. Ruether, *Gaia and God*, 31.

21. Ibid., 252.

22. Ibid., 252–53.

23. Judith Ress, "Ecofeminism and Panentheism," an interview with Ivone Gebara, in *Readings in Ecology and Feminist Theology*, ed. Mary Heather

MacKinnon and Moni McIntyre (Kansas City: Sheed and Ward, 1995), 208.

24. Ivone Gebara, *Longing for Running Water: Ecofeminism and Liberation (Biblical Reflections for Ministry)* (Minneapolis: Fortress Press, 1999); and idem, *Out of the Depths: Women's Experience of Evil and Salvation* (Minneapolis: Fortress Press, 2002).

25. For a description of the episode of the Vatican silencing of Gebara, see Ann Patrick Ware, "Foreword," in Gebara, *Out of the Depths*.

26. Ivone Gebara, in Ress, "Ecofeminism and Panentheism," 209.

27. Gebara, *Longing for Running Water*, 2.

28. Ibid., 83.

29. Ibid., 85–87.

30. Ivone Gebara, "Eco-feminism: An Ethics of Life," in *Sacred Earth, Sacred Community: Jubilee, Ecology, and Aboriginal Peoples*, ed. Canadian Ecumenical Jubilee Initiative (2000): 33. (The journal is published in Toronto.)

31. Ibid.

32. Ibid., 45.

33. Gebara, *Longing for Running Water*, 101, 111–12.

34. Ibid., 114.

35. For Gebara, "to speak of pan-en-theism is to consider the potentialities of the universe, the potentialities of life, and the potentialities of human life as always open-ended. Thus we escape from the closed circle of immanence and transcendence, of 'being in itself,' to become part of the reality we call the process of life, in which transcendence and immanence are mere expressions that point to the dynamics that draw us forth" (ibid., 124).

36. Ibid., 187.

37. Ivone Gebara, "¿Quién es el Jesús liberador que buscamos?" in *Palabras claves sobre Jesús de Nazaret*, ed. J. J. Tamayo and J. Bosch (Estella, Navarra, Spain: Editorial Verbo Divino, 1999), 158–60. Translation mine.

38. Ibid., 178.

39. Ibid., 184.

40. Gebara, "Eco-feminism," 37.

41. Ibid., 39.

42. Gebara, *Out of the Depths*, 4.

43. Ibid., 88–90.

44. Ibid., 124–28.

45. Ibid., 116.

46. Gebara, *Longing for Running Water*, 129.

47. Ibid., vii.

48. Gebara, *Out of the Depths*, 131.

49. Gebara, *Longing for Running Water*, 14.

50. *Con-spirando: Revista latinoamericana de ecofeminismo, espiritualidad y teología* 1 (March 1992): 2–5. (The journal is published in Santiago, Chile.)

51. Delores S. Williams, *Sisters in the Wilderness: The Challenge of Womanist God-Talk* (Maryknoll, NY: Orbis Books, 1993); Rita Nakashima Brock, *Journeys by Heart: A Christology of Erotic Power* (New York: Crossroad, 1991); Joanne Carlson Brown and Rebecca Parker, "For God So Loved the World?" in *Christianity, Patriarchy, and Abuse*, ed. J. Carlson Brown and C. Bohn (Cleveland: Pilgrim Press, 1989).

52. Delores S. Williams, quoted in R. Solari, "Just Another Conference?" sidebar in "In Her Own Image," *Common Boundary* (July/August 1995): 18–27.

53. Brock, *Journeys by Heart*, 56.

54. *Desarmar la violencia*, *Con-spirando* 8 (June 1994). See the entire issue, specifically, Ute Seibert, "Tanto amó Dios al mundo: Violencia y abuso en la tradición cristiana," 2–8.

55. "Afectos y poderes," *Con-spirando* 16 (June 1996). In this issue see particularly Bridget Cooke, "Nuestra relación con las/os niñas/os: Más allá del palo y la zanahoria," 18–25; and Ute Seibert, "Dios: Poder en relación?" 40–43.

56. *Sistematización: Más allá de la violencia: solidaridad y ecofeminismo*. Summary of the Shared Garden workshop held in Santiago, Chile, January 27–February 8, 1998 (Santiago: Con-spirando, 1998).

57. Josefina Hurtado, "Por sus símbolos los conoceréis," *Con-spirando* 19 (March 1997): 2–9.

58. Ibid, 7.

59. Yeta Ramírez, "El poder de los símbolos," *Con-spirando* 19 (March 1997): 35–35.

60. Paulo Freire, *Pedagogy of the Oppressed* (New York: Herder and Herder, 1970).

61. *(Trans) formación y cambio cultural*, *Con-spirando* 26 (December 1998).

62. *El ecofeminismo: Reciclando nuestras energías de cambio*, *Con-spirando* 4 (June 1993); *Etica y ecofeminismo*, *Con-spirando* 17 (September 1997); and *Ecofeminismo: Hallazgos, preguntas, provocaciones*, *Con-spirando* 23 (March 1998).

63. Throughout 2003 ten grassroots teams in Latin America researched the Marian feasts in their region and discovered images hidden behind the Virgin Mary. See *Vírgenes y diosas en América Latina: La resignificación de lo sagrado*, ed. Veronica Cordero et al. (Santiago: Colectivo Con-spirando, 2004).

64. For more about the Inanna myth, see Diane Wolkstein and Samuel Noah Kramer, *Inanna, Queen of Heaven and Earth: Her Stories and Hymns from Sumer* (London: Rider and Company, 1984).

65. "Final Report: Third School of Ecofeminist Spirituality and Ethics" (Santiago: Con-spirando Collective, 2002), 6.

5. Charting the Change

1. M. Judith Ress, *Lluvia para florecer: Entrevistas sobre el ecofeminismo en América latina* (Santiago: Colectivo Con-spirando, 2002).

2. All quotations from the women are taken from Ress, *Lluvia para florecer*. The translations from the Spanish are mine.

3. Sandra Duarte da Souza, *Ecofeminist Theory, Ethics and Spirituality: An Analysis of the Discourse*, Ph.D. dissertation, São Bernardo do Campo, Universidade Metodista de São Paulo, Brasil, 1999 (in Portuguese).

6. Challenges for the Future

1. An unpublished poem in Madonna's notebook at the time of her death in Chile in January 2000. The poem is entitled *Ularu*, after the aborigine sacred rock in Australia.

2. Thomas Berry, *The Dream of the Earth* (San Francisco: Sierra Club Books, 1988), 81.

3. Ivone Gebara, *Longing for Running Water: Ecofeminism and Liberation (Biblical Reflections on Ministry)*, trans. David Molineaux (Minneapolis: Fortress Press, 1999), 101, 111–12.

4. Ivone Gebara, private correspondence with author.

5. Rosemary Radford Ruether, *Gaia and God: An Ecofeminist Theology of Earth Healing* (San Francisco: HarperSanFrancisco, 1992), 252–53.

6. Ivone Gebara, *Out of the Depths: Women's Experience of Evil and Salvation* (Minneapolis: Fortress Press, 2002), 131.

7. Ivone Gebara, "Presentación," in M. Judith Ress, *Lluvia para florecer: Entrevistas sobre el ecofeminismo en América latina* (Santiago: Colectivo Conspirando, 2002), 15.

Selected Bibliography

Adams, Carol, ed. *Ecofeminism and the Sacred*. New York: Continuum, 1993.

Aquino, María Pilar. *Our Cry for Life: Feminist Theology from Latin America*. Maryknoll, NY: Orbis Books, 1990.

Bateson, Gregory. *Steps to an Ecology of Mind*. New York: Ballantine, 1972.

Berman, Morris. *The Reenchantment of the World*. Ithaca, NY: Cornell Univ. Press, 1981.

Berry, Thomas. *The Dream of the Earth*. San Francisco: Sierra Club, 1988.

———. *The Great Work: Our Way into the Future*. New York: Bell Tower, 1999.

Biehl, Janet. *Rethinking Ecofeminist Politics*. Boston: South End Press, 1991.

Boff, Leonardo. *Cry of the Earth: Cry of the Poor*. Maryknoll, NY: Orbis Books, 1995.

Canadian Ecumenical Jubilee Initiative. *Sacred Earth, Sacred Community: Jubilee, Ecology and Aboriginal Peoples*. Toronto, 2000.

Capra, Fritjof. *The Web of Life*. San Francisco: Anchor, 1996.

Clifford, Anne M. *Introducing Feminist Theology*. Maryknoll, NY: Orbis Books, 2001.

Comblin, José. *Called for Freedom: The Changing Context of Liberation Theology*. Maryknoll, NY: Orbis Books, 1998.

Con-spirando: Revista latinoamericana de ecofeminismo, espiritualidad y teología [Santiago, Chile] (1992–present).

Colectivo Con-spirando. *Diosas y Arquetipos: En memoria de Madonna Kolbenschlag*. Santiago: Con-spirando, 2000.

Daly, Mary. *Outercourse: The Be-dazzling Voyage*. San Francisco: HarperSanFrancisco, 1992.

Davies, Paul. *The 5th Miracle: The Search for the Origin and Meaning of Life*. New York: Simon and Schuster, 1999.

———. *The Mind of God: The Scientific Basis for a Rational World*. New York: Simon and Schuster, 1992.

Diamond, Irene, and Gloria F. Orenstein, eds. *Reweaving the World: The Emergence of Ecofeminism*. San Francisco: Sierra Club Books, 1990.

Duarte da Souza, Sandra. "Ecofeminist Theory, Ethics, and Spirituality: An Analysis of the Discourse." Ph.D. dissertation, São Bernardo do

Campo, Universidade Metodista de São Paulo, Brasil, 1999 (in Portuguese).

Eisler, Riane. *Sacred Pleasure: Sex, Myth, and the Politics of the Body*. New York: HarperCollins, 1995.

Ellacuría, Ignacio, and Jon Sobrino, eds. *Mysterium Liberationis: Fundamental Concepts in Liberation Theology*. Maryknoll, NY: Orbis Books, 1993.

Ellis, Marc H., and Oto Maduro, eds. *Expanding the View: Gustavo Gutiérrez and the Future of Liberation Theology*. Maryknoll, NY: Orbis Books, 1988.

Gebara, Ivone. *Longing for Running Water: Ecofeminism and Liberation*. Minneapolis: Fortress Press, 1999.

————. *Out of the Depths: Women's Experience of Evil and Salvation*. Minneapolis: Fortress Press, 2002.

Gimbutas, Marija. *The Civilization of the Goddess: The World of Old Europe*. Edited by Joan Marler. San Francisco: HarperSanFrancisco, 1991.

Hollis, James. *The Archetypal Imagination*. College Station: Texas A and M Univ. Press, 2000.

Irarrázaval, Diego. *Inculturation: New Dawn of the Church in Latin America*. Maryknoll, NY: Orbis Books, 2000.

Johnson, Elizabeth. *She Who Is: The Mystery of God in Feminist Theological Discourse*. New York: Crossroad, 1992.

Jung, Carl. *Man and His Symbols*. New York: Doubleday, 1964.

————. *Memories, Dreams, Reflections*. Edited by Aniela Jaffé. New York: Vintage Books, 1965.

Kolbenschlag, Madonna. *Eastward toward Eve*. San Francisco: HarperSanFrancisco, 1997.

Korten, David. *When Corporations Rule the World*. West Hartford, CT: Kumarian Press; San Francisco: Berrett-Koehler Publications, 1995.

Latinamerica Press/Noticias Aliadas [Lima, Peru] (1982–present).

"The Legacy of Marija Gimbutas." Special issue of the *Journal of Feminist Studies of Religion* 12, no. 2 (Fall 1996).

MacGillis, Miriam. "Genesis Farm Links Holistic Living with Envisioning a New World Order." In *IDOC Internazionale* [Rome] (July-August, 1990).

MacKinnon, Mary Heather, and Moni McIntyre, eds. *Readings in Ecology and Feminist Theology*. Kansas City: Sheed and Ward, 1995.

Macy, Joanna. *World as Lover, World as Self*. Berkeley, CA: Parallax Press, 1991.

Maturana, Humberto, and Francisco Varela. *The Tree of Knowledge*. Boston: Shambhala, 1987.

McFague, Sallie. *The Body of God: An Ecological Theology*. Minneapolis: Fortress Press, 1993.

————. *Models of God: Theology for an Ecological, Nuclear Age.* Philadelphia: Fortress Press, 1987.

————. *Super, Natural Christians.* Minneapolis: Fortress Press, 1997.

Mellor, Mary. *Feminism and Ecology.* New York: New York Univ. Press, 1997.

Merchant, Carolyn. *The Death of Nature: Women, Ecology, and the Scientific Revolution.* San Francisco: Harper and Row, 1980.

————. *Radical Ecology: The Search for a Livable World.* New York: Routledge, 1992.

Mies, Maria, and Vandana Shiva. *Ecofeminism.* London: Zed Books, 1993.

Nakashima Brock, Rita. *Journeys by Heart: A Christology of Erotic Power.* New York: Crossroad, 1991.

O'Murchu, Diarmuid. *Poverty, Celibacy, and Obedience: A Radical Option for Life.* New York: Crossroad, 1999.

————. *Quantum Theology: Spiritual Implications of the New Physics.* New York: Crossroad, 1998.

————. *Reclaiming Spirituality.* New York: Crossroad, 1998.

————. *Religion in Exile.* New York: Crossroad, 2000.

Ortega, Ofelia, ed. *Women's Visions: Theological Reflection, Celebration, Action.* Geneva: World Council of Churches Publications, 1995.

Plant, Judith, ed. *Healing the Wounds: The Promise of Ecofeminism.* Philadelphia: New Society Publishers, 1989.

Ponting, Clive. *A Green History of the World: The Environment and the Collapse of Great Civilizations.* New York: Penguin Books, 1991.

Primavesi, Anne. *From Apocalypse to Genesis: Ecology, Feminism, and Christianity.* Minneapolis: Fortress Press, 1991.

Rasmussen, Larry. *Earth Community, Earth Ethics.* Maryknoll, NY: Orbis Books, 1996.

Ruether, Rosemary Radford. *Gaia and God: An Ecofeminist Theology of Earth Healing.* San Francisco: HarperSanFrancisco, 1992.

————. *Women and Redemption: A Theological History.* Minneapolis: Fortress Press, 1998.

————, ed. *Women Healing Earth: Third World Women on Ecology, Feminism and Religion.* Maryknoll, NY: Orbis Books, 1996.

Sagan, Carl. *Cosmos.* New York: Ballantine Books, 1980.

Sahtoris, Elisabet. *Gaia: The Human Journey from Chaos to Cosmos.* New York: Pocket Books, 1989.

Shiva, Vandana. *Staying Alive: Women, Ecology, and Development.* London: Zed Books, 1989.

Shlain, Leonard. *The Alphabet versus the Goddess.* New York: Penguin, 1998.

Spretnak, Charlene. *The Resurgence of the Real: Body, Nature, and Place in a Hypermodern World.* San Francisco: Addison-Wesley, 1997.

————. *States of Grace: The Recovery of Meaning in the Postmodern Age*. San Francisco: HarperSanFrancisco, 1991.

Stevens, Anthony. *Archetypes: A Natural History of the Self*. New York: Quill, 1983.

Sturgeon, Noel. *Ecofeminist Natures: Race, Gender, Feminist Theory, and Political Action*. New York: Routledge, 1997.

Swimme, Brian. *The Canticle of the Cosmos*. Twelve-part video series. Berkeley, CA: Holy Names College, 1988.

————. *The Earth's Imagination*. Eight-part video series. Mill Valley, CA.: Center for the Story of the Universe, 1998.

Swimme, Brian, and Thomas Berry. *The Universe Story*. HarperSanFrancisco: 1992.

Tamayo, Juan-José, and Juan Bosch, eds. *Palabras claves sobre Jesús de Nazaret*. Navarra, España: Editorial Verbo Divino, 1999.

————. *Panorama de la Teología Latinoamericana: Cuando vida y pesamiento son inseparables*. Navarra, España: Editorial Verbo Divino, 2001.

Tamez, Elsa. *La sociedad que las mujeres soñamos*. San José, Costa Rica: DEI, 2001.

"Teología feminista desde América Latina." *Cristianismo y Sociedad* 135-36. Guayaquil, Ecuador, 1998.

"Teología latinoamericana: Evaluación, Retos y Perspectivas." *Alternativas* 18/19. Managua: Editorial Lascasiana, 2001.

"Teología con Rostro de Mujer." *Alternativas* 16/17. Managua: Editorial Lascasiana, 2000.

Vuola, Elina. *Limits of Liberation: Praxis as Method in Latin American Liberation Theology and Feminist Theology*. Helsinki: Suomalainen Tiedeakatemia, 1997.

Williams, Delores S. *Sisters in the Wilderness: The Challenge of Womanist God-talk*. Maryknoll, NY: Orbis Books, 1991.

Index

All references to the twelve women interviewed for Chapter 5 are indexed by their first names rather than their surnames.